The Secrets to
Good Grades

THE

Secrets to Good Grades

JAMES KEOGH

FAWCETT BOOKS

THE BALLANTINE PUBLISHING GROUP

NEW YORK

Contents

A Fawcett Book
Published by The Ballantine Publishing Group

www.randomhouse.com/BB/

LIBRARY OF CONGRESS CATALOGING-IN-PUBLICATION DATA
Keogh, James Edward, 1948–
    The secrets to good grades / James Keogh. — 1st ed.
        p.   cm.
    ISBN 0-449-00310-8 (tr : alk. paper)
    1. Education, Elementary—Parent participation Handbooks, manuals, etc.
2. Homework Handbooks, manuals, etc.   3. Study skills
Handbooks, manuals, etc.   I. Title.
LB1048.5.K453   1999
372.13'0281—dc21   99-12947
                                                                        CIP

Text design by Ann Gold
Cover design by Cathy Colbert

Manufactured in the United States of America

First Edition: August 1999

10 9 8 7 6 5 4 3 2 1

A Fawcett Book
Published by The Ballantine Publishing Group

www.randomhouse.com/BB/

LIBRARY OF CONGRESS CATALOGING-IN-PUBLICATION DATA
Keogh, James Edward, 1948–
    The secrets to good grades / James Keogh. — 1st ed.
        p.   cm.
    ISBN 0-449-00310-8 (tr : alk. paper)
    1. Education, Elementary—Parent participation Handbooks, manuals, etc.
2. Homework Handbooks, manuals, etc.   3. Study skills
Handbooks, manuals, etc.   I. Title.
LB1048.5.K453   1999
372.13'0281—dc21   99-12947
                                                              CIP

Text design by Ann Gold
Cover design by Cathy Colbert

Manufactured in the United States of America

First Edition: August 1999

10 9 8 7 6 5 4 3 2 1

Contents

Introduction

Being a parent of a grammar-school child can become frustrating at times, especially when you're asked to help with homework. Homework should be a breeze for us since we know how to read, write, and solve arithmetic problems. However, our job isn't to do the homework assignment, but to get our kids to do it, and that's where the frustrations set in.

You have probably attended PTA meetings or seen presentations on television where parents are told they must help their child with schoolwork. I've heard the same lectures, yet no one ever told me how to help my child.

I'm not a trained educator and neither are you. However, school officials expect us to explain grammar, reading, geometry, decimals, and an array of other subjects to our child. Quite honestly, I don't remember half the lessons I learned in grammar school. How am I expected to explain these lessons to my child?

I set out to find an answer to that question. I reviewed my daughters' first- through sixth-grade curriculum and determined the information I needed to help my kids with homework assignments. Then I asked many professional educators to tell me the best way to explain those lessons to my daughters. You'll find my results throughout the chapters in this book.

You'll notice my approach is different from other books that simply tell you what your child should learn in school. My objective is to show you how to effectively explain those lessons and to motivate your child to learn without nightly arguments over homework.

I was fortunate, because for more than a decade I was a member of the board of education that ran our school system. This gave me the insight to realize that you and I must take control of our children's education. We can't assume schools will do the job without our help.

You've read in the press how school officials can't meet the needs of our kids because of the lack of money, unqualified faculty, and a barrage of social issues. I know some of these excuses are true and others contrived, but talking about these problems doesn't accomplish anything.

Your child still must learn all the lessons planned for her by the school district. If she doesn't, she won't be able to compete with other kids around the country for college and jobs. However, no one in your school district makes sure your child masters each lesson, and if *you* don't, then she could fall through the cracks without anyone knowing until it is too late.

In this book I'll show you how to keep tabs on your child's education and how to make up any missed lessons. The techniques I show will work without costing you a dime to implement. And they will work within any public- or private-school system.

My first book, *Getting the Best Education for Your Child,* showed how to use the rules of your school system to make sure your child receives a good education. Techniques discussed in that book were developed during the years when I was a school-board member, where I discovered the secrets vital to working with the educational community.

I take a different approach in this book. I show you how to be your child's coach and how to use techniques of professional educators to effectively communicate with your child, motivating her into making good grades in school.

The book is presented in two sections. The first section provides insight into

- how your child is graded;
- how to get your child psyched for homework;
- strategies for combating objections to doing homework;
- how to be an effective coach to your child;
- how to stand up for your child's rights in school.

The second section of the book is devoted to showing you specifically how to help your child make the grade in first through sixth grades. These are the formative years when basic skills are taught to form the foundation on which is built the rest of her education. The last chapter of the book shows you how to use computer resources and the Internet to help with homework assignments.

I thought I knew my daughters like a book until I spoke to a few educators who opened a whole new world to me. They taught me how to recognize behavioral clues. For example, once you identify your child's problem or deficiency, you can use this information to coach her into a better performance in school. Performance depends on conditioning your child. If, as a child, you cringed when you heard the word *homework*, then you've been conditioned to think homework is a negative activity. After reading this book, you'll use the same conditioning technique to make homework something you and your child look forward to each night.

My kids could be great lawyers. No matter how hard I tried to motivate them into starting homework, they'd counter with very convincing arguments why they shouldn't. It was frustrating, to say the least. I typically ran out of patience to play opposing counsel, then bullied them into doing the right thing.

Let's face it, none of us wants to spend all day doing something only to come home and do more of the same. Your child is no different and can contrive all kinds of excuses for avoiding homework. This leads to evening homework hassles.

I will take you through the obstacle course created by your kids to impede homework. You'll learn how to successfully handle any argument your child poses for not doing homework.

It amazes me how a professional football team goes from nearly last place to the league champs in a matter of a year simply by changing coaches. The players didn't change. The opposition didn't change. Only the coach.

You are your child's coach when it comes to homework. *You* can change a losing school year into a winning year by using proven techniques to improve your child's attitude about homework and motivate her into achieving excellent results. You need to know yourself and your child, then use effective communication to rekindle the excitement in her about school.

"The teacher never taught us how to solve this problem."
"The teacher is never available for help after school."

You've heard these excuses, but did you consider them to be true? Most parents don't and immediately accuse their child of being lazy. However, some excuses are true. This places the child in a difficult situation, because no one believes what he's saying.

We have to fight for our child's rights in school. From my years on the school board, I learned that teachers, the principal, and the administration can cause situations that make learning nearly impossible for our kids.

I'm going to take you behind the scenes to see how the system causes problems for your child and show you how to do something about it.

Although curriculum varies among school districts, there remains a core of skills in language, reading, and math that is central to all schools. Some of these skills are intuitive for you to explain to your child. Others are less obvious.

In *The Secrets to Good Grades*, you'll walk through the difficult lessons of grades one through six. You'll learn what skills your child is expected to learn and how to coach her through those lessons. You'll learn the techniques necessary to relate abstract concepts to someone your child's age.

Your school district cannot guarantee that every student will master every basic skill. Neither can I. However, most students have the capability to learn, but are not given enough time to learn. Instead of always playing catch-up, your child can build up a safety net of learning skills that will prevent her from falling behind in class. She'll learn good basic concepts in reading, grammar, and math, using tricks professional educators rely on to teach children K–6.

The Secrets to
Good Grades

"Johnny's mom went to school with the teacher. That's why he gets good marks."

"The teacher is just getting even because you always complain to the principal about him."

And the mother of all excuses, "The teacher never taught us what was on the test."

Yes, we've all experienced this panic. I'd study like there was no tomorrow and even recruited Mom as a study partner. It was like getting psyched for the Super Bowl. Then the moment of truth was at hand. I peered down at the big exam confident I had this one bagged. Then reality hit. Nothing, I mean nothing I studied was on the test. Another D was coming and there was nothing I could do.

At the end of every marking period, your child's teacher has to summarize each child's performance into a single grade. This isn't easy to do. Teachers realize so much is riding on the decision. A low grade could have Mom knocking down the principal's door, forcing the teacher to support her claim.

Giving too many low grades brings the teacher's performance to the attention of school officials. That's like opening a Pandora's box. No one wants his performance to be scrutinized by his boss.

Of course, giving everyone in the class high marks will keep parents at bay, but this, too, might raise the curiosity of the principal. It is quite unusual for any class to have all straight-A students.

So experienced teachers follow the bell curve. A small percentage of the class will have low marks; a similar percentage will have high marks; and most of the students receive grades in the middle range. Where does your child fit on the bell curve?

We'd like to think our child's position is the recognition of hard work. However, in some situations, position on the bell curve depends on many factors outside of the classroom, including the excuses we'd hoped would save us from Mom's evil eye. And one little-known factor— your child's grades in other classes.

It is not unusual to find some teachers giving your child the same range of grades as your child received from previous teachers. If your child received low grades in other classes and you didn't complain, then low grades become acceptable to you, the principal, and the teacher. Your child isn't expected to perform at a higher level.

So the safest and simplest way to grade your child is for the teacher to continue the trend set by your child's former teachers. Is this fair? Of course not. This demoralizes your child. Not every teacher adheres to this job-saving rule. However, even the best teachers can fall into this trap at your child's expense.

Grades your child receives in school do not represent anything more than your child's teacher's unscientific assessment of your child. Typically, no one in your school district questions or oversees the way the teacher determines your child's grade unless you complain.

The grade your child receives does not tell you what lessons your child learned and what lessons your child still needs to learn. In fact, if you are like most parents, you were never given a list of facts and skills your child is expected to learn during the school year. I call this your child's master plan. Educators refer to this as course proficiencies.

TALES OUT OF SCHOOL: NO. 356

Kids concoct intriguing ways to avoid preparing for tests. I thought I'd heard them all until a few years ago on the day before a final exam.

This day a student stayed after class to show the teacher an obit from an out-of-town newspaper. The child's aunt had passed away and the family was leaving for the funeral that evening, so he wouldn't be available to take the final exam.

The teacher had a problem. There wasn't any time left in the school year to make up the final exam. School would be over before his family returned from the funeral. A dilemma, just as the youngster anticipated. He was told not to worry. The teacher would handle matters.

Party time! School was over, no cramming for finals. What more could a guy ask for? He was celebrating in his room when the doorbell rang. He could hear voices from downstairs.

"We're the crisis-intervention team from your son's school. He told us about your loss. Please accept our condolences. We're called out anytime a close family member has passed away,

to help your son and the rest of your family
tragedy."

Then the words that brought the party to a scree
"What? No one died in our family."

Summer school, here he comes.

Your Child's Master Plan

Throughout the years I spent in school, I never realized someone painstakingly planned the skills and facts I learned—or more correctly, was supposed to learn. It wasn't until I changed roles and became a parent, then was elected to my community's board of education that I realized a master educational plan exists for every child.

Here's a little insight into how your child's master plan is created. The school board assigns the professional staff to devise a list of skills and facts children in the school district should learn by the time they complete high school. This is the district's curriculum. In some states, a core curriculum is specified by the state education department and is enhanced by local school districts. The combination becomes the district's curriculum.

The list is quite long and is divided into shorter lists, each of which is assigned to a grade level, becoming your child's master plan for the school year. The *course proficiencies*, as these lists are also called, are presented to the school board for review, comment, adjustment, and approval.

Once approved by the school board, the course proficiencies become law-enforceable in the courts. Teachers cannot waver from this master plan, even though they may disagree with it. If they do, they could be fired—even if they are tenured.

Your child's teacher translates the course proficiencies into daily lesson plans. A lesson plan shows how the teacher intends to teach your child the course proficiencies and includes plans for homework assignments, tests, and other activities.

Making Sure Your Child's Master Plan Is Followed

Moments after taking the oath as a member of the board of education I was transformed from being just another parent to having near-godfather status in the school district. And talk about some royal butt-kissing! Now every administrator, principal, and teacher couldn't do enough to help me. These were the same people who tied me up in red tape when I was a parent and made a simple request.

Being on the inside with this "super" power gave me access to information you and other parents are not permitted to see. It was like being a fly on the wall at all those secret meetings I imagined happen in government: those smoke-filled rooms where deals are cut, decisions regarding my child's education are made, and 75 percent of my property taxes is spent. Of course, smoking is no longer permitted.

The first time I learned that a master plan for my child's education existed, I requested to see it. The plan was in simple English, on a few sheets of paper that any parent could understand, and was public information to anyone upon request.

However, I learned that many school officials prefer to keep course proficiencies a treasured secret. The reason became apparent when I suggested replacing report cards with the course proficiencies and requiring teachers to check off proficiencies learned by each child.

Course proficiencies are the list of obligations of your school district. Each year your school district and your child's teacher promise to teach your child those skills. No one uses the course proficiencies as a checklist to make sure obligations are fulfilled. No one knows if the goods you paid for were really delivered.

Demand to see the course proficiencies for your child at the beginning of the school year. Don't take "no" for an answer. And don't accept the sanitized version school officials sometimes hand out to parents. Make sure you receive the actual pages approved by the school board.

You can get an official copy of your child's course proficiencies from the central office of your school district. Ask for a copy of the *school board's policy* that specifies the course proficiencies for your child's grade.

Policies are rules that govern your school district and contain very specific wording that must be followed by the faculty and staff. The sanitized version of the policy contains someone else's words, and their interpretative version could be misleading.

Throughout the school year, ask your child's teacher to check off proficiencies your child has learned. Do this after you receive each report card.

Keep an eye peeled for proficiencies that haven't been checked by the end of the school year. They signify your child is missing important educational building blocks that must be made up before your child begins the next school year.

Course proficiencies are better than report cards for monitoring your child's progress. For example, the letter *B* on a report card simply tells you some course proficiencies were not learned by your child— but you don't know which ones are missing.

There is nothing preventing the teacher from checking off all the course proficiencies at the end of the school year even though some of the lessons were not taught. That's to be expected. However, eventually the missing lessons will become apparent in later years when another of your child's teachers realizes your child is missing the prerequisites for learning new lessons.

You have heard teachers complain, "How can I teach them to solve word problems when they don't know how to multiply?" If this happens to your child, review your previous course proficiencies to find out which teacher taught your child how to multiply. You have the paper trail that leads you and school officials to the teacher who did not live up to her obligation.

You've also caused another little-known event to occur. Peer pressure by colleagues can motivate the teacher into cleaning up her act, because her work is preventing other teachers from doing their jobs. This is far more effective than actions taken by your school board.

Time on Task

Why does your child miss lessons? I've asked many school officials, administrators, and teachers this question. The answer: not enough time in the school year for your child to learn all the skills she is required to master.

The school year hasn't changed much since you and I sat in the classroom. It is still about 180 days, depending on the state in which you live. However, this is deceiving. I calculated the days my child was taught by her regular teacher and discovered her school year was actually 144 days. I then surveyed the rest of the school district and found the worst case to be 90 days of school.

Children in my school district had between 90 days and 144 days to learn all the lessons planned for 180 days of school. Obviously, there will be missed lessons. The reasons for the shortened school year are many:

- your child and your child's teacher out sick;
- teacher conferences during class time;
- shortened class periods for faculty in-service training;
- inclement weather;
- half days counted as legal full days of school.

You can read more about this topic in my book *Getting the Best Education for Your Child*. Your school district is likely cheating your child out of an education just as the potato-chip industry sells large bags of potato chips with contents that barely fill the bottom of the bag.

PROCEDURE:
How to calculate the actual time your child spends learning in school

1. Get a notebook.
2. Carefully track the number of school days that your child has her regular teacher and days that a substitute teacher takes over the class. Let's face it, substitute teachers are little more than baby-sitters. I usually get into trouble by saying this, but it's true. You and I always looked forward to having a substitute because it was like a day off from school.
3. Note the days you kept your child out of school. Regardless of how sincere the reason is for the absence, the time still must be deducted from the 180 days of school.

4. Keep track of half days of school, too. Very little learning takes place when kids know they'll be in school only a half day.

5. Track the number of party days and other events that take away from lessons. You remember those times when a mom convinced the teacher to hold a birthday party in class for her child. The party was scheduled for lunchtime; however, it always managed to conclude just about the end of the school day.

6. Tally the number of whole and partial days your child was not taught.

7. Subtract those days from the total days in the school year.

8. Review the course proficiencies and ask yourself if your child's teacher has enough time to teach the class. If not, then it is likely your child will miss lessons, lessons that the school district has no intention of making up.

9. Share the results with other parents and your school board so new policies are enacted—or existing ones enforced—to assure your child is given sufficient time to learn.

Monitoring Your Child's Performance

The best way to assure your child makes the grade is to make sure she learns *all* her lessons. I underscore the need for all lessons, because each lesson is a building block and all the building blocks fit together to give your child a good start in life.

However, when lessons are missed, your child won't be able to keep up with the class. Demands will be made that she will be incapable of meeting. Think for a moment how you would feel sitting in the class when everyone except you can whiz through a multistep math equation.

Serious problems such as a loss of attentiveness and a feeling of inadequacy can arise as your child falls further behind. She could lose interest in school and begin to get into trouble. Yelling and making threats won't get her back on track. The only way to avoid these problems with your child is by making sure your child doesn't miss lessons.

PROCEDURE:
Making sure your child doesn't miss lessons

1. Get a copy of the course proficiencies for the current school year.
2. Make sure you fully understand the skills and facts your child is expected to learn.
3. Ask your child's teacher or the principal for clarification if any of the proficiencies escape you.
4. Plan to meet regularly with your child's teacher, ideally at the end of a marking period.
5. Ask the teacher to check off proficiencies learned during the period. If you get resistance, don't argue with the teacher. Instead politely ask the principal to join the conversation. And if you still get resistance, then elevate the issue to the chief school administrator and finally to your school board. Don't hesitate and don't accept any excuses from school officials. It is your legal right to know. Your child's future is at stake. Read my book *Getting the Best Education for Your Child* for specific instructions on how to complain to get results.
6. Monitor the lessons the teacher presents to your child.
7. Scan through your child's notebooks and exercise books.
8. Carefully review tests. Don't accept the excuse that the teacher won't let your child take home the test for your review. Follow up with a call to the teacher and arrange to see the test.
9. Pay careful attention to homework assignments.
10. Look for indications that each of the course proficiencies is being taught.
11. Check off the proficiencies when you have seen evidence that the proficiency is being taught. All of the proficiencies on your list should have two check marks alongside them: one you made and the other made by the teacher.
12. Bring to the teacher's attention the fact that you haven't seen evidence that all the proficiencies are being covered in class. You might learn that the teacher plans to cover the material sometime in the future before the school year is over.

13. A frank discussion with your child's teacher quietly puts the teacher on notice that you are carefully monitoring the progress of your child's education. Very few parents know how to take such an active role in their child's education. And that's why I believe some school officials and educators can get away with cheating students out of a full education.

Homework and Making the Grade

How do you help your child make up missed lessons? I suggest a two-stage attack. First, complain to school officials. Let them know your child needs additional help. Keep the pressure on until they come to her aid. Complain all the way up to the school board and you're bound to get results.

Your child's education needs more of a shoring up rather than a complete makeover. The place where you can become most effective is with helping your child with homework assignments. Homework can be transformed from a chore into an activity allowing your child to catch up with the rest of the class and make up those missed lessons.

Homework has a negative feeling among students—and former students like you and me. We looked at homework as a punishment rather than a challenge or a way to maintain our competitive edge.

For parents, homework signifies a nightly battle that typically culminates in the child stubbornly going to bed following a half hour of screaming threats by Mom. (Somehow Dad manages to remain neutral by watching television and pretending not to hear a word—although Mom can hear the slamming windows coming from the neighbor's house.)

So homework is the second tool toward making up those missed lessons. You can avoid the negative connotations—and those dreaded fights with your child—by creating a positive spin on homework. Throughout the remaining chapters I'll show you techniques used to make homework an activity your child and you look forward to each night.

Homework is also required by policy of your school district. Teachers must give your child a specific number of hours of homework every night. Visit your school district's central office and ask for a copy of the school board's homework policy. This is public information that cannot be withheld from you. Compare the policy to your child's homework assignments to make sure the homework is in compliance with the policy. Bring to the attention of the principal any serious discrepancies.

Remember that homework is to be done at home and not in school. Be alert for teachers who substitute homework for classroom exercises. Your child needs both classroom exercises and homework exercises to master her skills.

Homework as a Safety Net

Every one of us learns at a different pace. Some students, like me, require time for lessons to sink in. Others, like my wife, catch on quickly to new things. The teacher's job is to present material at a pace that allows most students to grasp each lesson, and then she moves on, leaving slower learners to fend for themselves.

There isn't enough time in the school year to make sure everyone in the class masters each lesson. This is an educational reality and there is very little a school district can do to change the situation.

When I talk about slow learners, I'm not referring to children who have learning disabilities. Special remedial programs are available and mandated by law to assure those students have sufficient time to learn.

In the ideal school district, a teacher will have one student and can tailor the curriculum to the learning style of the child, who has sufficient time to master each lesson.

A more typical school groups youngsters together based upon their perceived ability to learn. You and I know these groupings as the class of A students, B students, and C students. Educators call the grouping *tracking*.

At first glance, tracking makes sense. A teacher can better adapt lessons to children who learn at relatively the same pace. However, tracking unjustly categorizes and stigmatizes students.

Students in the A class tend to develop a superiority complex, when in reality they are average kids. C students are looked upon by other students, teachers, and themselves as slackers, unable to keep pace with the other students. In reality they, too, are average kids. Many school districts have moved away from tracking students for this reason.

Your attitude about school and homework plays a critical role in whether or not your child keeps pace with her schoolwork. If you take homework seriously and work with your child, you'll be strengthening your child's ability to learn. You don't need to be a genius to help your child. With a little coaching from the teacher and applying techniques I talk about in this book, any parent can give their child a leg up in school.

You can use homework as a safety net. Homework gives your child a second chance to learn when your child is unable to understand lessons taught in the classroom.

Mastering or Master of Taking Tests?

I thought I started World War III when I asked a principal why youngsters didn't master long division by the sixth grade. The course proficiencies indicated the topic was taught. However, the results of a standardized test revealed that most of the students could not solve the long-division problems.

"No one told us you wanted the children to master long division," the principal responded.

You can imagine my reaction. The presumption you and I make is that our children will become proficient in their schoolwork. Never make assumptions. I learned school officials design a curriculum with one of three objectives in mind:

- Students will have a basic understanding of the subject.
- Students will master the subject.
- Students will have knowledge to pass standardized tests.

School districts score high in standardized tests because they train students to pass those tests. However, tests prove very little. The result of any test indicates only what your child knew at the moment the test was taken. Test results do not take into consideration factors such as your child

- panicked when taking the test;
- was ill;
- didn't understand the questions;
- had problems understanding the instructions;
- was overly cautious and ran out of time to complete the test.

Those who support standardized tests, like test publishers, claim everyone taking the test is under the same constraints. However, that may not be true. A case in point involved a sixth-grade class who were required to take a statewide test. They did poorly on the test, the results of which were published in the county newspaper. Parents were up in arms, screaming at school officials for doing such a poor job of educating their children.

However, the sixth graders had been scheduled to learn the test material four weeks *after* the test was given. State education officials assumed all school districts would have taught all the material by the time the test was given.

The Hidden Benefits of Homework

Homework does more than give your child a chance to catch up to the rest of the class. Homework is the first time in your child's life when she takes on the responsibility to complete an assignment. It is your child's responsibility—not yours—for making sure directions are followed and homework is completed accurately and on time.

My mom would say homework builds character, independence, and accountability—a solid foundation for becoming a successful adult. Of course, I thought homework was just busywork that got in the way of important things like television. I didn't know any of my mom's friends who did homework after working all day. They just sat around, popped a few cans of soda, and sat back for an evening of television.

If coached properly, your child will slowly learn to plan ahead, manage time, and develop patience to solve homework problems—or any other kind of problem. You'll need to provide nurturing support. In upcoming chapters, I'll give you some tips I received through my years of speaking with educators.

Another important but frequently overlooked benefit of homework is its diagnostic capabilities. Your child has much to understand. Besides reading, writing, and arithmetic, kids need to learn how to focus on a problem and be attentive to think through to a solution. Children need to learn how to learn and how to avoid becoming frustrated when quick remedies don't work.

I believe that everyone can become anything they strive for—a doctor, lawyer, plumber, electrician—as long as they know how to learn and have the maturity to persevere and work through problems.

Whenever your child sees a whiz kid perform what seems to be a miracle, remember there must be a trick involved. Your child just needs to learn the trick, too, to become a whiz kid—and those tricks are taught in school.

Homework enables your child's teacher and you to look for clues of trouble that interfere with your child's ability to learn. There are a number of obstacles that can keep your child from learning. Problems can range from physiological and psychological factors to less severe conditions that are easily overcome by special educational programs that your school district is required to provide.

Homework Can Be Trouble

The press always tells us that you and I need more quality time with our children. I'm sure homework time in your house doesn't meet the criteria for quality time. In most homes, the word *homework* is synonymous with trouble. That's with a capital *T*, my friend.

The question you must ask yourself and your child's teacher is, why is your child having difficulty doing homework assignments? Is she not properly psyched to deal with schoolwork at home? Could the problem stem from a more serious, underlying problem that is manifesting itself during homework time, but really is the reason for your child's low performance in school?

Clues of trouble can be masked by your closeness to the problem. All of us get personally drawn into the ardent task of our child's homework. We want our child to succeed so much that we lose patience and make demands that our child can't fulfill.

I remember back when I was busy jabbering with the guy next to me when the teacher was showing the class how to solve a word problem.

The teacher didn't catch me, so I thought I got away with skirting the rules.

Then a similar problem appeared on a homework assignment. Obviously I was in trouble. No matter how much time I took to read the problem, I couldn't get the answer. Then Mom came in and looked over my shoulder. She, too, couldn't solve the problem, but she wouldn't let on.

It was like a symphony. She began with encouraging remarks. As the evening progressed, her frustrations vibrated in her voice. There I was, between a rock and a hard place. I didn't know how to solve the problem and I dreaded Mom's next visit. The final crescendo was reached at the same time almost every evening. By 11 P.M., both of us were tired and frustrated. She would scream that she'd like to shove the solution into my head. I began to cry. We both gave up and headed for bed.

This whole experience was a symptom of a problem. Fortunately, goofing off during class caused the problem. However, the same symptom could have signaled other, more serious difficulties. These include poor academic skills or simply not knowing how to study.

Then there could be more serious problems such as attention deficit disorder, which means your child is unable to keep focus on a task for any length of time. Special help is required from your school district to work with this condition. Likewise, there could be other underlying learning factors that need correction.

These symptoms can also indicate problems in the classroom with the teacher. Not every teacher your child will have will do a bang-up job. You and I remember that a few of our teachers had trouble keeping the class in line, let alone teaching lessons.

Homework problems can be caused by inappropriate assignments. Assignments should give a child the ability to succeed, much like doing a connect-the-dots puzzle. These puzzles are designed to challenge, yet be fair so your child can complete them within a reasonable time.

Not all teachers adhere to this philosophy of homework. One of my children's teachers believed in assigning homework problems covering topics not taught in class. He wanted the kids to struggle and try to find the solution, knowing that practically none of the students would succeed.

My wife and I were frustrated to no end. We read the assignment and searched the textbook for clues to no avail. The problem stemmed with the teacher, not our child. Take it from me, my child didn't learn anything from the homework.

TALES OUT OF SCHOOL: NO. 542

No matter how much you think you understand, you still get it wrong—and you don't realize you're wrong until it's too late. This happens to all of us, including me back when I was in kindergarten. Admittedly, I don't remember much from those years, but certain events seem to be etched in my memory for life.

I was one of those five-year-olds who wasn't too thrilled to leave the comforts of home and spend a day in a strange building with kids I didn't know. Especially when I discovered Mom was going to leave me by myself.

I guess you could say I had a mind of my own and things that made sense to me didn't make sense to the teacher. And it was almost impossible for this five-year-old to change the teacher's mind.

Trouble began the first rainy day. All the kindergartners at Horace Mann Public School had practically the same color raincoat and were storing them in the same closet. Well, almost all of them. I wasn't going to lose my raincoat in that mess. I planned to keep it on during class. No one would notice.

The teacher didn't agree with me. Let's say we were at a stalemate. I wasn't going to take off the raincoat and she wasn't going to start class until I removed it. That was fine with me. I had no place to go until Mom got back anyway. Then she yelled out the window to Mom, who had just started to walk home with the other mothers.

Mom had a way of avoiding arguments with me. She simply ripped the coat off my back and hung it in the closet as she mumbled some juicy words leaving the classroom. This was embarrassing, but what's a guy to do?

Trying to smooth a few ruffled feathers, the teacher asked me to lead the class in the Pledge of Allegiance.

"I pledge allegiance for Richard Stands," I began loudly.

"That's 'for which it stands.' "

I gave the teacher that look—the one that normally got me banned from watching TV for a week if Mom was around.

"Why is she changing the words? Wait till the principal hears about it," I thought.

The class finished the rest of the Pledge of Allegiance for me. After class, the teacher asked me why I pledged allegiance for Richard Stands.

"He's the principal!"

So I was a little confused. I thought that each morning the class was paying honor to our principal, Richard Stands. How was a little guy to know about these things? However, I was right about the raincoat. The rest of the class left the room by the time I finished my chat with the teacher. Just as I expected, one of the kids walked off with my raincoat.

Your Role

I remember the times my wife and I sat quietly rooting for my daughter to complete her homework. She had five word problems to solve and like most of us was losing patience when the answers didn't come quickly. She wanted to solve the problem herself without our help. So my wife and I kept our distance—something very hard to do when you know you can help. You don't like to see your child struggle. Every so often, my wife made up some excuse to walk by to note her progress.

"Do you want a glass of soda?" My wife was going to the kitchen anyway.

Normally the only response was a look of frustration that shouted, "Can't you see I'm busy? Don't bother me."

We sat in the next room, pretending to watch TV. Each of us wanted to lend a hand. We listened for clues for assistance. You know how it is. Your kid knows she's in a bind and wants you to bail her out, but is too proud to ask. So she sighs loudly and rustles papers in hopes of gaining your attention.

But no sighing. No rustling. It was time for the next recon mission. I used the ploy of trying to find missing papers that I had left on the table. This just happened to be around the area where my daughter was doing her homework. I got the same look as my wife.

Finally, two hours passed when an "I got it!" reverberated from my daughter. Finally, she stumbled onto the method for solving the word problems. The insurmountable obstacle was overcome.

Probably the hardest thing for you and me as parents is to see our child in need and not run to help. Yet, we know that we can't be there to help our child all the time. Part of growing up is for our youngsters to learn how to solve problems without assistance from Mom and Dad. And that's one of the benefits of homework assignments.

You and I have an important role in our child's homework assignments—and the role is not to solve homework problems for them. We must avoid the natural tendency to do our child's homework. For one thing, we might come up with the wrong answer. I've done that a few times myself.

For another, you're sending the wrong message to your child: hem and haw and put off doing homework, and then someone else will do it for you. No matter how long it takes and whatever excuses your child conjured up, *don't do your child's homework assignment.*

Kids are very clever. They know just how to manipulate us. And if we are not careful, we can be suckered into doing the homework assignment without realizing it. You're bound to have the experience I had with my daughter.

She'd lay out on the table all the material she needed to do homework, then begin with the first problem. The look in her eye should have told me what was in store. It took a few minutes, but the trap was laid. First, she neatly rewrote the problem on a sheet of paper before calling me over.

Then she baited me with, "I'm not sure how to do this problem. Can you show me?"

The trap was opened and I was walking smiling into it. What dad would avoid the opportunity to become a hero in front of his daughter?

What a sucker. I fell for it every time. I sat down and worked out the problem for her.

"Now this problem is solved a little differently, isn't it?" she'd ask innocently.

What would any dad do? So I showed her how to solve the next problem. I ended up doing all the problems under the pretense of showing her how to arrive at the solutions.

Later in the book I'll give you tips on how to avoid the traps of our offspring and tips on how to coach your child through homework. For now, here are some dos and don'ts that will help to define your role.

PROCEDURE:
How to define your role in your child's homework

1. Do a portion of a homework problem to get your child started in the right direction, but stop long before the solution becomes apparent.

2. Do step in and help your child think through tough problems that can become frustrating. Homework is easier to complete when calm heads prevail—both yours and your child's.

3. Do help your child organize the time allotted for homework. Have your child divide homework assignments into the no-brainers and the I-have-no-idea-how-to-solve-it categories. My suggestion is to begin with a no-brainer so your child gets a feeling of success the first time at bat. Difficult problems should be tackled early in the evening when your child will have a clearer mind and not feel fatigued. After a couple of difficult problems, switch to a no-brainer to break the pace and give your child a feeling of success again.

4. Don't help or encourage your child to avoid doing part or all of the homework assignment. No excuses are acceptable even if doing so jeopardizes your child's grades. Grades give your child an indication of success. Unearned grades camouflage reality.

5. Don't become your child's teacher. That's not your role, and

your method of teaching might conflict with techniques used in the classroom.

6. Don't correct your child's homework. Make sure your child gives a best effort, but allow for mistakes. Mistakes provide clues to your child's teacher as to which lessons must be reinforced. Your child's teacher has no way of knowing that your child has not learned the lesson if she hands in mistake-free work.

Your Child's Role

Your child's job is to hoodwink you into doing the homework assignment—or at least conspire to avoid doing it herself. You and I made the same attempts when we were confronted with mounds of assignments that interfered with more important activities.

Kids are clever and parents are suckers. It goes with the territory. However, your child, with coaching from you, must attack homework head-on with a can-do attitude. Homework shouldn't be looked on as a chore, but as a way for your child to prove lessons have been learned—and as a way of being competitive.

Unfortunately, most kids—and parents—think sports is the only competitive activity in school. Hours are spent after school and on weekends polishing athletic skills, making sure techniques are learned to win the game.

Few of us ever stop to realize that those athletic skills rarely turn into job skills. The student body and sometimes the community focus on kids who are super athletes. They are hailed as heroes and given professional-athlete treatment in the press.

Then high school graduation arrives—and the bubble bursts. No longer are they superstars. They must now compete in the real world. Superstars are in for a shock if they don't make the grade in the classroom. And the key to this success is hitting the books just as hard—or harder—as hitting the ball field.

When I was in high school, school officials managed to keep our focus on both schoolwork and athletics. Kids had to make the grade in the classroom before they could even think about heading for the ball field. Coaches demanded study practices where the team got together to hit the books. Fellow students tutored athletes. It was a team effort to make grades.

Then there were the school sweaters, which were the most visible sign that academics and athletics were equally important. At the end of junior year, kids who excelled in sports or academics were awarded letterman sweaters—bright white sweaters bordered with blue for sports and gold for academics. A big blue or gold letter was imprinted with the symbols of their accomplishment. The sweater was a badge of honor aspired to by every underclassman.

Now your school may not motivate your child the way my school did, simply because of lack of finances. Sweaters cost money, money that is frequently allocated for school supplies and other necessary expenses. However, you can create your own incentive plan (I'll show you how in later chapters) to motivate your child into making the grade.

Your child has a job to do. And it's your job to make sure your child knows how to do this job. Here are a few tips that will keep your child on track for making the grade.

PROCEDURE:
How to define your child's role in homework

Your child should

1. Know the objective of each lesson and homework assignment. It is very difficult for any of us to work hard to solve what seems to be a meaningless assignment. Our attitude changes once the clear objective is acknowledged.

2. Know all the steps required to reach the objective. Identify milestones along the route to learning the lesson. This helps your child know if progress is being made—and when the end is near.

3. Know the way to achieve the objective. A youngster must learn how to multiply before solving a word problem requiring multiplication.

4. Speak up if a roadblock is encountered. All of us find it dif-

ficult to ask for help, since it exposes our weaknesses. However, solutions come more easily if your child calls you, the teacher, or friends for help.

5. Know how to think through a problem. Sometimes help isn't available immediately, therefore your child needs to know how to research possible solutions until help arrives.

6. Know how to properly confront the teacher when there is a disagreement or confusion about an assignment. Some kids are apprehensive about approaching an adult to clarify an issue. There is a tendency for youngsters not to question authority. You and I probably have the same apprehensions. However, you must show your child how to overcome this mental block. The youngster must know there is a right and a wrong way to raise an issue.

7. Know you are willing to intervene if conflicts arise between her and the teacher. Your child must be confident that you won't prejudge either side of the issue and that you will look fairly at the facts before reacting. Let your child know you will support her if the facts prove the teacher isn't being fair and that you'll support the teacher if your child is mistaken.

2.

Conditioning Your Child for Doing Homework

- Things You Probably Don't Know about Your Child
- A Peek inside Your Child's Head
- Avoiding the Condition for Failure
- Setting the Stage for Homework
- Pick a Good Time to Do Homework
- Pick a Good Location to Do Homework
- Plenty of Supplies on Hand
- Set Down the Law

Something strange occurs between kindergarten and first grade. I've seen this happen with my youngest daughter on her first day of school. The few hours after supper in our home are reserved for homework. This is the time I spend writing books, my oldest tackles school assignments, and my wife works on her college class.

Sitting alongside of my oldest daughter was our youngest, who with pencil in hand scribbled on some paper. We chuckled and asked her what she was doing.

"My homework," she responded with a look that said don't bother me.

Homework in kindergarten? That's hard to believe. My feelings were confirmed in a call to my daughter's teacher. However, the conversation was enlightening. This is why I always recommend you open a dialogue with your child's teacher, because she has a wealth of information about your child and is eager to share it with you.

I was told my daughter was carefully observing the family's routine. She heard the term *homework* talked about in relation to my oldest daughter. She knew homework was performed on a school night after supper. And since she started school today, she obviously needed to join with the rest of the family doing homework.

Her enthusiasm to do schoolwork at home waned by the next school year, of course. This seemed strange, for nothing had changed in our routine between kindergarten and first grade.

What we experienced is not unusual. Many children lose interest in doing homework as they mature. Schoolwork becomes more difficult. Outside interests grow. Classmates become more influential than parents. This is especially true in single-parent homes and homes where both parents are away during after-school hours.

It seems that you and I start losing control of our children when they begin school. Each year we lose progressively more control and influence until we are practically ignored by the time our kids reach high school. Don't become too alarmed. Think back to when you and I were growing up. How much influence did our parents have on us, as we grew older? We survived, so there is every reason to believe your child will also survive.

What can you and I do to keep alive the thrill experienced by most five-year-olds when they begin kindergarten? The answer lies with conditioning at an early age. Conditioning instills your child with sets of procedures that show her ways to succeed.

We condition our children every day—showing them how to take care of bathroom needs; properly dress for the day; behave in school and exhibit manners when interacting with family, friends, and strangers. Conditioning requires certain behaviors to be repeated until the steps are performed subconsciously.

The effects of conditioning linger with you and me and our children throughout our lives. Remember your first back-to-school night? You joined other parents sitting in your child's classroom listening to the teacher. Were you listening objectively or did something in your mind say, "I hope she doesn't ask me any questions or give us a test"?

I experience flashbacks every back-to-school night. It begins when

I open the door to the school. The familiar smell of the hallways triggers memories. I am the student again scurrying around to find my classroom—my daughter's classroom, I should say.

As the teacher speaks, I find myself taking notes. For what, I don't know. It's a habit and I'm not the only parent doing it. None of the parents attempts to leave until the teacher dismisses us. I also notice the teacher falling into a similar pattern by standing in front of the classroom and lecturing to us as if we were students.

Our conditioning has a negative effect. We don't think of ourselves as equals with our child's teacher, which interferes with holding a frank conversation about our child. Avoid this by discussing your child with her teacher on neutral grounds and not in the classroom or an office. Classrooms and offices are set up to give the teacher the psychological advantage. Try

- a conference room;
- a remote table in the cafeteria;
- even a stroll around the block.

Your job is to condition your child at an early age with procedures that give her a leg up in school. Our moms browbeat into us good cleanliness and social rules, which we instinctively pass along to our children. You and I must do the same with good homework skills and a can-do attitude that helps them make the grade.

Things You Probably Don't Know about Your Child

You and I like to find easy solutions to complex problems. We expect all murders to be solved within fifty minutes—without commercials. We expect professionals like physicians and teachers not to make mistakes. We expect to quickly condition our kids to be excited about homework and approach every assignment enthusiastically. Unfortunately, the real world doesn't work this way.

We take for granted that educators know how our children learn. We send our kids to school and somehow they return educated. However, the way our children learn is complex and not a precise science. Those who study learning and related disciplines have generally settled on several theories that help explain how your child learns. Teachers apply these theories in the classroom. You and I can use the same theories to help condition our youngsters for homework.

There are five theories teachers find useful when dealing with children. These are the learning theory, the model theory, the system theory, the humanistic theory, and the behavior-modification theory.

I thought I'd need a degree from Columbia's Teachers College to understand these theories. I was wrong. They are not difficult to understand, and with a little common sense you can immediately apply them to your child.

I remember my high school days when Mom took one look and declared I was born unorganized and a slob. No offense was taken. You can't argue with the truth. And little did I know Mom's comments were truer than she even realized. According to the *learning theory*, children are born unorganized. Organization skills that give kids structure in their daily routines must be learned.

I quietly panicked when my child's teacher told me about the learning theory. The implication was that my child was unorganized, which was not the case. The teacher said that most parents teach their children organizational skills naturally through conditioning. You and I have been applying the learning theory each time we nag our kids to clean their rooms.

Kids catch on quickly, which is the whole idea of the learning theory. Once their daily routine is organized, then your child subconsciously organizes the rest of her life without your help. You've taught her the skill of how to organize.

Mom would sound off with a few choice words whenever a crazy driver cut her off. I just stared in shock the first time this occurred. I'd have my mouth washed with soap if I used those words. She caught the look and felt embarrassed, then she came back with a statement only a mom can get away with saying: "Do what I say, not what I do."

Unfortunately, Mom's truism contradicts the well-established *model theory*. Our children do what we do, not what we say. This is probably the most valuable educational theory you and I should master. You've probably seen examples of the modeling theory, like when your four-year-old playacted with toys mimicking nearly everything you do around the house. If you're like me, you thought this behavior was cute. In reality your child was learning from you.

The modeling theory is one of the reasons your child's teacher looks forward to meeting parents on back-to-school night. It's a kind of game teachers play. Match the kid with the parent.

TALES OUT OF SCHOOL: NO. 974

One Saturday afternoon I was sitting in the barbershop getting a trim when my hair stylist was called to the phone. I heard one side of the conversation, but that was enough for me to guess what was happening on the other end of the line.

"Mom," the stylist said, "you can't do that anymore." Pause.

"I know you don't mean to, but the kids are repeating it in school."

Mom was from Italy and baby-sat for the kids after school. Trouble came with a call from the teacher. She had returned a low-scored test to one of her students, and then the youngster got mad and startled the teacher by saying, "I'm going to kill yea."

The hair stylist couldn't understand where the child picked up the expression. No one in her home used such language. But when she picked up the kids, she heard Grandma slam a drawer closed, yelling, "I'm going to kill yea."

The modeling theory is complemented by the *system theory*. The system theory states that our kids grow up in a system of relationships that begins with our family. If the system functions properly, then our kids function well. If not, then problems within our family can appear as problems with our kids.

Your family provides a foundation from which your child explores the world outside your home. Your family also provides a secure, safe haven where your child can return to receive love even when things aren't going well in school and with friends.

Kids need a stable home life if they are to deal successfully with the topsy-turvy world of school. And by stable, I don't mean your home must be like the *Brady Bunch*. Even a single-parent home can provide continuity that gives the feeling of security.

Nearly half of the youngsters in my child's school come from single-parent homes, yet most have no problems learning. Kids easily adjust to new situations as long as there is a basic degree of stability at home.

Latchkey kids, for example, are conditioned to go home to an empty house, knowing that Mom will arrive around 5:30 P.M. and neighbors are available until then for help. Problems arise when Mom doesn't come home on time. The routine is broken and creates a situation the child isn't conditioned to handle.

In retrospect, the system theory hit home for me when I was in the third grade. My home life up until that point was stable. Mom stayed home with me while Dad worked. Toward the end of the second grade, things changed radically. Dad lost his job and started drinking heavily. Mom's concerns for him quickly turned from sympathy, to anger, to fear.

Soon this seven-year-old found more stability at school than at home. Something was wrong and I didn't understand what was happening. My emotions triggered life-threatening asthmatic attacks. My home life went from bad to worse by the third grade when my parents separated. I was out sick for most of the school year and was forced to repeat the third grade.

It wasn't until the fifth grade that things stabilized at home. Mom settled into a job that paid just enough to keep us afloat. I fell into the latchkey-kid routine. For me, things were normal and once again I subconsciously looked at home as a secure and loving place. And my schoolwork improved dramatically.

The *humanistic theory* repeats what my mom and yours have been saying to us for years: you accomplish more with a compliment than you do with a slur.

You and I—and your child—instinctively react to situations based upon how we interpret clues. If under attack, we go into a defensive mode. If being taught, we go into a learning mode.

Clues indicate the kind of situation that we're experiencing. When you display a snarling face and speak angrily, your child instinctively goes on the defensive, which is counterproductive to learning. An excited tone in your voice and a similar expression foster a learning situation.

I'll admit having mixed feelings about the benefits of the humanistic theory. Sweetness and candy can go just so far. Sometimes kids need something to shake them up and get them back on track. Once on track again, the humanistic theory can be used to stroke your child's ego and rebuild your child's self-esteem.

Alternating between sweetness and anger is characteristic of the *behavior-modification theory*, where positive behavior is treated with sweetness and negative behavior is treated with anger. Teachers have warned me that this carrot-and-stick approach doesn't last too long. You'll find your child deciding the punishment is acceptable and doing the negative behavior anyway.

TALES OUT OF SCHOOL: NO. 142

I thought I'd seen everything after twelve years on the school board. I was mistaken.

A group of students protested at one of our meetings, demanding we overturn a decision to expel a student. No one cared too much about the protest, because the kids conducted themselves appropriately. They were told they could address board members; however, law prohibited the board from discussing the case.

What came next shocked us all. A big student athlete stood up and claimed the school board wasn't playing fairly. The student who was expelled for fighting thought the punishment was a one-week suspension—which is what the student athlete received when he beat up the kid earlier in the school year.

There was no remorse about either incident. Both kids felt they could do the time, so they did the crime, but they weren't expecting expulsion. Board members were astonished. We didn't realize the kids were so calculating and didn't know right from wrong.

A Peek inside Your Child's Head

So why do many kids dislike homework? This is a question you and I ask about our children—and our moms asked about us. Homework and schoolwork contradict the way children naturally learn. For the first five years of life children learn by doing. They are free to pick and choose the skills to learn and when to learn them.

I remember when my two-year-old toddled over to our prized covered bowl to search for treasures. Looking back I realize her exploration was a learning experience, one which she controlled. She decided the topic—searching the bowl—and she decided when to learn the topic—when Mom and Dad weren't looking.

Something disturbing happens when your child starts school. The way he learns dramatically changes. Constraints are placed on a child's learning—by Mom and Dad, the classroom, and the teacher. The next thirteen years are spent memorizing, secondhand, from books and lectures, and not by doing. Our kids follow in our footsteps and those of our parents. Most of the day is spent behind a desk. They don't choose the topics they're interested in, nor decide when to learn those topics.

Exploring the world yourself is much more conducive to learning than reading about the world in books or hearing about the world from teachers.

I always complained about having to learn Shakespeare at 8:30 in the morning. No one, including the teacher, wanted to read Shakespeare so early in the day, and most of the kids didn't want to read Shakespeare *any* time of the day. We just muddled through and didn't learn much until a three-person Shakespearean company performed in the auditorium. The entire student body was drawn into the performance. Those actors made Shakespeare come alive.

This theory of learning, though logical, won't cut it in the real world. You and I are conditioned to overcome the natural way of learning, by doing things when they need to be done. And we must condition our youngsters to do the same.

The question then is, how do we condition our kids? There is no easy answer, because we must tailor our conditioning technique to complement our child's personality traits (table 2–1).

TABLE 2–1
PERSONALITY TRAITS OF YOUR CHILD

Personality Trait	Characteristics
Introvert	Likes to work alone and may be shy to ask for help.
Extrovert	Likes to work in a group and may be uncomfortable working alone on a project.
Pragmatist	Likes assignments that require a set of procedures to complete. Uncomfortable working on projects that have few directions.
Creative	Likes assignments with few directions. Uncomfortable with structured assignments.

Some kids like to learn on their own and solve problems with minimal assistance. Educators call this kind of student an *introvert*. Group activities such as joint homework assignments with other kids go against the natural grain of a youngster who shows introverted traits. Parents need to give such a child private time to work on homework, but must also closely monitor the youngster's progress, for it is not in the child's personality to ask for help.

On the other side of the spectrum are kids who perform well in a more social setting than working out problems on their own. Educators call these kids *extroverts*. They are children who are likely to be the first in the class to suggest group homework assignments and who encourage parents to work with them. Their social prowess is also a trait that cleverly leads you and me into the trap of doing the homework for them.

Two other personality traits that you might find in your child are pragmatism and creativeness. A *pragmatist* likes homework assignments that are real and practical. Math homework is a pragmatist's dream. There is a set of procedures to follow that always results in the same answer.

These children become unsettled if they are asked to perform a less structured assignment, such as drawing a picture that best describes their summer vacation. The assignment is vague and provides little direction. The pragmatist typically responds by asking a battery of questions to get answers that reduce the amount of free thinking required.

"How big should the picture be?"

"Do you want me to show family members or the landscape?"

"Do you want me to use pencil or crayons?"

A youngster who is a pragmatist can spend hours repeating sets of procedures to complete an assignment without becoming bored or frustrated, yet finds it difficult to complete assignments that have no prescribed way to complete the project.

The opposite of a pragmatist is a youngster who is *creative* and likes the freedom to complete homework assignments without using a standard set of procedures. Math problems turn them off because they are repetitive and boring. Drawing pictures and writing essays excite them because there are no rules.

My children have a mixture of all four traits. They're extroverted and pragmatic on the ball field, yet introverted and creative doing homework. Personality traits can change with our child's moods and maturity.

Your child's homework cannot be tailored to complement your child's personality traits. There are simply too many combinations of personalities in a class for the teacher to modify homework for each student. So the child will likely end up with homework assignments that conflict with her personality.

You can take countermeasures that will help your child overcome any problems by being flexible in the way you condition your child for homework. You'll need to provide hands-on help for homework assignments that do not complement your child's personality.

PROCEDURE:
How to provide hands-on help for homework assignments

1. Identify your youngster's personality traits at homework time. Keep in mind traits change throughout the day and as your child matures.

2. Review the homework assignment and determine if the assignment is procedural, such as math, or creative, such as writing an essay.

3. Determine if your child's personality traits complement the assignment. The results will determine if you should give more help to your child with homework.

4. Give less help at the onset with assignments that complement your child's personality. A youngster who is creative is less likely to require much prodding to write an essay or to draw a picture than a child who is pragmatic.

5. Give more help to a youngster whose homework assignment does not complement the child's personality. You'll need to give a child who is a pragmatist guidelines to follow to begin an unstructured homework assignment. Likewise, you may find yourself giving a child with a creative tendency a push to get started doing math homework.

6. Give an introverted child private time to do her homework assignments. However, make sure you stop by regularly to check your child's progress and to provide some unwanted but needed help. There is nothing wrong with a youngster quietly doing homework.

7. Closely monitor the homework of a child who seems to be an extrovert. Extroverts perform well in a social atmosphere. However, most homework assignments are completed independently, leading some youngsters to quickly lose focus.

Avoiding the Condition for Failure

Your child is conditioned without your realizing it. Think back to the preschool days. How much did you teach your child and how much was learned from observing and mimicking your behavior? My kids learned more from observation than from my wife's instruction. And these observations conditioned our kids to behave in a certain way.

You and I must prevent ourselves from negatively conditioning our children. This occurs when the clues our youngsters pick up from their observations lead them to draw the wrong conclusion. We see this happen all the time as adults. We hear bits and pieces of a conversation, draw a conclusion, then make decisions based on what probably is the *wrong* conclusion.

My wife and I tried to be aware of sending the wrong message to our kids when our youngest became a toddler. Our kids were treated equally. We made it obvious there were no favorites. Rules applied to everyone.

However, that's not the way our kids saw it. The oldest claimed our youngest was getting away with everything. The youngest felt we paid too much attention to our oldest. A little sibling rivalry at work, we thought, until my older daughter's teacher said miscommunication was taking place—miscommunication that could result in negative conditioning if we didn't correct the situation.

Kids quietly pay close attention to our actions and reactions. You and I are probably not conscious of our behavior at home. We joke around; talk in incomplete sentences; say things we won't say in public; and do things without thinking how our actions appear to others. Yet, we're in a fishbowl, with our kids studying our every movement.

Our situation wasn't too much different from yours. My wife and I are quick to praise our kids when they do something good and sound a few discouraging words when they do something wrong. I never realized the sequence of praise and displeasure is recognized as a pattern by my kids, which they use to draw a conclusion.

My youngest brought this to light when she claimed my wife and I didn't like her. Impossible, we thought. So we asked her how she reached her conclusion. She listed incidents where my wife and I yelled at my youngest for doing something wrong and praised our oldest.

She was correct in her observation, but wrong with her conclusion. My oldest was bringing home high marks on school assignments, which we encouraged. My youngest seemed to be always getting into mischief since she was home with my wife all day. The oldest wasn't an angel all the time, but didn't get caught because she was in school all day.

An unbiased observer could conclude after reviewing the facts that we preferred one daughter to the other. We straightened out the situation immediately. If we hadn't, we could have inadvertently conditioned our youngest into believing she wasn't wanted by us.

We were fortunate that our youngest was willing to tell us about her conclusion. According to educators, some kids are not vocal. However, kids do provide clues that indicate trouble is brewing. One of the most telling clues is a child's performance.

A sudden drop in performance could indicate that certain recent changes in your child's life are affecting her behavior. A preschooler's loss of interest in play or a radical decline in grades for a school-age child are causes for concern.

A gradual drop in grades is also an indication of trouble in school. Lessons missed in previous years could be causing your child to fall behind the class. If this situation is not remedied immediately, your pride-and-joy could feel inferior, lose self-esteem, and be conditioned for failure.

PROCEDURE:
What to do if your child is showing signs of trouble

1. Contact your child's teacher at the first sign of trouble and see if the teacher agrees. The teacher may put you at ease by acknowledging your concerns, but may find the symptom is not of any significance. Some behavior we consider a serious problem is really a sign of immaturity, which resolves itself as your child grows older.

2. Discuss the clues with your child to ensure you are not drawing the wrong conclusion. Ask an open-ended question, then listen carefully to the youngster's response. You might be able to defuse a potentially dangerous situation.

3. Ask your child's teacher to join with you to resolve any problems you encounter with your child. (Teachers have the skills and knowledge to understand what is going on in your child's head.) Then enlist the professional staff of your school to devise a plan to fix the problem.

4. Don't overreact. It is easy for us to see clues that appear to form a pattern, when in reality no problem exists.

TALES OUT OF SCHOOL: NO. 402

Kids can be cruel by harassing a classmate who doesn't seem to be quick to answer questions in class. This happened to a fourth grader who always hesitated when called upon. The youngster got nervous and kept saying "da" while searching her mind for the answer. It was an unconscious, nervous habit. Unfortunately, the fourth-grade teacher normally lost patience and moved on before the youngster could respond.

Almost like clockwork the same scenario played time and again during the school day. She'd get called on, become stymied, then sit down, never answering any questions correctly. The youngster was devastated and humiliated in front of her friends.

Events took a turn for the worse in the fifth grade. Wise guys in the class nicknamed her Da and teased her every chance they got. Before class, at recess, on the way home from school, she was constantly under a barrage from the kids.

Each day she dreaded being asked questions in class. Some of the kids poked fun at her aloud while she tried to answer the question.

"Da . . . I don't da know."

The teacher usually chastised the teasers, then quickly moved to another topic. Disaster struck in the sixth grade. The youngster ignored the teacher anytime she was asked a question. She wouldn't stand for the spelling bees. She guessed at questions on tests. She simply gave up on herself. Her classmates conditioned her to failure.

You would think her parents and her teachers would have identified clues that something was wrong—but the clues were missed. The youngster was embarrassed to tell her parents about the problem. Each night she suppressed her feelings and acted as if nothing was wrong in school. She looked like a normal kid to her parents.

Her fourth- and fifth-grade teachers wrongly assumed the teasing didn't bother her, because she didn't complain and sat quietly doing her schoolwork. It wasn't until the sixth grade when her dramatic change in behavior alerted the teacher to this deep-rooted problem.

School officials provided intense counseling. More than a year passed before she regained her self-esteem.

Setting the Stage for Homework

Much of what your child knows of the world comes from you. You are your child's first teacher and probably have done an excellent job. Don't stop now. There's more work to be done. The next step is to get your youngster on the right track for learning from others in school.

Your child is conditioned for a successful home life. She knows how to behave around the house, in the neighborhood, in the mall, and with relatives and friends. You've trained your child to know right from wrong through trial and error—which is the fundamental technique of conditioning.

She makes a mistake, you correct her. If the same mistake is made again, you follow with the same corrective action. The pattern continues until your child catches herself before the mistake is made the next time. Your child is conditioned.

The same technique is used for schoolwork. Your child's teacher conditions her for classroom assignments. It's your job to condition her for homework assignments.

There is really no right or wrong way to do homework. Some kids need total silence. Others require the radio blasting. I like doing homework after supper, while my kids prefer tackling assignments after school.

The best homework technique is the one that works for your child. Once you've found the right formula, then make it consistent. Keep the same routine each day. Consistency is the conditioning tool your child needs to successfully complete schoolwork at home.

I've talked to a number of teachers who have told me about homework techniques they find worth considering. I noticed there is a common theme among them. Each has these same fundamental characteristics:

- Homework is organized into a schedule and performed at the same time every day.
- Homework is done in a location conducive to learning.
- Adequate supplies are on hand to complete homework assignments.
- Rules are established to focus attention on completing assignments correctly and in a timely manner.

Pick a Good Time to Do Homework

What is the first thing you do when you enter the bathroom in your home? If you're like me, you lock the door. And you do so even when no one else is home because you've been conditioned to do so.

Conditioning causes us to perform steps without consciously thinking about them. You and I drive our car on automatic pilot most of the time. You've probably driven safely for hours, stopping for traffic lights, giving the right-of-way to other vehicles, and parallel parking without giving it a second thought. Your body just seems to take over, reacting to situations faster than if you took time to think through each traffic problem.

Emergency crews are conditioned through training on how to behave in a crisis. They jump into action immediately, getting the job done in situations where you and I would be frozen in fright. They react swiftly, with little thought, and perform with a high degree of success because a team of instructors conditioned them to do so.

You're an important member of the team of instructors whose job it is to condition your child with skills required to get good grades. Your child's teacher is the team leader and exposes your child to successful ways to learn in the classroom. You take over when it comes to homework, a major component of getting good grades.

Homework has been given a bad rap since long before you and I were in school. You need to give homework a positive spin in your home and condition your child that homework is a challenge just like a game.

My approach is to break homework into two pieces: the task of doing homework, and the lesson to learn. The task of doing is a conditioned response much like you and me driving a car. The lesson to learn is a conscious effort similar to our following directions to find an unfamiliar destination.

Begin the conditioning process by fitting homework into the family's schedule. I mention the family's schedule rather than your child's schedule because homework is a family activity. Reserve time in the schedule for your child's homework.

PROCEDURE:
Setting up a homework schedule

1. Don't allow your child to decide when to do homework. You have the responsibility to set the schedule and to make sure your child follows the schedule.
2. Schedule homework for early in the evening or after school when you and your child are less tired and more receptive to facing a challenge.
3. The same time each day must be reserved for homework.
4. Be sure homework time coincides with your availability. You don't need to sit in the same room as your child, but you should be on call to lend a helping hand.
5. Be sure to set the start and end of homework time. Homework period cannot be endless. There is definitely a cutoff period after which your child and you are probably not in a good state of mind to continue working. A word of caution: Don't fall sucker for the stall. Your child knows how to tell time and can easily hem and haw until time runs out. End on time, but make sure to get your child up a little earlier the next morning to complete the assignment. Try this technique for a week and there is a good chance homework will be completed on time for the rest of the school year.
6. Allow sufficient time for your child to complete the homework assignment.
7. Review the homework schedule with your child. Allow your child to recommend adjustments to the schedule; however, make it clear that *you* have the final say on setting the schedule.

8. Review homework assignments with your child before work begins. This gives you the chance to see the lessons your child is learning. You are also demonstrating to your child that you are in charge of the homework schedule. This is similar to the classroom where the teacher is in charge, but the kids work independently on assignments.

9. Review your child's homework as the last step in the homework schedule. Make sure your review is sincere and more than a cursory glance. The quality time you spend reviewing your child's work implies to your child the high degree of importance you place on homework.

10. Each night allocate the amount of the schedule for each homework assignment. The schedule always begins with your review of the assignments and ends with your review of your child's work.

11. Let your child help allocate time in the schedule. First and second graders need to give you input, but expect to complete the allocation yourself. Your role will diminish as your child matures and takes on greater responsibility. At some point your child will allocate time without your help.

12. Make sure the allocated schedule is written and prominently displayed so your child can monitor the time while working on assignments.

13. Be sure a clock is available so your child can practice the skills necessary to keep on schedule.

14. Don't let any activity except an emergency supersede the time allotted for homework. All incomplete assignments must be completed the next morning or the next homework session even if the teacher does not require this.

TALES OUT OF SCHOOL: NO. 48

A few years ago, more years than I want to remember, my wife and I showed up at our high-school reunion. The gang hadn't changed much. Of course, there were a few that no one could recognize, but that's part of getting older.

One of the guys, known as Moose in grammar school, was one of the few who was well dressed and in top-notch shape. We greeted each other and exchanged pleasantries, then politely snooped a little.

"What are you doing these days?"

"I work for the federal government," Moose cautiously replied.

"Where in the government?"

"The justice department," he replied.

This led to other questions. Finally, he revealed he was an FBI agent. I did what any red-blooded American is conditioned to do: I took one step back. It was an instinctive move. I was joking and even laughed as I continued the conversation.

Well, apparently I wasn't the only one who was conditioned that way. After the third person greeted Moose, he'd only say he worked for the justice department. No one flinched and no further questions about his occupation were answered.

We are kicking ourselves now because Moose later became the greatest success story of the class. He became a federal prosecutor, federal judge, and director of the FBI.

Pick a Good Location to Do Homework

I never realized the effects of conditioning until I thought about how you and I act when we go to the movies. Our voices automatically become hushed—even before the movie begins. We sit elbow to elbow with a total stranger and ignore each other as if a brick wall were between us—unless we war over the armrest. Yet, we won't dream of ignoring each other if the same two people sat together in a mutual friend's living room watching television.

Our behavior is dictated by our surroundings and how we are trained to react within the surroundings. Your kids won't think twice of making noise or turning on the TV while you're reading a book in the living room, but they'll talk quietly and walk softly if you are reading the book in the library.

If you create surroundings conducive to doing schoolwork, then your child will be subconsciously influenced into cooperating. Change the surroundings to a play area and your child will know it's playtime.

When I was in school, I used the kitchen table, blasted the radio, and downed bags of chips while doing homework. This worked for me. You can say this made me well rounded—not in the educational sense. Somehow I don't think that's what my daughter's teacher had in mind when I asked for advice on creating the proper surroundings for doing homework.

Initially I was concerned that I needed to set aside a room in my home for homework. This would be impossible for me to do. My home isn't spacious and I had no intentions of moving. With a little creativity from my wife we temporarily rearranged things to set the stage for homework and placed everything back to normal when homework was completed.

At first I thought this was a waste of time. I was wrong.

PROCEDURE:
How to set up a place conducive to doing homework

1. Avoid using an entertainment area of your home, such as your living room. There are too many temptations, and family members probably want to watch TV.

2. Find a spot where there is a large table and a comfortable chair out of the main traffic flow of your home. The table allows your child to spread out books and supplies needed to complete the assignment. I found the table in the kitchen met this requirement. My wife and I also found an old artist's desk

at a garage sale that fit perfectly into the corner of our attic. Our oldest used the artist's desk while our youngest took over the kitchen table.

3. Make temporary changes to an area of your home to create a place to do homework. In our house everything on the kitchen table is removed and my wife places a clear tablecloth on the table. The tablecloth is a symbol to my daughter that the table has been transformed into her homework table.

4. The location should have minimal distractions while your child is doing homework, so family members need to get snacks and finish washing the dishes before homework begins on the kitchen table.

5. Your child should have privacy, but still be able to yell for help while doing homework. Our kitchen met these requirements for my youngest. However, our attic provided only privacy. My oldest walked down several flights to ask for help—until she discovered she could call us on the second phone line.

6. Proper lighting is crucial for doing homework. I use an unscientific method that works very well to determine if proper lighting exists. I call it the magazine test. If I can read a magazine comfortably, then chances are good that my child has sufficient lighting to do her homework. I use a magazine because poor lighting causes glare on the magazine's glossy pages. Glare can cause eye strain and lead to fatigue.

7. Temperature and humidity are two factors you must consider when creating a place for doing homework in your home. No one—including your child—can concentrate if the area is uncomfortable. Make sure the area is well ventilated, cooled in the summer, and heated in the winter.

Plenty of Supplies on Hand

Just when everything seems under control, my daughter speaks those words that bring tears to my eyes. It's 7 P.M. Sunday night and she says, "I have to make a family tree out of green construction paper."

And we're out of supplies. So I volunteer to pick up some paper tomorrow.

"But it's due tomorrow!"

What transpires next is played out in my home—and probably yours—every school year.

"Why didn't you tell me about this yesterday?"

Silence with an I-don't-know expression.

"Where do you think I'm going to find green construction paper tonight?"

The trap is set and I'm slipping fast. My guilt trip has started. I go into a sweat as my daughter sits calmly by. The entire house is searched for a piece of construction paper. My wife and I are the only ones searching, of course. I'd pay anything for a lousy sheet of green construction paper.

"Why did the teacher give you such a short deadline for the assignment?"

A shrug followed by a dumb look. A dead giveaway the project was probably assigned a month ago, but she waited till the last minute to begin work.

Eureka! It took a half hour, but I found a hunk of orange construction paper. Now she can complete the assignment.

"I need green construction paper, not orange."

We all know how this story ends. Now let's look at some ways to prevent the story from happening another day.

PROCEDURE:
How to avoid running out of homework supplies

1. Don't take ownership of your child's homework assignment. This is a trap. It's your child's problem—not yours—if supplies are unavailable. Don't be afraid to let your child sweat a little. It's all part of the learning experience.

2. Plan ahead by asking your child's teacher at the beginning of the school year for a list of supplies that would help your child complete homework assignments. Your child's teacher will be

careful not to give you the impression that these supplies
are required to do homework assignments, since all required
supplies must be provided to your child free of charge by the
school district.

3. Prepare a homework kit that consists of assorted markers,
   pencils, pens, crayons, colored pencils, writing paper, construction paper, erasers, glue, correction fluid, paper clips, a
   stapler, a hole punch, tape, scissors, index cards, report fold-
   ers, and rubber bands.

4. Place all homework supplies in a container, perhaps an inexpensive plastic toolbox.

5. Make sure the homework kit is placed in the homework
   location every night and returned to the storage area once
   homework is completed. Homework supplies must be used
   only for homework. This gives a special meaning to the homework kit and cuts down on the use of supplies for play.

6. Enhance the homework kit with other items as your child
   moves into the upper grades. You'll probably need a dictionary, almanac, atlas, thesaurus, compass, and inexpensive
   calculator.

7. Ask the teacher at the beginning of the school year if you can
   substitute materials. Contrary to what your child tells you, the
   teacher is likely to agree.

8. Don't purchase expensive supplies. My wife and I normally hit
   the discount and warehouse stores a month before school begins. We also scan ads for special sales. Office stores are con-
   venient places to buy inexpensive school supplies.

9. Ask the teacher for an alternate assignment if the one given to
   your child requires special equipment that's unavailable. One
   of my daughter's classes was instructed to videotape inter-
   views with family members. A great exercise if parents owned
   a camcorder. A nightmare if they didn't. School officials are required by law to either loan equipment for the assignment or
   provide an alternative assignment.

Set Down the Law

Our job as parents is to help our children develop good habits. And the job isn't easy, as you can probably attest. We know what we want our youngsters to do, but getting them to do it will test the patience of a saint.

First establish clear rules for your child to follow and rigorously enforce them. These are rules that define how your child should complete homework assignments.

Create sets of procedures for each kind of homework assignment. My wife and I created procedures for practicing printing and writing, reading, math, and in later years ways to study from a textbook. This made it easy for my daughter to know how to approach and work through any assignment.

Also create a framework within which your child can perform those procedures. Table 2–2 contains the procedures we use in our house. They should help you create your own homework procedures for your child.

TABLE 2–2

A FRAMEWORK FOR DOING HOMEWORK

Prepare the homework location.

Review the homework assignment.

Create a homework schedule.

Follow procedures to complete each assignment.

Review the results of the homework.

Clean up the homework location.

You must provide a structured environment for doing homework. Establish rules, then enforce them. Remember, rules that aren't enforced are not rules.

PROCEDURE:
How to create and enforce homework rules

1. Signal when your child must prepare for homework. Take a strong lead until she gets used to doing homework.

2. Police the area for signs of interruptions until the entire family accepts the new procedures.

3. Be flexible. Give your child time to try the procedure. Be ready to modify the procedure if it isn't working.

4. Ask your child's teacher to help you create homework and study procedures. Teachers are an untapped resource parents frequently overlook.

5. Be constructive in your comments to your child and avoid criticism. Don't compare one child with another. Understand your child's problem before you rush to judgment. You want to reinforce success, not failure.

6. Ask your child to help design homework procedures. Procedures are designed to make it easier for your child to solve problems and complete assignments. When you sincerely welcome participation from your child, you're making it easier for your child to buy into the process.

7. Don't be overly strict. Expect your child to daydream and use up unspent energy by fidgeting.

8. Make sure you schedule breaks at regular intervals. Allow for a diversion or a snack, but not entertainment such as video games or TV.

9. Call a time-out whenever you and your child are butting heads over a problem. Be sure to talk to each other about pleasant matters during the break. This shows that your concerns don't reflect any long-term feelings.

10. Be sure your child keeps pace with the schedule of assignments. Don't let your child rush ahead. Some kids like to speed through homework assignments, giving little care to the quality of work. Their work is typically incomplete and unacceptable. Slow things down by enforcing the schedule.

If she finishes an assignment before the next is to begin, then use the time as a break.

11. Set penalties for not adhering to the schedule or the rules. The penalty must fit the maturity of your child and the violation. For example, start homework time earlier tomorrow if the homework couldn't be completed on time. Forgo TV for the rest of the evening if you find your child rushing through homework.

12. Don't change procedures that work. Change only those that aren't working.

13. Break up assignments into spurts. Some kids find it difficult to work on a long assignment, such as one hundred addition problems. Divide the assignment into small groups, say groups of ten. Review the results of each group as your child completes them. Groups become milestones that build confidence. Increase the size of the group in subsequent assignments until your child becomes comfortable working straight through the assignment.

3.

Answers to Why Your Child Can't Do Homework

- Won't Do Homework
- Unable to Do Homework
- Takes Too Long to Do Homework
- Homework Is a Mess
- Whiners
- The Top Ten Excuses and Responses

I heard the rattle of a chair and scurrying of footsteps as I made my way up the attic steps to check on my daughter's progress with her homework assignment. Something was amiss and it didn't sound like much homework was being done.

"What do you want?" she asked.

Obviously I was intruding and breaking her concentration. So I made a cursory review of her assignment and stood by waiting for her to continue. She went back to work, then stopped and gave the I-can't-work-while-you're-looking-at-me look.

I did feel a bit out of place, and then sheepishly I asked if she needed any help. She silently stared me down and I retreated downstairs.

I noticed a red light on our telephone when I reached the kitchen. Strange. Only the two of us were home. So I used a trick my daughter taught me—hold down the mute button while removing the handset.

"He's gone. I'm sure he won't be back for a while. He thinks I'm studying this stuff. Just don't forget to make an extra copy of the homework for me tomorrow, otherwise I'm screwed."

Won't Do Homework

It is hard to imagine there was a time when your child couldn't wait for school to begin. Anticipation began with the preschool rituals of being dragged to the malls to buy new clothes, notebooks, pencils, pens, and other doodads. There was a sense of excitement that filled houses throughout the neighborhood, for a new school year brought a new classroom, a new teacher, and a fresh start.

I remember those moments. First I'd admit to myself that I wasn't the greatest student last year. I'd then promise myself I'd buckle down, hit the books running, and prove to everyone I could make the grade. All those troubles of last year—and the year before and the year before that—were history.

I'm sure there were a few years when you, too, made such resolutions. Somehow new-school-year resolutions follow suit with New Year's resolutions. Within the first week of school when the teacher starts piling on homework assignments, old habits return.

Some parents face a terrible time getting kids to do homework. What do you do with a kid who outright refuses to do homework? I've posed this question to many educators. Their response: There's no easy answer.

Teachers told me that it is common for every youngster to challenge parents. This is a sign of maturity and a way for kids to declare their independence. Their defiance is usually passing. Once they've made their point, kids get on with the homework assignment.

There are a number of youngsters who don't fit this model. They simply won't concede to parents under any terms. Over the years they have developed a reputation for being strong-willed and noncompliant. Every attempt to adjust their behavior has met with failure.

Educators told me the behavior of these kids is actually a sign of a more serious and complex underlying problem. Their defiant attitude is really a cry for help. So how do you render assistance if your child shows such behavior? The first step is to thoroughly understand the situation.

PROCEDURE:
What to do with a child who is defiant

1. Avoid a rush to judgment. Your child's response is not addressed to you personally, although this is hard to believe.
2. Let your child know you are not taking those remarks personally. Communicating your feelings defuses an explosive situation and shows that punishment is not forthcoming.
3. Take your child away from the place in your home where homework is done. Kids have a tendency to subconsciously associate this place with a negative feeling. Try a walk around the block or to a local park away from friends and relatives.
4. Ask your child to talk about the problem. Structure questions so there is no blame or punishment for an honest response. Leading questions are great for setting the tone of the talk and give direction to which way you want the conversation to proceed.
5. Make sure you listen. Let your child do the talking. You may need to take several of these walks before both of you open up to each other.
6. Don't agree to anything. Convey to your child that you think you understand the basis of her views and you'll see what you can do to change the situation. Don't negotiate. Don't draw any conclusions.
7. Discuss the situation with your child's teacher and previous teachers. Teachers will describe your child's behavior and academic performance in school. They'll also give you an insight into your child's social activities. All of these are clues to her underlying problem.
8. Share with your child's teacher the information you gathered.
9. Piece together the clues. Use common sense and keep an open mind during your review.
10. Put yourself in your child's position and see the facts as your child sees them.
11. Piece together a day in your child's life, from wake-up until

bedtime. Lay out what she experiences during a typical day. Pay careful attention to schoolwork, especially if her behavior away from schoolwork is normal. Educators have told me that when a child refuses to do homework assignments, the youngster may be unable to complete the assignments and is embarrassed to admit this. See the "Unable to Do Homework" section in this chapter if you suspect this is the case.

Defiant behavior can also be a sign of a learning disability. Whenever I heard the term *learning disabled* I immediately conjured images of a physically challenged youngster in the classroom. However, I was wrong. Many physically challenged youngsters have no inability to learn once given the necessary accommodations.

There are some physically capable youngsters who have difficulty learning. Your defiant child might be one of those children without your realizing it. Your child's frustration with learning lessons and completing homework assignments could be psychologically and physiologically based. You can read more about learning disabilities in books such as *Learning Disabilities and Your Child* by Lawrence Greene.

Raise the possibility of a learning problem with your child's principal and ask that the school's child-study team examine your child. The child-study team is a group of professionals from a variety of backgrounds that includes teachers, a physician, and a psychologist. They'll examine your child and determine if a learning disability is present. This won't cost you any money. A special program will be created if your child is diagnosed with a learning disability.

Unable to Do Homework

One look at your child's homework assignment, and you'll have an idea how long the assignment should take to complete. I do this all the time when I review my child's homework. However, educators have told me that most parents arrive at the wrong time estimate. You and I set the time limit for the assignment based on *our* experience and *our* capabilities and not those of our child.

What happens if your child doesn't live up to your unfounded expectation? You assume your child is slacking off. The solution? Turn up the pressure and threaten punishment. All of us have used this technique and end up making a serious mistake.

Instead of helping the situation, we make the situation worse. Homework assignments require your child to work with a clear head. Doing a difficult assignment naturally clouds the mind, and when you exert pressure, those clouds turn into dense fog. You must refrain from a knee-jerk reaction and recognize that some children are unable to complete all the homework assignments. Here are some of the reasons:

- Your child was not in the class or not paying attention when the lesson was taught.
- Your child did not grasp the lesson and never asked the teacher for help.
- Your child left the necessary books in school.
- Your child missed previous lessons needed to complete the assignment.
- Your child is too tired.

Once you've recognized that your child's dilemma isn't concocted, then you need to fix the problem. The solution must be developed by a team that includes your family, your child, and your child's teacher. It is important that your child become an active member of this team. Don't treat your child as if she is insignificant to the solution.

PROCEDURE:
How to deal with a child who is unable to complete a homework assignment

1. Review the list of the skills your child is to learn this school year.

2. Ask your child's teacher to check off those skills that your child has learned.

3. Show your child the checklist and tell her check marks indicate accomplishments. Skills unchecked still need to be learned. Thus she is not a failure, but still needs to learn a few more lessons.

4. Develop a plan with your child's teacher for making up those missed lessons.

5. Ask the teacher to modify homework assignments to complement the situation. It doesn't make sense to continue the same lesson plan if your child has fallen behind.

6. Begin with an assignment that uses skills your child has already learned. This guarantees success on the first try and builds self-esteem.

7. Demand that school officials provide remedial help to your child.

8. Make sure your child isn't embarrassed in school because she isn't keeping up with the class. Acceptance by classmates is more important to her than making up missed lessons.

9. Ask the PTA to help organize a network of students, friends, and relatives who could be called upon in the evening to answer questions about your child's homework.

10. Be prepared to hire a tutor for more formal instruction. An upperclassman recommended by your child's teacher is a good candidate.

11. Monitor your child's progress each day. Make sure you and the teacher change strategies if little or no progress is seen.

Takes Too Long to Do Homework

"Just one minute." This was my favorite answer to Mom's prompts to get me started with homework. Actually, this was my response to most all of her requests that involved my doing something I preferred not to.

My philosophy was simple: why do something now when it can be postponed for another time.

Most kids adopt this philosophy. It's strange how attitudes change with age. I find myself cracking down on my children when they postpone the inevitable—like homework.

Some kids take forever to begin homework assignments and even longer to complete them. They work at a snail's pace although they know how to do the lesson. They tend to daydream instead of working on assignments. Homework is just not important to them.

There's nothing to worry about if your child seems to procrastinate about homework. This behavior is not unusual and can be improved by your taking offensive action.

PROCEDURE:
How to motivate your child to do homework

1. Make sure your child is capable of doing the assignment. The problem may be more complex than a lack of motivation.
2. Develop a homework plan with your child. I show you how to do this in chapter 2. Make sure the plan clearly defines the start and end times for each assignment.
3. Divide homework assignments into smaller assignments, which don't seem too imposing.
4. Post the homework assignment schedule in view of your child so she realizes there is a schedule of tasks that must be performed before bedtime. Each assignment should be clearly identified with the start and end time and a sentence that describes the assignment.
5. Place a clock in the area where your child does homework so your child can't lose track of time. I recommend using a clock that doesn't tick too loudly. The ticking is distracting.
6. Set down the rules once the schedule is posted. It is your child's responsibility to complete each assignment on time.
7. Establish penalties for missing deadlines and rewards for

meeting deadlines. Each assignment for the evening has a deadline, a penalty, and a reward. Treats such as cookies and praise are the rewards.

8. Remove all distractions from the area.

9. Crack down hard on delays. State your concerns in a clear, unwavering tone. Your demeanor must convey a no-nonsense approach to homework.

10. Check each assignment. Be thorough, but sincere, with your criticisms. You set the standards to which your child must aspire.

11. Let your child cross off completed assignments on the schedule once the assignment meets your expectations. This will give your child a sense of accomplishment.

12. Ask your child's teacher for long-range homework projects, which are typically forgotten by your child until the day before they are due.

13. Divide long-range projects into tasks, then place those tasks on the nightly homework schedule. This shows your child how to manage time.

14. Post the schedule in an obvious place in the house. My wife and I use the refrigerator door and sometimes the back of the bathroom door. We leave subtle reminders to our kids in their lunch, book bag, and anywhere else they are likely to look.

Homework Is a Mess

Back when Mom looked over my homework I can remember saying, "Yeah, I know you'd be embarrassed to hand in this homework, but I'm not you. I'm not embarrassed at all." Of course, I said this to myself. I was sloppy, not stupid. She'd given the assignment the once-over, looking for things that didn't meet her expectations—and there were plenty.

Mom always picked out misspelled words in my homework. When she found one, she'd give me an impromptu spelling bee using the word I spelled wrong. If I knew how to spell the word correctly, I would not have gotten the word wrong on the homework.

The ending was predictable. She'd ask why I didn't take the time to look up the word in the dictionary. How could I look up the word if I didn't know how to spell it? Now the roles have changed. My wife and I are the homework inspectors in search of misspelled words and messy homework.

Why would kids consider handing the teacher messy homework assignments? A more pressing question is, how can you and I change this behavior? These were two questions I posed to my child's teachers as soon as I discovered my daughter was following in her father's footsteps.

Her teachers told me messy homework is a sign your child isn't concentrating on details of the assignment. Focusing on the fine points of a task must be learned through careful coaching from you and your child's teacher.

Preschoolers have a tendency to be unaware of details. They scribble in a coloring book thinking the result is a perfectly colored picture. This performance becomes unacceptable as your child matures. However, your child must learn this. You must teach your child neatness by showing her how to stay within the lines and select complementary colors. Through trial and error and your guidance, she masters how to focus on the details.

All your hard work seems to be for naught when your child rushes through assignments. Homework papers are filled with errors. You're ready to pull out your hair because your child won't take the time to produce accurate results.

Educators point out your preschooler's life radically changes when she begins school. She's no longer a baby. Activities outside your home increase. School, homework, new friends, and after-school activities all compete for her time and energies.

Schoolwork becomes increasingly demanding. New skills to learn. New rules to follow. Your preschooler is shocked into the realities of growing up. Children tend to prefer activities they find entertaining and easy to perform. Playing with their friends after school falls into this category. Schoolwork is rarely entertaining. Schoolwork is a challenge. Schoolwork is also a roadblock to the fun stuff.

So what do you do if your child submits sloppy homework assignments?

PROCEDURE:

What to do with a child who produces sloppy homework

1. Limit the number of activities in which your child participates.
2. Make sure adequate time is scheduled for homework. Homework must have a fixed, unmovable place in your child's daily schedule.
3. Set and enforce priorities. I'll admit this recommendation is difficult to implement. It is nearly impossible to tie down your star goalie to do homework an hour before the game when you don't have the strength to endure the consequences if you don't let her play.
4. Establish a model of a perfect homework assignment for your child. The model gives her a clear picture of what you expect from her.
5. Don't waver from your standards. Homework is either neat, accurate, and acceptable, or it is not.
6. Avoid destructive criticism. Comments you make that are not specific to the quality of your child's work can be counterproductive. Don't say, "You're a slob." It's better to say, "You know how to print better than this."
7. Give constructive criticism. Focus on aspects of your child's work that are unacceptable. Show her where mistakes occurred and help to correct those mistakes.
8. Praise every success. This builds self-confidence. Your child's homework assignments have many pieces. Some of those pieces will be completed accurately and others will not. Make sure you tell her you recognize the correct ones.
9. Compare your child's work to other work she has performed successfully. If she printed her name sloppily, question whether or not she had actually concentrated on doing it. Show her another of her assignments where the name was neatly printed. The difference will be obvious.
10. Check your child's work frequently during the evening. Let her do a page of an assignment, then check the page for accuracy and neatness. Require corrections to be made immediately.

Whiners

"But, do I have to do it now? It's too hot. I'm too tired. My arm hurts."

Sounds familiar? And so another evening of homework begins.

Every kid moans and carries on occasionally. My kids go through this exercise until they settle down and realize there is no way to avoid homework. Their complaints diminish as they begin to focus on completing assignments.

You may not be so lucky. Your child may rarely stop whining during homework. She needs an audience and intends to ruin the evening if you don't show for the performance. You're expected to sit by and resolve all her problems as soon as they appear.

The scenario is predictable. You answer the cries with help until you realize you're not helping. Instead, you're being used as her servant. Next, you try to change the rules. You insist she solve problems without help. She responds with louder whining. You're left with a choice: either scream, yell, and threaten bodily harm, or comply. Most parents of whiners simply give in. They'd rather do the homework themselves than listen to the moaning.

What do you do with a whiner? Educators gave me some hard answers that you can implement if you have a lot of patience.

PROCEDURE:
How to handle a whiner

1. Don't give in to your child's whining. Remember when she fussed as an infant when you placed her in the crib. You ignored her and eventually she learned to quiet down and change her behavior.
2. State the rules when homework begins. Help, but don't respond to moaning. A request for help must be made in a normal, polite tone.
3. Ask your child if she sees any difficulties with the assignment. This will focus her attention and give you the opportunity to help before homework begins.

4. Keep to the homework schedule. Don't return until the end of the time limit for the first assignment. Don't come running at her beck and call.

5. Leave the homework area immediately. My wife sits on the front porch, in the backyard, or in a different part of the house where she's out of earshot of our child. This gives our daughter the feeling of being alone and having to address the problems herself.

6. Review the assignment for accuracy and neatness when the time limit for the assignment has expired. This is the time for your child to ask for help.

7. Review the next assignment with your child, then repeat the same process until all the assignments are completed.

8. Don't extend the homework schedule. If assignments are incomplete at the end of the evening, the assignments remain incomplete. Let your child suffer the penalty for wasting time whining and not concentrating on doing the work.

9. Don't expect your efforts to be a total success right away. Things will improve gradually over time.

10. Expect tears to be shed and homework assignments to be incomplete for the first few nights. This is fine. Tell your child's teacher your strategy and ask for support.

11. Return to a normal homework routine only when your child no longer whines.

The Top Ten Excuses and Responses

I'll admit to having a black book of excuses for avoiding school and homework when I was growing up. A few worked, but most failed. My list was complete, I thought, until I took an informal poll of educators from around the country. I asked, "What are the ten best excuses for not doing schoolwork, and how should a parent respond?"

The list they gave me was very long and interesting. I could have devoted a whole book to excuses! However, I've narrowed the list to the best and most outlandish excuses educators gave me.

I'm not smart.
Examine your child's situation very carefully. Youngsters tend to look for justification for being unable to overcome obstacles, and one of the most compelling reasons is the feeling of inadequacy. You and I use the same excuse when we can't do something such as fixing household plumbing. Here's what to do:

- Acknowledge your child's concerns, but don't accept the excuse.
- Identify the problem that led her to voice her concern.
- Make sure you and your child's teacher work closely together to overcome the problem.

The teacher doesn't like me.
Youngsters are quick to rush to a conclusion based upon only a few clues. I've seen this with my own children. If I say good-bye to one and not the other, I'm accused of favoritism. The same kind of situation happens in the classroom. However, her perception could be accurate, because at times there is a personality conflict between a student and teacher. Here's what to do:

- Investigate the situation with an open mind.
- Speak with your child's teacher about her concerns. Get a feel for the teacher's personality and determine if a clash could exist.
- Ask the principal to transfer your child to a different class if a conflict exists.
- Devise a plan with your child's teacher to change your child's perceptions if personality isn't a problem. Your child's teacher should know how to remedy the situation.

You won't help me with my homework.
What is your child's definition of *help*? You'll likely be accused of not helping her anytime you don't do her homework for her. Help your child complete school assignments independently—gradually decreasing your assistance as she becomes capable of handling matters on her own. Here's what to do:

- Ask your child to provide you with examples of where you're not helping. This defines her definition of *help*.
- Don't modify your behavior to meet your child's definition. Your objective is to *change* her definition.
- Explain your approach and reassure her you'll lend assistance once she makes an attempt to complete the assignment on her own.

Schoolwork is too hard.

The skills your child learns are a challenge. Third grade is more demanding than kindergarten. Sixth grade is more demanding than third grade. The degree of difficulty becomes evident if she is unable to maintain pace with the class. Here's what to do:

- Identify when your child first determined school is too difficult.
- Explore the situation with your child's teacher.
- Review her course proficiencies for the current year and previous years to pinpoint difficult lessons.
- Ask your child's teacher to modify your child's lessons, giving her time to catch up with the class.
- Seek extra help for your child from your school so that she can strengthen weaknesses.
- Don't leave this condition unattended since this could lead to serious academic and emotional problems in the future.

I'm too tired to do homework.

Kids have more energy than you and I, but they're more active than we are, too. So there might be some truth when your child complains about being too tired to do homework. However, fatigue isn't simply caused by a busy schedule. Other factors such as medical conditions can have the same effect as being exhausted. Here's what to do:

- Make sure homework is scheduled for after school or during the early part of the evening when your child is likely to have energy left.
- Don't overbook your child's schedule with too many after-school activities.
- Be alert to the activity that precedes homework. Video games and

working on the computer for too long can lead to eye strain and
fatigue—something you don't want to occur before tackling homework assignments.

- Call for a fifteen-minute recess several times during homework to
break up the session.
- Be cautious if there is no obvious reason for your child to become
tired. The problem could stem from a physical condition such as
poor eyesight.

I don't have any homework tonight.
Chances are good this excuse is more wishful thinking than true.
Homework is an important ingredient for making the grade. You know
this and so does your child's teacher. Occasionally a night slips by without an assignment, but this is more the exception than the rule. Here's
what to do:

- Call your child's teacher and find out the truth.
- Ask your child's teacher for a copy of the assignments for the
week and the due dates.
- Show the list the next time that your child claims there's no
homework.
- Get a copy of your school board's homework policy and complain
to the principal if the teacher is not following this policy.

I left my books and homework assignment in school.
If the assignment and books aren't home, then your child feels she
avoided homework. You and I have a lapse of memory occasionally and
forget something, but again, this is more the exception than the rule.
Your child will inadvertently leave homework assignments in school on
occasion, too. However, you must take action if forgetfulness becomes
a habit. Here's what to do:

- Become friends with parents of your child's classmates at the beginning of the school year.
- Form an informal network where each parent will help other parents with homework.

- Call other parents in the class and ask them for the missing assignment.
- Arrange to borrow books when the other youngster has finished the assignment.
- Ask the teacher to inventory your child's book bag before leaving class. It'll take only a few seconds and your child will soon get the message.

This is not the way the teacher told us.

Conflicts typically brew between you and your child whenever you attempt to show how to solve a homework problem. Your child's teacher may have shown your child a different way to solve the problem than you were taught in school. Both methods arrive at the same answer, but your child's teacher is looking for the way your child learned to solve the assignment. Here's what to do:

- Admit there is more than one way to solve the problem. Your method isn't wrong and neither is the teacher's. Your child must learn to solve the problem the way the teacher shows the class.
- Don't argue with your child if you disagree with the teacher's method.
- Call your child's teacher and discuss the dilemma.

It's my life and I don't want to do homework.

This excuse is a sign of maturity. Your child has had a taste of independence and is starting to make decisions without your input. She realizes she has the power to avoid things that are displeasing. It makes sense to her that she decides when to do homework assignments. Here's what to do:

- Try to reason with your child before taking a harsh approach.
- Explain there are activities we can choose to do and activities we are required to do.
- Point out that this rule applies to all of us.

I'm never going to use this stuff anyway.

It is hard to argue with the truth. Some lessons taught in school are of no practical value. How many times have you used geometry since you were in school? Yet, there are lessons that seem to be irrelevant now that play an important role in future classes. Here's what to do:

- Acknowledge that some lessons are not very useful outside the classroom. This statement recognizes that your child's observation is not necessarily wrong.
- Mention that some lessons will become important in the future.
- Make it clear there is at least one reason for learning the lesson— to pass a test.
- Call your child's teacher and ask for an explanation of the relevance of the lesson.

4.

Be Coach
Mom and Dad

- Knowing Yourself
- Knowing Your Child
- Communicating with Your Child
- Motivating Your Child
- Learning How to Help

Whenever someone talks about coaching I run the other way. Be a coach? Not me! That's for those other guys. Coaching is a thankless job. Parents look to you as an unpaid baby-sitter. Kids see you as a gym teacher who likes only those kids who perform well. And your spouse feels you've become a Walter Mitty being the athlete you never were.

I've attended my kids' games and realize a coach puts a lot of time and effort into making the activity worthwhile. A coach plans activities, scouts the other teams, comes up with winning strategies, and trains the kids.

You and I can duck out of being a Little League coach, but we can't quit as our kid's homework coach. This is a job that only a mom or dad—or both—can fill. You're the one who plans to address homework activities, scouts what the teacher really wants, comes up with a way to meet the teacher's goal, shows your child techniques for solving assignments, then lets your child do the work. And it goes without saying you're always the unpaid baby-sitter.

Coaching your child requires the skills of a teacher, a child psychologist, and a saint. You must fill all those roles and more. You're the

- lawmaker creating rules for your child to follow;
- homework police looking for violations of those rules;
- judge who objectively looks at the facts of a situation and determines if your child is goofing off or if this is a simple case of miscommunication with the teacher;
- defense lawyer who fights the system for your child when she has been wronged;
- twenty-four-hour teacher who shows your child how to solve any problem;
- doctor who makes all your child's troubles go away;
- cheerleader who roots for your child even when all hope for success is lost.

Homework coaching requires you to reach a few very clear objectives. First, you must establish the homework routine in your home. I've discussed these techniques in previous chapters. You must create an atmosphere for learning and studying. By this I mean more than creating a comfortable place for your child to do homework.

A learning environment includes the proper attitude about school and studying. When the rest of the family members consider education important, then your child will follow suit.

You and I tend to develop our attitudes about school and education from our days sitting behind the desk. We see education as a positive experience if we had a good experience in school. Yet, we are quick to reject school if those years left us with a bad taste.

We have to distance ourselves from our school experiences if we are to become a top coach for our child. Our experiences are not relevant to our child's experiences in school. Hard for me to believe, but true. My children are taught by different teachers than those who taught me. Different textbooks are used, and the whole atmosphere of school has changed since we attended.

We must look objectively at our child's education. And that's a key goal of being a coach. Identify the facts, then interpret them objectively so you can devise a winning strategy for your child.

PROCEDURE:
How to coach your child

1. Have a nightly conversation about school with your child.
2. Avoid simply asking "How was school today?" because you probably respond to whatever she answers with "That's nice," but you're not really listening. Your actions tell her you're not interested in her education.
3. Demonstrate that you and family members use the skills your child is learning. Let her see you read a book and write correspondence. Show that math learned in school is used to balance your checkbook and tally the grocery list. Don't make a big production out of this; instead bring it up naturally.
4. Ask your child's teacher for advice on how you can supplement the educational plan for your child. He's your child's head coach and you're the assistant coach responsible for homework.
5. Teach your child skills necessary to study and complete homework assignments.
6. Don't do homework assignments for your child. The coach can't get into the play even when doing the assignment yourself is more efficient than standing on the sidelines shouting directions.
7. Motivate your child into doing a good job by giving her encouragement. Encouragement begins by treating your child with respect, just the way you'd like to be treated. Don't be surprised when you receive the same respect in return. Kids tend to use our behavior as the model for their behavior. Encourage your child with a thumbs-up, high five, or the old pat on the head. A hug is even better.
8. Check off homework problems correctly solved rather than

looking for mistakes. The results are almost the same, except you're telling her you're looking for successes, not failures. Say "Great! Six right. Only four to go," rather than "You got four wrong."

9. Build your child's self-esteem. Children who have a high perception of themselves have a positive attitude toward undertaking new challenges.

10. Let your child know she is truly needed and capable of making a significant contribution to the family and her school.

11. Allow your child to influence her situation. Explain problems to her, then give her a limited number of solutions from which she can choose to solve the problem.

12. Make mistakes something good instead of bad, because mistakes show your child what she needs to learn. Once mistakes become acceptable, she focuses on learning from those mistakes to improve and will not fear failure.

13. Teach your child interpersonal skills such as self-discipline, cooperation, negotiation, listening to others, being a friend, and how to have empathy for others.

14. Show your child how to evaluate situations, to decide a course of action, to know the consequences of those actions, and to understand she will be accountable for her actions.

15. Handle conflicts objectively. Keep an open mind. Gather facts before drawing a conclusion.

16. Don't take your child's actions personally. Kids become frustrated with assignments and release their frustration toward parents. You and I feel we're being disrespected and retaliate.

17. Be a third party to redirect your child's focus by calmly saying, "Let's see what the teacher wants you to do." This maintains your role as an assistant coach while empathizing with your child.

18. Maintain a positive attitude.

19. Don't argue with your child. Walk away and cool off as soon as you lose your temper. Reestablish your position as coach when both of you have regained composure.

20. Listen carefully to your child and make a sincere effort to identify each of her points. Reiterate them once she's finished to show that you understand her position.
21. Give your child tips on how to overcome her frustrations by working through a problem.
22. Point out to your child how you think she mishandled the situation and how her actions made you feel bad. Calmly let her know that you've been hurt by her actions.
23. Let your child have the last word.
24. Apologize to your child if your misunderstanding caused the problem and admit you, too, can make mistakes.

TALES OUT OF SCHOOL: NO. 902

I hated the times I was called upon in class to answer a question. So I always found a remote desk in the classroom, the desk that was the farthest from the teacher's view, but my strategy rarely worked. Teachers noticed everyone. I wasn't afraid of the teacher, I just didn't want to be embarrassed by giving the wrong answer in front of my friends.

Then I came across a sensitive teacher who was careful not to embarrass anyone in the class. He peppered students with questions and called on everyone. However, he responded to a wrong answer with "I know what you meant to say," then he gave the correct answer. No one was afraid to participate in class.

Knowing Yourself

I'm not mechanically inclined, yet I rarely admit it. When our bathroom sink clogs I step in, grab a plunger, and go to town. A nasty odor usually precedes the gunk that spits out of the drain. The sink becomes covered with the black, smelly goo, and the water that once trickled down the drain stops altogether. Of course, I do my handiwork with the bathroom door closed, but the smell brings the family outside the door.

"Is everything all right?" My wife knows better than to ask.

"Nothing to worry about. I have things under control." In my dreams.

I move to plan two—opening the trap, a simple job. I'd watched Norm and the guys do it all the time. Just unscrew the bend in the pipe, all the gunk flows into the bucket. I'm never sure if you turn it clockwise or counterclockwise to open. It usually never matters since the screw doesn't budge anyway.

After a few frustrating hours and in Tool Time style, I'd proudly open the door and ask my wife for the Drano guy's phone number.

None of us wants to admit we have weaknesses nor do we want to let our kids know we can't solve all their problems. Yet, this lack of honesty can hinder our performance as coach.

A coach needs to identify facts, then use those facts to come up with a strategy to solve a problem. Unfortunately, you and I sometimes deem fact-finding as unnecessary. As soon as we see a few facts falling into a pattern, we jump to a conclusion. What you don't know can hurt you.

Being a good coach requires you to take a hard look at all the facts.

I fear that my child will fail because I'm not a good parent.
The fear is legitimate, but the underlying premise is not, according to educators. Most children are successful in spite of our mistakes. Failure is subjective. My definition is a rather simple one. If my daughters learn a skill to earn a living, are able to put food on the table, keep a roof over their heads, and have the wherewithal to raise their own families, then my wife and I have not failed. You and I can try to instill habits that won't lead to failure. However, it is up to our kids to adopt those good behaviors. If they don't, then our kids have failed—not us.

My child's problems should be hidden from everyone.
No parent wants to admit their child is less than perfect. In reality, no child is perfect. All kids have faults and need help. You treat your child with home remedies whenever she gets a cold. However, you don't hesitate to call a physician when your treatment no longer works. Yet, many parents are embarrassed to get the same level of help from their school district.

I lack self-assurance.

You're probably like me in assuming every parent knows how to raise kids. I recall many times sitting at a parents' assembly where administrators described a new approach to math or some other subject. Technical buzzwords flew in all directions. Parents began studiously nodding. Each one assumed the other had a firm grasp on the topic. I soon realized none of the parents knew what the administrator was talking about, but they were too embarrassed to ask.

I found myself having a similar experience when it came to my child's homework assignments. Even when I didn't understand the instructions, I blamed my child for not paying attention in class. I lost confidence in my own common sense. The reality is if the assignment isn't clear to you, then it probably isn't clear to your child and the rest of the class.

I compare my successes with my child's.

We sometimes look at our child as our competitor. We're rooting for them to succeed, but feel inadequate if their accomplishments surpass our own. This is just a passing feeling for most of us. However, some parents find themselves discouraging their kids from activities that could overshadow their own success. Sometimes we become too personally involved with our child's success. We try to make up for our own lack of achievement in school by pushing our child into directions she either does not want to go or where she isn't capable of achieving.

My kid inherited my skills.

We tend to assume our ability to learn is inherited. If you're an excellent speller, so should be your child. If you performed poorly in history, then it's acceptable for your child to fail also. Academic performance is not passed down through genes.

My family will negatively influence my child.

Family situations have a dramatic effect on your child. Some children who are brought up in a family environment where the relationship between Mom and Dad is strained use homework assignments as a way to bring the family together. These kids purposely make errors and cause problems to attract attention, then elicit help from Mom and

Dad. Kids also make mistakes to be noticed. Good behavior rarely draws attention.

TALES OUT OF SCHOOL: NO. 82

It's embarrassing when parents lose touch with reality when it comes to expectations for their child. This happened to a couple when they told friends and relatives that their son was going to be a physician.

In his junior year of high school, they took him on weekend visits to colleges the caliber of Georgetown, Columbia, and Yale. They'd walk around the campus, inspect dorm rooms, and interview faculty members. They looked down on parents who were simply hoping their child would be accepted to a state college.

Their dreams were hit with a taste of reality during an admissions interview when the counselor told their son the list of courses required for incoming freshmen.

"English Comp! You mean I have to take English?" he questioned.

The final blow came when the admissions counselor asked those magic words, "What are your SAT scores?" The scores barely qualified him for a local state college.

Knowing Your Child

"If I could only get into your mind for just a few minutes, maybe I could understand you." My mom always uttered those words whenever she became frustrated with me for skirting a homework assignment. You've probably heard similar words from your mother. Sometimes our actions as kids defy logic.

Kids develop their own brand of logic as they grow up. Their actions give clues to what they're thinking. Unfortunately, these clues can easily lead us to the wrong conclusion.

Remember the times you actually forgot your homework at home?

No one believed you. Why? Because everyone thought they knew how you think and concluded you were trying to extend the deadline for the assignment. You knew the truth, but defending yourself was a losing battle.

Kids are complicated. Growing up is a challenge itself, and the challenge becomes increasingly difficult when your child starts school. Further complicating matters, she may lack the ability to describe her difficulty. Words come out of her mouth, but the meaning isn't clear. You need to turn on your parental ESP to see what is really bothering your child. Look at the situation as your child sees it, then the words might make sense.

It's a frightening world to your child. She knows how to respond by observing how you handle similar situations. She asks you to explain events that are confusing. However, in school, she is on her own with strangers. Mom and Dad are not around to help sort out this new experience.

Your child's natural reaction is to avoid the situation altogether— and that might be avoiding school. Kids will come up with creative reasons for not going to school. Your job is to treat the excuses as a symptom of an underlying problem, which you with the help of your child's teacher need to identify and resolve.

Kids begin school with the skills you've taught them: skills to take care of their needs, skills to communicate with others, skills to make friends. School is a social experience for your child where her friends become more important than lessons and family.

My wife and I were deeply concerned when our child started to make friends in school. We realized we were starting to lose control of our child. Will her friends be a good or bad influence on her? Is she being supervised when she is over at her friend's house? Does her friend's family have rules that conflict with our standards? These are unknown factors that could have a dramatic impact on our relationship with our child.

The teachers I've spoken to say that you should worry only about situations that affect the welfare of your child. Establish rules for safety and don't waver. Teach your child right from wrong and she will know when to break off a friendship if events turn for the worse.

As the homework coach, you need to get into your child's brain so you know how to give the correct advice. Obviously you're in the same predicament as your child's teacher. What do teachers do to solve this problem?

PROCEDURE:
How to deal with your child's moods

1. Your child's mind is in continuous change. What she thinks today might be completely opposite of what she will be thinking tomorrow. This makes piecing together clues very challenging.
2. Your child is in a world of her own, sometimes tuning out the rest of us. Your mom probably called this daydreaming. This is normal and educators suggest gently touching your child to bring her mind back to earth.
3. Don't take your child's aggression personally. When something annoys your child she tends to release her frustrations as verbal abuse. Your child's ability to control herself is at its lowest point at the end of the day, and saying "It's time to do your homework" typically sets off the abusive behavior. Be firm. Keep to the homework schedule. Call for a ten-minute recess to let you and your child cool down, then begin homework again. Once the frustrations are released, she'll realize the homework routine isn't changing and eventually your child's behavior will return to normal. However, in a small number of cases aggressive behavior is normal for the child. Contact your principal if you see a pattern is developing.
4. A child who is down could show the beginnings of childhood depression. Educators warn that childhood depression is a serious behavior with sometimes disastrous results. Kids are normally down after losing a game or getting discouraged by a problem they can't solve. You and I can help ease the loss with a few kind words. However, suspect serious trouble if her depressed mood doesn't swing back to normal over a few weeks. Take action immediately. Let your child know you are

concerned. Stay with her while she does homework and wherever she goes. Call the principal the morning after you recognize her depressive behavior and demand to have her examined by the child-study team that day.

5. Children can be frightened over events that they don't fully understand. Calm those fears with your behavior. Your composure tells your child how to react. Acknowledge that her fears are normal. Let her know you, too, become afraid of things you don't understand. Explain the event that frightened her. Be compassionate but honest in your explanation. Don't say there's nothing to fear. Instead explain the details of the event and how she can avoid the dangers.

6. A child without patience is going to have rough goings in school, because she has a natural tendency to misjudge time. Show your child how to be patient by demonstrating your own patience. Team up with her on a project that requires both of you to be patient, such as building a model, painting a fence, or cooking.

Communicating with Your Child

"If they can make penicillin out of moldy cheese, then I'm sure they can make something good out of you," Grandma always said to me. She probably picked it up from TV. I never took this as an insult. It was Grandma. She was always making cracks that seemed degrading, but she had good intentions. The words just didn't come out the way she'd intended.

The antics of my grandmother made for cute stories to tell my kids. However, Grandma's comments could have had a negative impact on her grandchildren. Adults are looked up to as authority figures by children. What an adult says, kids take seriously.

There is an effective way to communicate with children; however, many times you and I miss the mark. We say things at home we don't really mean. Yet, our kids take us at our word.

So I inquired about the techniques I needed to converse effectively with my children.

PROCEDURE:
How to talk effectively to your child

1. Be a good listener. Try to find what your child is really trying to say.
2. Be respectful when talking with your child. Speak as if you are speaking to a very young friend. Use words like *please* and *thank you* and mean it.
3. Choose appropriate places to hold conversations with your child. Discipline or criticism must take place privately. Don't embarrass or humiliate your child by chastising her in public.
4. Be clear in your conversation. Explain exactly what you want her to do and why she should do it.
5. Talk with a cool head. All too often we get tied up in our own problems and let our frustration out on our child. Avoid talking to your child when you're angry, because you'll say things you don't mean. No apology can mend hurtful words.
6. Talk about misbehavior rather than threatening punishment. Misbehavior is your child's way of communicating to you a problem. Threats alter her behavior, but after a while she will either ignore you or accept the punishment without changing the misbehavior.
7. Make sure you and your child are communicating. Keep in eye contact. Listen carefully to each other. Pay attention. Once your child finishes a thought, restate the facts so you are sure you comprehend what is being said.
8. Let your child finish her thoughts before you respond. Restrain yourself, otherwise you're signaling that her words are unimportant to you.
9. Converse at your child's level of understanding. Place yourself in her position. Look at the facts as someone her age would interpret them. Use vocabulary and sentences you're sure she comprehends.

10. Speak in a friendly tone. Your inflections imply the feelings with which you mean the words you speak. You and I tend to become frightened and go on the defensive whenever someone speaks to us in a harsh tone. We stop listening to the words, and communications break down.

11. Be sympathetic whenever your child approaches the conversation in anger. Avoid conflicts.

12. Let your child express her feelings.

13. Be assertive when enforcing rules or correcting behavior. Calmly identify the problem, then give your child firm direction showing what she needs to do to correct the situation. Make the penalty clear if she does not comply. Don't threaten. Simply state the directions and the punishment, then let your child make the choice. Follow through with the punishment if she doesn't comply.

14. Be truthful and require your child to be truthful. Let her know a lie isn't disastrous, but also is not acceptable.

15. Ask your child to write a note to you if she feels uncomfortable talking about a situation. Read the note privately, then use the note as a way to begin a conversation to explore the issue with your child.

Motivating Your Child

Les Brown is the best motivational speaker to listen to whenever you're feeling down. I'm a big fan of his PBS specials. Give a listen to Les for five minutes and you'll believe you can accomplish anything. Somehow Les uses the right words in the right sentences with a tone of voice that makes you overcome your inhibitions and fears of failure.

Each one of us—including your child—needs someone like Les to be in our corner when times get tough. Les probably won't be much help until your child becomes an adult. So until then you'll have to become your child's motivational leader.

Educators point out that all of us are motivated to learn when we are born. Only a few hours after her birth your child learns how to cry out for food and for a change of diaper. From that time on she instinctively seeks to learn new things. Within nine months she is watching your every movement, and by the end of the first year she's attempting to do the things you do.

Then something magically happens when your child begins school. Your child loses much of her learning motivation. Learning new things becomes less of a challenge and more of a chore. Learning isn't fun anymore.

You and I are unlikely to appreciate the dramatic changes our children face when they attend school. Most of us think of our child's school as a black box. We drop off our children in the morning and we pick them up midafternoon. We really don't know what goes on in school. Yet we need to be sensitive to our child if we are to be a good coach. We must keep our youngster's spirits high to meet her challenges head-on.

How do you motivate your child to learn in the atmosphere of school?

PROCEDURE:
How to motivate your child

1. Praise your child frequently.
2. Balance your criticism. Don't simply point out mistakes. Provide your child with a full critique of her work, which includes positive comments for things performed correctly and negative comments for things needing improvement.
3. Ask the question *Why?* whenever your child states she can't do the assignment.
4. Let other family members know of your child's successes. I think this is why they invented refrigerators and cute magnets. Post prizewinning assignments where everyone can see them.
5. Adjust praise to the degree of success. Rewards and praise quickly lose effectiveness when they are not metered in relationship to the success.

6. Praise and rewards must come immediately after the successful behavior. Any delays minimize the benefit of the acknowledgment.

7. Give meaningful rewards to acknowledge your child's success. I always thought candy or a gift is a good reward, but teachers have told me to avoid material prizes if possible. Instead, consider spending a few more minutes of quality time with your child, such as going to lunch or a ball game, or simply hanging out with her for the weekend.

8. Acknowledge your child's difficulties and work to resolve them. Children feel their inability to complete an assignment or make a good grade is their fault.

TALES OUT OF SCHOOL: NO. 501

I thought I heard all the clever ways to motivate a child, but I was wrong. Parents of a second grader came up with an unusual but effective method. Their child was having difficulty with simple addition. She always failed arithmetic tests. Then one day something must have clicked and she started to pass her math tests. They wanted a special incentive to recognize her accomplishment.

The night after receiving the results of a big test, the telephone rang. Mom and Dad were suspiciously busy, so their daughter answered the telephone.

"Hello, Caroline," a deep voice bellowed.

"Yes."

"I heard you earned an A on your arithmetic test yesterday."

The child was puzzled.

"Do you know who I am?"

"No."

"I'm Santa Claus. I know I haven't visited you for five months, but I've been keeping a close eye on your schoolwork."

The child was left speechless.

Learning How to Help

A call for help brings hordes of Good Samaritans who sincerely want to help. Good intentions aren't enough to do the job. In fact, assisting someone when you don't know what you're doing can be dangerous.

I thought I knew the best ways to assist my child until I overheard a parent ask a teacher for tips on how he could help his child. Here's what the teacher recommended.

PROCEDURE:
How to help your child in school

1. Have your child read each homework assignment to you; that way, you'll be assured she has read the assignment thoroughly at least once.

2. Question her about the assignment. Listen carefully for key words and concepts. Ask her to explain them to you. If she can clearly explain terms and concepts used in an assignment, then she is likely to successfully complete the homework assignment.

3. Ask your child to tell you what tools she needs for the assignment.

4. Give your child time to work out problems herself.

5. Show your child how to solve a problem rather than solving it for her.

6. Identify mistakes in the completed assignment. Ask your child to show you how to correct the mistakes.

7. Have your child teach you the lesson. The best way to learn is to be required to teach.

8. Be honest with your child if you can't help. Don't expect to help her in all her lessons. No one's a genius. However, don't leave her stranded either. Ask for assistance from other family members and her teacher.

9. Work on one assignment at a time. Schedule the assignments

---

as I describe throughout this book, and then keep to the schedule.

10. Discuss alternatives she can use to complete the assignment. Your role is to start the discussion, then let her come up with ideas. Give her time to think. Avoid rushing to speak when there is a pause in the conversation.

5.

Making the Grade in the First Grade

- Learning Letters
- Learning Words
- The Art of Pronunciation
- First-Grade Words
- First-Grade Sentences
- More about First-Grade Words
- Reading
- First-Grade Math
- Place Value
- Addition
- Subtraction
- Math Vocabulary
- Word Problems
- Fractions
- Telling Time and Using a Calendar
- Geometry
- Measuring Things

The first grade was an exciting time for my daughter and a breath of fresh air for my wife, the first time in six years she had both the mornings and afternoons to herself. We were one of the fortunate families who squeaked by on a single income, allowing my wife to be a full-time mom to my daughter for all but one of her preschool years.

There are tricks only a mother knows about getting her youngster to do things that seem impossible. And there are tricks only a teacher knows about how to help your first grader learn to read, write, perform arithmetic, and discover the world around her.

My wife and I knew the first grade was the beginning of our child's serious education. This is probably true for you, since in some parts of our country, kindergarten is not a requirement.

I never thought learning first-grade schoolwork was difficult. You're likely to have the same impression, because we tend to judge the degree of difficulty based on our own current knowledge. We know how to perform simple addition and how to read and write. Therefore, you and I assume our children can quickly grasp these skills.

We're mistaken. At least that's what I discovered talking to many first-grade teachers. Your child's education is an assemblage of building blocks of skills. Skills learned in the first grade become the foundation for skills learned in the second grade and so forth. However, many fundamental concepts are introduced for the first time in the first grade.

What is a number? What is a letter? How do numbers relate to things? How do letters come together to form words? These are some of the basics we take for granted, but your child must learn in the first grade.

Here's a way to appreciate the challenge facing your child, the first-grade teacher, and you when you help her with homework. You'll need another adult to help with this demonstration. Place a sweater on a table. Instruct the person to put on the sweater. However, assume the person knows nothing!

I give this challenge to my computer science students at my college. Not one has been successful. They usually begin by telling the person to pick up the sweater. However, the person doesn't know what a sweater is. Furthermore, the person doesn't know what *pick up* means. Nor what arms, hands, and fingers are.

My sweater demonstration is an exaggeration. However, it illustrates the difficulty your child's teacher has when teaching her basic skills. You're likely to have similar difficulty when helping her with her first-grade homework.

Throughout this chapter, I'll share with you the tips, tricks, and hints first-grade teachers have shared with me to help our children better understand schoolwork. I found these suggestions invaluable when my wife and I were called upon to coach our kids through the first grade.

Learning Letters

Typically your school district expects your first grader to recognize letters and numbers and be able to identify her printed name before beginning school. Her teacher will enhance these skills and have your child reading simple sentences by the end of the school year.

Expect your child to be tested the first several days of class. These tests aren't for grading; they determine a baseline of basic knowledge. The results tell the teacher how much review is necessary before the class is introduced to phonics.

Phonics is the association of a particular sound with the image of a letter, such as "sss" for the letter **s**. Once the image and sound are linked together in your child's mind, the teacher uses this skill to phonically spell simple words.

Your job as Coach Mom and Dad is to help the teacher by reinforcing the phonics at home. Avoid the mistake most parents make. Don't become your child's teacher. Think of yourself as the teacher's assistant.

There are several proven methods for teaching your child phonics. Her teacher has chosen one of those methods to use with your child. Don't confuse your child by using a different method at home.

PROCEDURE:
How to help teach your child phonics

1. Ask the teacher for his teaching strategy so you can use a similar strategy at home.
2. Find out the list of simple words used with each phonics lesson. Typically, the teacher will sound a letter, such as "mmm" while pointing to the letter **m** on an alphabet card, then show the letter in a simple word, such as **mom**, and phonically sound the word. Your child begins to associate the sound with letters and use those sounds to pronounce words.
3. Develop a nightly game where your child must find the "letter of the day" in a magazine, book, newspaper, or on any printed material. Of course, the letter is the one taught by her teacher that day in school. Give her five minutes to find as many occurrences as possible, then place the nightly score on the refrigerator door.
4. Give your child a spontaneous pop quiz. We do this around our home. My wife casually notices a letter displayed on my older daughter's sweatshirt, then asks my youngest to find and sound the "letter of the day" on the sweatshirt.
5. Ask your child to help you pronounce a simple word you find in the newspaper. Kids always like to help. Once our daughter knew the sound of several letters, we'd search the newspaper for a word that used those letters. I'd point to each letter and ask her how the letter sounded. She'd sound the letters over again until she recognized the word.
6. Phonically sound words used to instruct your child. For example, I'd ask my daughter if she wanted "ma - ii - ll - ka." I exaggerated the sound to simulate how she sounds out simple words on her homework.
7. Confirm the sounds of each letter with her teacher. Some letters have more than one pronunciation, such as the **e** in **end** and in **eat**. You don't want to contradict the first-grade teacher.

Learning Words

Take it from a parent of two. The first grade can be embarrassing for you and your spouse. It was around mid-school-year when my daughter briefed us on her homework assignment: practice the unvoiced consonants.

I gave one of those fatherly responses.

"Yes, unvoiced consonants. That's a topic right up your mother's alley."

"She said you knew all about unvoiced consonants."

"Yes, indeed," as I searched my mind trying to remember back to my elementary school days. I was sure consonants had something to do with reading.

"Why don't you just read them to me."

The master of all parental stalls, buying time in hopes something she says jogs my memory. However, she never seemed to cooperate.

I'm sure you'll play out a similar scenario with your first grader sometime this school year. It isn't that we are ignorant of our language. We can speak and read well. However, many of us don't remember the rules of English. Vowels, consonants, verbs, nouns, all those basics we learned many years ago are not fresh in our minds. So the challenge all first-grade parents face is to cram for your child's nightly homework.

I never want to look stupid in front of my daughters, so I quietly asked a few first-grade teachers to give me a short refresher course in first-grade language. It all came back to me quickly, and here it is.

- *Symbols* are used to represent letters of the alphabet.
- Words are formed by assembling letters.
- Letters are divided into two groups: consonants and vowels.
- *Vowels* are **a**, **e**, **i**, **o**, and **u**. All the rest are consonants.
- *Consonants* (table 5-1) are further divided into voiced and unvoiced.
- *Voiced* consonants require the sound of the letters to begin in your vocal cords, such as **r**, **v**, **m**, **n**, **y**, **w**, **b**, **d**, **g**, **th** (the), and **z**.
- *Unvoiced* consonants require the sound of the letters to begin in your mouth, such as **p**, **t**, **k**, **f**, **s**, **th** (fifth), **sh**, and **ch**.
- A word containing a consonant also requires a vowel, although the

reverse isn't true. A word containing a vowel does not require a consonant.

- Letters that are vowels are sounded by flowing air through your mouth.
- Vowel sounds are divided into three groups: short sounds, long sounds, and muted sounds.
- *Short sounds* are **aunt, bet, fig, lox, rub**.
- *Long sounds* are **make, weep, tike, tone**.
- *Muted sounds* are **bar, or, took, ball, tout, choice, better**.
- *Silent letters* don't have a sound when they are used with other letters. Table 5-2 contains a sampling of silent letters.

TABLE 5-1
THE SOUNDS OF CONSONANTS

Consonant	The Sound	Consonant	The Sound
b	boy	p	pull
c	come	q	quart
c	cyan	r	rang
d	drive	s	soak
f	four	s	cars
g	get	t	toy
g	geography	v	very
h	hat	w	walk
j	juice	x	wax
k	kite	x	excellent
l	like	x	ox
m	me	y	yellow
n	new	z	zebra

TABLE 5-2
THE SILENT LETTERS

Letter	As in	Letter	As in
b	comb	c	yacht
c	tick	d	ledger

Letter	As in	Letter	As in
g	lau<u>g</u>h	n	autum<u>n</u>
h	<u>h</u>onor	p	<u>p</u>neumatic
k	<u>k</u>now	p	<u>p</u>sychology
l	ca<u>l</u>f	t	Chris<u>t</u>mas
l	ta<u>l</u>k	t	wi<u>t</u>ch
l	ca<u>l</u>m	w	<u>w</u>rite

The Art of Pronunciation

I admire how television announcers seem to breeze through the pronunciation of any word the writers place before them. I thought they were geniuses until a conversation with a few first-grade teachers revealed their secrets.

There are two tricks of good pronunciation: phonetically spell the word, and properly position your lips and tongue when saying the word. I could teach my kids phonic spelling, but how on earth was I expected to explain lip and tongue movements to describe pronunciation? Kids quickly pick up on correctly pronouncing most letters, so you shouldn't be too concerned. There are a few letters kids have difficulty saying.

PROCEDURE:
How to pronounce difficult letters

1. Sounding **b** is done by holding your breath, closing your lips, and breathing out abruptly without saying anything, which is a good way to say to your child not to use her vocal cords.
2. The **d** sound is created by pressing the front portion of your tongue behind your upper teeth, then abruptly pulling down the whole tongue while breathing out and using your vocal chords.
3. Sounding the letter **f** is done by placing your tongue on the bottom of your mouth while breathing out, then quickly

placing your lower lip on the bottom of your upper teeth. Make this sound without using your vocal cords.

4. The letter **g** is sounded by placing the center of your tongue onto the roof of your mouth, then breathing out abruptly, using your vocal cords to make the sound.

5. Sounding **k** requires you to place your tongue in the same position as you did sounding the letter **g**, except this time don't use your vocal cords to make the sound.

6. You'll need to perform some tongue gymnastics to properly pronounce the letter **r**. Curl the front of your tongue toward the roof of your mouth and curl the sides so they slightly touch your upper teeth, then breathe out using your vocal cords to make the sound.

7. Sounding **p** is done by holding your breath, closing your lips, and breathing out abruptly without using your vocal cords to make the sound.

8. The letter **s** is pronounced by closing your teeth, placing the sides of your tongue by your upper back teeth, and the tip of your tongue below your lower teeth. Breathe out, making the sound without using your vocal cords.

9. The **t** sound is created the same way as you pronounce **d**, but pull down the tip of your tongue instead of your whole tongue. Don't use your vocal cords to make the sound.

10. The **th** sound at the end of a word, such as in **math**, is pronounced by placing your tongue between your upper and lower teeth while breathing out without using your vocal cords.

11. Sounding **th** at the beginning of a word, such as in **the**, is made the same way as you pronounce the **th** at the end of a word except you use your vocal cords to make the sound.

12. The letter **v** is sounded by placing your lower lip on the bottom of your upper teeth, breathing out as you open your mouth, making the sound with your vocal cords.

13. The **z** sound is created the same way you pronounce **s**, but use your vocal cords to make the sound.

First-Grade Words

Communicating with a first grader can be a challenge. They're quick to understand you, then at times you're ignored. However, you're never sure why you're being ignored. Could it be a medical condition or just a lack of understanding of your vocabulary?

My wife and I had such an experience with our daughter. Like many parents, we thought the worst: she had developmental problems. So we did what any parents would do, asked friends and relatives to help diagnose the condition.

Of course, this only confused the issue, and we eventually brought her to our pediatrician for a thorough evaluation. He put her through a battery of tests, then broke the news to us. She had what he called SH syndrome.

We were shocked. He said SH syndrome is common among first, second, and third graders. In fact, chances are good your child also has an undiagnosed case of SH syndrome. There were several cases of SH syndrome in my child's first-grade class.

The condition is more annoying than serious, our pediatrician reported. You see, the *SH* stands for *selective hearing*. Whenever our daughter doesn't want to do what we ask, she ignores us.

Selective hearing is one possibility for why you have problems communicating with your first grader. Another reason can be vocabulary, according to educators. Your child learns basic vocabulary during the preschool years by associating words you say with things you do.

For example, you speak the word *milk* many times when you give your child the white liquid. She quickly makes the connection, and the word *milk* becomes a permanent part of her vocabulary.

By the time she starts the first grade, she can associate many things and actions with the sound of related words. She still doesn't recognize the written word with the sound, however. This occurs when your child is introduced to reading in the first grade.

She learns basic, preschool vocabulary naturally, with little help from you and Bert and Ernie. Most of her vocabulary is acquired through observation. She watches actions, listens to words, then attempts to deduce the meaning without talking to you. She presumes her interpretation is accurate. And you probably don't realize she is quietly building this vocabulary without proper checks and balances.

Your job is to help your child develop a first grader's vocabulary and help her make the connection between the word sound and the printed word. Educators say the best method is to break the vocabulary list into two components: simple words called sight words, and complex words referred to as compound words.

Sight words are typically one-syllable words such as **can** and **boy** while *compound words* include **baseball** and **driveway**. Table 5-3 contains a sample list of vocabulary words your first grader should learn. Ask her teacher for the vocabulary used in her class since this is the list she is required to master. Here's how you can use the vocabulary list to help your child with reading and writing.

PROCEDURE:

How to use a vocabulary list to help with reading and writing

1. Ask your child to print vocabulary words on index cards—one word per card, so you can use them as flash cards.
2. Pick a word each night, and then have her find these words in the newspaper or magazine you're reading. This exercise reinforces the image of the word in her mind.
3. Print messages to your child using words on her vocabulary list.
4. Play the synonyms and antonyms game. *Synonyms* are words that mean the same, and *antonyms* are words that are opposites. For example, **look** and **see** are synonyms, and **go** and **come** are antonyms. Mix up flash cards, then ask her to pair off the synonyms and antonyms. Some flash cards can't be paired off because there isn't a matching word in the stack.
5. Play the picture game. Find pictures in magazines or in books, then ask her to search through her flash cards and find words that relate to the picture.
6. Locate compound words on her vocabulary list, such as **driveway**, then ask her to break up the word into smaller words—**drive** and **way**. This helps her recognize that some words are created by putting together two or more words.

7. Play board games like Scrabble with your child, but only use words on her vocabulary list.

8. Use the finger method to help your child sound out letters of words. A teacher showed me this trick. Ask her to point to each letter in the word, then make the sound of the letter. Ask her to increase the pace until she pronounces the complete word at normal speed.

TABLE 5-3
FIRST GRADER'S VOCABULARY

A
a, all, am, an, and, any, are, as, ask, at, ate, away

B
ball, be, big, black, blue, boy, brown, but, by

C
came, can, cat, come, could

D
did, dog

E
eat

F
find, for, four, from, fun

G
get, girl, give, go, good

H
had, has, have, he, help, her, here, him, his, how

I
I, in, into, is, it

J
jump, just

K
know

L
let, like, little, look

M
make, may, me, must, my

N
new, night, no, not, now

O
of, old, on, once, one, open, our, out, over

P
play, please, pretty, put

R
ran, red, ride, run

S
said, saw, say, see, she, so, some, stop

T
take, than, thank, that, the, them, then, there, they, this, three, to, too, two

U
under, up

W
walk, want, was, way, we, well, went, were, what, where, white, who, will, with

Y
yellow, yes, you

First-Grade Sentences

All the experiences your child has during her preschool years come into play in the first grade when she begins to assemble words into formal sentences. By the time she was two, she could sound words to describe her needs, such as "milk" and "cookie." In the next few years, she combined words to form complete thoughts, like "more milk" and "I want cookies."

Now in the first grade, she learns the rules of organizing words into sentences to complete an idea. Your job is to help guide her through this new learning experience, and if you're like me, you'll panic the first time she comes home and asks you to write an imperative sentence. An imperative sentence?

We already know how to write various kinds of sentences, though you might have forgotten the technical terms used to describe these sentences. So let's brush up on sentence rules so you can sound like a whiz in front of your child.

There are four kinds of sentences: declarative, exclamatory, imperative, and interrogative. A *declarative* sentence tells about something. First graders know this as a "telling" sentence. The *exclamatory* sentence says something surprising. In some first grades, this sentence is known as the "surprise" sentence. An *imperative* sentence gives a command and, therefore, has the simple moniker of a "command" sentence. An *interrogative* sentence asks a question and is known as an "asking" sentence.

You can tell your child there are two ways to determine the kind of a sentence: by listening to the context of the sentence, and by looking at the punctuation at the end of the sentence. The asking and surprise sentences are easy for her to recognize. One asks a question and ends with a question mark, and the other talks about excitement and ends with an exclamation mark.

My kids had difficulty distinguishing between a telling sentence and a command sentence. Both end with a period, so there aren't any distinguishing marks when the sentence is printed. Kids must ask themselves, Does the sentence tell you or someone to do something, or does the sentence tell you or someone about something? If the answer to the first question is yes, then the sentence is a command sentence, otherwise the sentence is a telling sentence.

Check with your child's teacher to find out if all four sentence types will be taught to your child in the first grade. Some school districts teach only the telling and asking sentences and leave the command and surprise sentences for the second grade.

A sentence expresses a complete idea and has two parts: a subject and a verb. First graders need only to understand that the *subject* of a sentence is the person or thing talked about in the sentence. Take, for instance, the sentence **"Jack runs."** **Jack** is the subject. A *verb* is better known as an *action word*. **Runs** in the previous example is the verb.

If a sentence doesn't have a verb, then it is not a sentence. **"Jack."**, for example, is not a sentence, because a verb is missing and no complete idea is being expressed. However, **"Run."** is a complete sentence, because **run** is a verb and completes an idea.

This is all the review you'll need to successfully coach your first grader in her efforts to learn sentences. Here's what some first-grade teachers recommended to me for reinforcing lessons on sentences taught in the classroom.

PROCEDURE:
How to reinforce lessons on sentences

1. Ask your child to print you a message. This gives her a chance to use her new skill of constructing sentences and a special way to show off in front of you and the family.

2. Print a few sentences with mistakes and ask your first grader to correct your work. I'd create sentences missing the verb or subject. Sometimes I'd leave out punctuation or capitalize the wrong word.

3. Mix correct sentences with incorrect sentences, and then ask your child to find and correct the incorrect sentences.

4. Show your child a picture from a magazine or book and ask her to write a sentence describing the picture. Make sure she uses proper capitalization and punctuation and properly uses the subject and verb.

5. Ask your child to sort her flash cards into two stacks: subjects and verbs. This helps her recognize words that are used as subjects in a sentence and words used to describe action.

6. Have your child create sentences using flash cards. You'll probably need to make flash cards for punctuation marks and

create another set of flash cards where the first letter of each word is capitalized. My kids looked at this exercise more as a game than schoolwork.

More about First-Grade Words

Your first grader will learn a bit more about words than how to place them in order to complete an idea in a sentence. She'll also learn that words can be placed in another kind of order—the alphabetized order.

Alphabetizing words doesn't seem like too much of a challenge, but it is quite a challenge for a first grader. Alphabetizing brings together two skills: knowing the order of the alphabet, and vocabulary words.

Most first graders are expected to place only three words in alphabetical order using only the first letter of the word. You can help reinforce this skill by mixing up flash cards, then asking her to place them in alphabetical order.

Another skill your child learns is how to capitalize the first letter of every sentence and to capitalize other words regardless of their position in the sentence, such as the days of the week, the months of the year, the names of people, and the word *I*.

Our daughter's first-grade teacher introduced the capitalization rules toward the end of the first grade when he added the days of the week and months to our child's vocabulary list. Check with your child's teacher and find out when these rules will be taught so you know when to introduce them at home.

Probably our toughest first-grade lesson was helping our daughter learn the difference between singular and plural and making sure only one is used in a sentence. Even you and I have problems with using singular and plural correctly, because of the inconsistencies in the rules.

Many words are made plural by placing an **s** at the end of the word—for example, **cars** and **boats**. However, the rules change with words that end with the letter **y**, such as **copy**. Whenever a word ends with the letter **y**, the letter **y** is removed and is replaced by **ies**, such as in **copies**. The exception to this rule is when the letter **y** is preceded by a vowel (**a**, **e**, **i**, **o**, and **u**), as in **boy**; the **y** remains and the letter **s** is added to the end of the word to make it plural, such as **boys**. Words ending in the letter **h**, such as **lunch** and **fish**, are made plural by placing **es** at the end of the word, as in **lunches** and **fishes**.

All of the words I just mentioned are called *regular plurals* because the spelling of the word doesn't change much when the word is changed from singular to plural. There are *irregular plurals*, which are words whose spelling is changed when made into a plural, such as **man** to **men, mouse** to **mice**, and **I** to **we**.

When a subject is plural, so must be the verb. For example, changing the sentence **"The boy is here."** to plural requires both the noun and the verb to be plural, as in **"The boys are here."** As you'd expect, there are exceptions to this rule where it is assumed the verb is plural, as in the case of **"The boy ran."** and **"The boys ran."**

The rules for changing a word to plural can be hard to remember. Here's the method my wife and I used when coaching our daughter.

Meet with your child's teacher and ask him to give you the rules he'll be covering in class. Some school districts gradually introduce the topic over two grades so as not to confuse young students.

Avoid using technical terms such as *regular* and *irregular plurals*. This tends to become confusing. Instead, start with words that can be made plural by adding the letter **s** at the end, then introduce the rule for words ending in **y**. Follow up with words made plural by adding the letters **es**. Finally, use singular and plural words in a sentence and show how to make the noun and the verb agree.

Here are a few tips you can use to make it fun for your child to learn alphabetizing words, capitalizing letters, and properly using singular and plural words.

PROCEDURE:
How to make learning about words fun for your child

1. Ask your child to cut out headlines from a newspaper, and then place the headlines in alphabetical order. This exercise shows your first grader that words learned in school are also used in publications.

2. Have your youngster search through a magazine or one of her books to find words that are singular and plural.
3. Print several sentences using words in her vocabulary list and make subjects and verbs disagree, then ask her to correct your work.
4. Read aloud simple sentences where the subject and verb disagree. Your child should catch your errors immediately because the sentences will sound wrong. This technique tunes her ear to disagreement between subject and verb.
5. Mix correct and incorrect subjects and verbs and capitalizations in printed messages you leave for your child. Ask her to find the mistakes.

Reading

My wife and I were a little disappointed when we looked at our daughter's first-grade reading book. The pictures were large and the words sparse. How could she learn to read if there weren't a lot of words? This was the question I posed to the first-grade teacher. Then I became the pupil and learned a little about what it takes to teach six- and seven-year-olds how to read.

Reading is more than recognizing the meaning of a group of words printed on the paper. The purpose of reading is to understand the ideas conveyed by the author. First-grade reading books are designed to blend both word and idea recognition without becoming overbearing for your child.

The first-grade teacher has the challenge of first showing your child that letters are assembled to create words that represent things, such as **cat** and **dog**. And these words can be placed in an order to convey an idea like "The cat jumps high."

The first-grade reading book emphasizes more word recognition than idea recognition in the text. Word recognition includes both sounding out the word and identifying the meaning of the word while reading the sentence in the book.

Your child at first concentrates on pronouncing the word correctly and identifying the meaning of the word. She spends little time linking together the meaning of the words in the sentence. However, the picture supplements the sentence by conveying the idea of the sentence.

As her word recognition and pronunciation skills improve, she will begin to identify the meaning of the sentence. The picture is then used to confirm her interpretation of the sentence.

Once you know the logic behind first-grade reading, you can direct your coaching efforts to conform with the way your child learns to read. Don't push too hard to increase her reading speed. Children need time to develop reading skills. Some first graders catch on quickly while others require more time to master reading. Here's what first-grade teachers suggest.

PROCEDURE:
How to help your child read

1. Encourage your child to read. Don't demand it.
2. Select reading material containing words in her vocabulary. Reading is a challenge unto itself, so there is no need to increase her frustrations by introducing words she hasn't yet learned.
3. Enforce speed control when your child reads. Some first graders tend to benchmark their achievement by the number of pages read rather than the number of pages understood.
4. Have your child read a sentence, then stop and explain the sentence to you. You'll be focusing her attention on the context of her reading.
5. Ask your child to read aloud to you so you can monitor her performance and help her link the words together to understand the meaning of the sentence.
6. Select a picture from your child's book. Make up and print three sentences with only one of them describing the picture. Be sure the sentences comprise words she understands. Ask her to pick out the sentence that best describes the picture.

7. Ask your child to draw a conclusion to a story. For example, "John threw the ball to Jane. The ball went into the air. What do you think happens?" Your child is expected to say, "Jane catches the ball."

8. Have your child identify characters in the story and explain what the characters are doing. This helps you to know if she is properly comprehending the story.

First-Grade Math

First-grade math seems insultingly simple to you and me, but this is a whole new and challenging world for your child. Your first grader probably knows how to print numbers from 0 through 9 and can say those numbers in order.

This school year she begins to do something with numbers. She'll learn the meaning of numbers and how to perform addition and subtraction. Her teacher will introduce fractions and geometric shapes. And you'll be expected to coach your child through these lessons.

My wife and I discovered being a math coach is more difficult than we expected. The job appeared easy—after all, how difficult is first-grade math? Then we quickly realized our job had nothing to do with solving math problems. Instead, we had to show a six-year-old how to understand the abstract concept of math.

Our first stop was the school and an informal conference with our child's first-grade teacher. He spent a few hours showing us his plan and the technique he and other first-grade teachers use to introduce math to students.

I'll save you a trip and share with you what we learned. Your initial task is to relate the number with a group of objects. This is an interesting approach to teaching first graders basic math since it reinforces the concept that numbers represent real things in a way a six-year-old can easily understand. Here's a simple exercise to try with your child.

PROCEDURE:

How to introduce your child to math

1. Place an apple on the table, point to the apple, and say, "One apple."
2. Place another apple on the table, point to each apple, and say, "One apple, one apple."
3. Point to both apples and say, "Two apples." We've all done this with our kids, but probably never appreciated the importance of this exercise. This is the first time your child associates the sound of a number with objects.
4. Place flash cards with the number 1 in front of each apple to associate the object with the printed number 1.
5. Use a flash card showing the plus sign and the equal sign with the apples to introduce the concept of an equation. An *equation* is a way of saying numbers on each side of the equal sign are equal $(5 = 2 + 3)$.
6. Place two apples on the table and ask your child to count the apples, then place the appropriate flash cards in front of the apples to reinforce the relationship between objects and printed numbers.

Place Value

Another challenging concept for your first grader to learn is place values. *Place value* gives meaning behind the position of digits in a multi-digit number. My daughter had a rough time learning this. She knew how to count from 1 to 100, but really didn't appreciate why 10 had a 0 in the right column and a 1 in the left column.

Honestly, I wasn't much help. I was becoming frustrated explaining the concept in a way a six-year-old could understand.

PROCEDURE:
How to explain place value to a first grader

1. Take a lined piece of paper and draw columns and mark them appropriately with ones, tens, hundreds, and thousands. Start in the ones column and write each number down the column. Make sure the first number is 0. Numbers actually begin with 0 and not 1 (table 5-4).

2. Ask your first grader to point to each number on the paper and count down the column.

3. Stop when she reaches the last number, which is 9. Since there are no more numbers, she must place a 1 in the tens column, which indicates the number of times she counted all the numbers in the first column, and a 0 in the ones column indicating she's ready to start counting again.

4. Take a clean piece of paper and cover up all but the first row of numbers.

5. Ask your youngster to tell you the number she sees on the paper. The number is 10 and helps her to relate the number 10 to place values.

6. Continue another round of counting in the right column. Afterward ask your child to erase the 1 from the tens column and print the number 2 in its place since this is the second time she counted all the numbers in the right column. Again cover up the rest of the numbers and see if she recognizes the number 20.

7. Let her continue counting until the number in the tens column is 9. You'll need some patience for this exercise. On the next round of counting, have her replace the 9 with a 0 and print a 1 in the hundreds column, as shown in table 5-4.

8. Move on to four digits once she is comfortable with the ones, tens, and hundreds columns.

TABLE 5-4
THE PLACE-VALUE TABLE

Thousands	Hundreds	Tens	Ones
	1	0	0
			1
			2
			3
			4
			5
			6
			7
			8
			9

Addition

Adding numbers together isn't difficult for your child to comprehend once she understands the apple exercise I talked about earlier in the chapter. The object now is to replace the apples with numbers.

You need to make a smooth transition from adding together fruit to adding together numbers. Modify the apple exercise by creating an expression consisting of only apples on the kitchen table (2 apples = 1 apple + 1 apple). As before, place flash cards with the equal sign and the plus sign between the apples, but don't use any flash cards with numbers.

Ask your child to build another expression below the apples using the numbered flash cards. Expect her to place the appropriate number below each apple (2 = 1 + 1), which shows her both expressions are the same, except numbers are used in the second expression to represent the apples.

Once she understands that numbers represent real things, set up the apple expression again, however leave off the apple to the right of the plus sign (2 apples = 2 apples +). Challenge her to insert the missing number.

I tried this exercise with my daughter. She stopped at this point and claimed I made a mistake. It took me an hour to explain how zero is the number to represent nothing. Zero can be a difficult concept for first graders to grasp because they become used to relating numbers to objects.

Within a few weeks of adding together apples, my daughter solved simple addition problems using numbers. I then introduced column addition. Don't try this until your child understands place values, otherwise she'll have a difficult time understanding why she needs to align numbers in columns.

Begin with single-digit numbers, such as shown in figure 5-1, and be sure there is no carrying. The concept of carrying a value from the ones column to the tens column is not introduced until the second grade. Table 5-5 contains the values that can be added together without causing a value to be carried over.

$$\begin{array}{r} 3 \\ + 6 \\ \hline 9 \end{array}$$

FIGURE 5-1. ADDING TWO SINGLE-DIGIT NUMBERS WITH NO CARRYING

TABLE 5-5.
NUMBERS TO USE IN SINGLE-DIGIT ADDITION THAT WON'T PRODUCE A CARRY VALUE

First Number	Second Number
0	0 through 9
1	0 through 8
2	0 through 7
3	0 through 6
4	0 through 5
5	0 through 4
6	0 through 3
7	0 through 2
8	0 and 1
9	0

Increase the complexity of the addition problem only when you're sure she has mastered single-digit column addition. Many educators I've spoken to have warned about the dangers of pushing a child too fast when introducing them to the basic concepts of math.

The next degree of complexity requires her to add together three single-digit numbers as illustrated in figure 5-2. Again avoid carrying values. Once mastered, move on to two-digit column addition shown in figure 5-3.

$$\begin{array}{r} 1 \\ 3 \\ +\,2 \\ \hline 6 \end{array}$$

FIGURE 5-2. ADDING THREE SINGLE-DIGIT NUMBERS WITH NO CARRYING

$$\begin{array}{r} 32 \\ +12 \\ \hline 44 \end{array} \qquad \begin{array}{r} 23 \\ +\,1 \\ \hline 24 \end{array}$$

FIGURE 5-3. ADDING DOUBLE-DIGIT NUMBERS WITH NO CARRYING

Subtraction

My kids loved learning subtraction because I used miniature Tootsie Rolls instead of apples. I'd set up the equation just like the addition equation and substitute the minus-sign flash card for the plus sign and the Tootsie Rolls for the apples.

The first equation subtracted one Tootsie Roll from two Tootsie Rolls. And the easiest way to make this meaningful is to let her eat one Tootsie Roll, then count those remaining to determine the difference. Make sure you have a large bag of Tootsie Rolls handy just in case your first grader needs extra work with subtraction. My wife substituted baby carrots whenever she coached the exercise. Within a short time, the food was replaced by numbers.

Follow the same graduated steps used to introduce addition when helping your child learn to subtract numbers. Start off using things in an equation, then move to single-digit column subtraction, as shown in figure 5-4, followed by two-digit column subtraction (figure 5-5). Be sure to avoid carrying values, by always subtracting a smaller number from a larger number in both the ones and tens places.

$$
\begin{array}{r}
3 \\
- 2 \\
\hline
1
\end{array}
$$

FIGURE 5-4. SUBTRACTING TWO SINGLE-DIGIT NUMBERS WITH NO CARRYING

$$
\begin{array}{r}
32 \\
- 12 \\
\hline
20
\end{array}
\qquad
\begin{array}{r}
23 \\
- 1 \\
\hline
22
\end{array}
$$

FIGURE 5.5. SUBTRACTING DOUBLE-DIGIT NUMBERS WITH NO CARRYING

Math Vocabulary

It is amazing how a first grader can take simple everyday math and make it sound scientific. I discovered this when my daughter came home from school and talked about addends and sums. For a moment I didn't know what she was talking about, yet all she was doing was describing addition.

Which number is the addend? It's been a long time since I used the proper terminology to describe components of a math expression. I'm sure you'll find yourself in the same position. So let's jog your memory and review a few terms you're likely to encounter.

There are two kinds of numbers spoken about in the first grade. These are cardinal numbers and ordinal numbers. *Cardinal numbers* are digits used in math problems (e.g., 0, 1, 2, 3, 4). *Ordinal numbers* are first, second, third, etc.

Addition has its own terminology. Numbers being added are called *addends*, and the result of addition is called the *sum*.

The result of a subtraction problem is called the *difference*.

In division, the number being divided is called the *dividend*, and the number used to divide the dividend is called the *divisor*. The result is the *quotient*.

In multiplication, the number being multiplied is called the *multiplicand*, and the number multiplying the multiplicand is called the *multiplier*. The result is called the *product*.

Your first grader will also use special symbols to compare two values. These are the *less than* symbol ($<$) and the *greater than* symbol ($>$). The expression **5 < 6** states that the value 5 is less than the value 6. Likewise, the expression **7 > 4** says the value 7 is greater than the value 4.

Word Problems

A man drives his car 5 miles from his home, up a 45-degree incline for half the distance. How old was he when he arrived at work? Who cares! I hated word problems when I was in school, especially those that led to the wrong answer if you misread the problem.

You'll find word problems on your child's homework; however, these problems are straightforward and require one-step solutions such as addition or subtraction.

There are two kinds of word problems first graders are expected to solve: picture problems and traditional word problems. A *picture problem* combines a picture with a one-sentence question. For example, Jane is pictured in the park with several dogs. Beneath the picture is the question "How many dogs are playing with Jane?"

The object is for your child to read and understand the question, then find and count the dogs in the picture. Picture problems are the first word problems she'll encounter because they help to bridge the gap between counting things and reading a word problem.

Picture problems also lead to traditional word problems, where there aren't any pictures to help your child solve the problem. Here's a typical word problem: Bob buys soda for 60 cents and a bag of pretzels for 30 cents. How much money did Bob spend?

Word problems can confuse any first grader, especially when the problems appear on a homework assignment and the teacher isn't around to give hints. It's your job to assure she uses the proper techniques for solving the problems. Here are some tips given to me by teachers.

They'll come in handy the first time you're faced with a first grader's word problem.

PROCEDURE:
How to solve a word problem

1. Make sure your child takes her time reading and understanding the problem. Many kids rush to a solution without fully understanding the problem.
2. Divide pieces of the problem into three categories (table 5-6): (1) pieces needed to solve the problem; (2) pieces not needed to solve the problem; and (3) pieces your child is unsure of. In the previous example, the soda, pretzels, buying, and the person's name won't help solve the problem. The money amounts will, as will the question "How much . . . spend?"
3. Deduce from the needed pieces the step required to solve the problem. In this example, the step is addition because the problem asks how much was spent.
4. Set up the problem on a piece of paper, then ask her to perform the math.

TABLE 5-6
DIVIDE THE WORD PROBLEM INTO THREE CATEGORIES.

PROBLEM:
Bob buys soda for 60 cents and a bag of pretzels for 30 cents. How much money did Bob spend?

Needed to Solve Problem	Not Needed to Solve Problem	Unsure If Needed to Solve Problem
60 cents	Bob	
30 cents	buys	

Needed to Solve Problem	*Not Needed to Solve Problem*	*Unsure If Needed to Solve Problem*
How much money did Bob spend?	soda	
	bag of pretzels	

Fractions

When my daughter told me we were going to do fractions for homework, I went into an anxiety attack. I saw flashbacks of Sister Combo's class.

Fractions are confusing, especially those involving mixed fractions. However, first-grade fractions are easy to understand and easy to explain to your child. There are typically four fraction facts she'll learn:

- A fraction is a part of something.
- The fraction ½ indicates the whole is divided into two pieces.
- The fraction ⅓ indicates the whole is divided into three pieces.
- The fraction ¼ indicates the whole is divided into four pieces.

Your child's math book contains pictures of a pie or fruit cut into pieces to illustrate each fraction fact. This is an abstract way of teaching fractions since they can't be touched. Your child must divide and assemble the pictures in her mind to fully appreciate the concept.

You can make fractions come alive by using real things around the house. My wife asks my daughter to cut the pie in half, then into quarters. You can also use snacks such as carrots or a candy bar. Pieces don't have to be the same size. For example, a candy bar can be divided into thirds, each piece a different size (figure 5-6).

FIGURE 5-6. A WHOLE CANDY BAR DIVIDED INTO THREE
UNEVEN PIECES

Telling Time and Using a Calendar

Time has a different meaning for young children than it does for you
and me. Kids tend to have little concept of time, which I discovered
when I promised to take my daughter to the park. I said in an hour. Five
minutes later she asked, "Is it time yet?"

Children formally learn about time in the first grade. They'll learn
that a clock and a watch are used to tell the time and they learn how to
read hours and half hours. Minutes and seconds are topics covered in
other grades. The most difficult aspect of teaching your child to read
time is showing her which hand points to the hour and half hour. You'll
figure the best method to solve this problem yourself.

Your child also learns there are seven days in a week and how those
days relate to the calendar. This is where the "Thirty days hath Septem-
ber. . ." rhyme is memorized.

I've found it useful to bring in a little science to answer the battery of
questions from an inquisitive six-year-old, such as "What is a day? Why
is it hotter in August than January?" You might find this a valuable exercise to use with your child.

You'll need an inexpensive globe and a flashlight to answer these
questions. Shoot the beam of light right over the area of the globe
where you live. This is twelve noon. Ask her to touch that spot, then
slowly rotate the globe to the right. The light fades and her finger falls
into darkness until light returns again. This is a day.

Next, place the flashlight over the center of the globe, then tilt the
globe forward so her finger is close to the light. This is the summer.
Tilt the globe backward away from her finger. This is the winter. Her
finger should be a little warmer in the summer than in the winter.

Geometry

Geometry is another subject that brings horror stories to mind. So when my daughter's teacher told us he'd be covering geometry in the first grade, I thought he was losing his mind. All I could imagine was how on earth my wife and I were going to brush up on geometry within a few months.

Fortunately, first-grade geometry has very little to do with high school geometry. Many school districts are attempting to change the image of geometry by introducing the basic concepts in the first grade, then gradually introducing other concepts such as angle measurements in later grades.

Geometry defines the relationship lines have when forming shapes. First graders learn very simple geometrical concepts, such as flat and solid shapes and open and closed shapes. No measurements are required.

Flat shapes include a square, a rectangle, a triangle, and a circle. Solid shapes are a sphere and a cube. These shapes are closed since lines defining the shape are connected. If one line is missing, the shape is considered open.

Another geometrical concept your child will learn is *inside* and *outside* a shape. You'll probably find a picture of a sphere inside a cube in your child's math book to illustrate this concept.

Measuring Things

You've taught your first grader the concept of big and small before the school year began. Now it's time for your child to learn how to better describe size by measuring things. Measuring is one of those tasks that you and I know how to perform. We know inches are combined to make a foot, and feet form yards and miles. We also know ounces make up pints, quarts, and gallons.

However, I was surprised to learn my daughter was also taught the metric system. I assembled a small table (table 5-7) to help you better understand both systems of measurement.

TABLE 5-7
HELPFUL MEASUREMENTS

U.S. Standard Measures	Metric Equivalents	Metric Measures
1 inch =	2.54 centimeters	1 centimeter
12 inches = 1 foot =	0.3048 meters	1 meter = 100 centimeters
5,280 feet = 1 mile =	1.6093 kilometers	1 kilometer = 1,000 meters

6.

Making the Grade in the Second Grade

- Second-Grade Words
- Prefixes and Suffixes
- Abbreviations
- Reading
- Second-Grade Math
- Number Exercises
- Addition and Subtraction with Thousands
- Two-Digit Addition and Subtraction with Carryover
- Checking Answers
- Multiplication and Division
- Measures
- Arabic and Roman Numerals
- Geometry—Lines and Line Segments
- Geometry—Symmetry
- Second-Grade Word Problems
- Biology

D id you ever do something that made the family history books? I'm talking about an event that was so extraordinary—and stupid— that the story is told time and again at every family gathering. One of my classics took place when my daughter began the second grade.

Every parent wants to give their child just a little more than what they experienced as a child, and I'm no exception. I always watched Leonard Bernstein's *Young People's Concert* on television when I was growing up, but never had the opportunity to go in person. When my daughter turned seven, I noticed that Lincoln Center was reviving the series. This was my chance to give my daughter an experience I missed—even if she wasn't interested in music.

The first sign of trouble came when my father-in-law looked at the tickets.

"This starts at two!"

"So, it's a Saturday."

"You're not taking your wife?"

"It's a father-daughter outing. No moms allowed."

"What happens when she needs to go to the bathroom?"

The bathroom? He was right. The concert started after lunch just when she makes a pit stop. No one told me about taking her to the bathroom. The stage was set for disaster. I could see it all happening. We're in the concert and she breaks the news she has to use the facilities. She's too little to use the ladies' room by herself and too old for me to take her into the men's room. What's a dad to do?

Well, we did go to the concert with a little improvisation from my wife and me. First, my daughter's lunch consisted of a small sandwich and a few sips of water and ended with many trips to the bathroom before leaving the house. I also think my wife had a mother-daughter talk explaining why dad was panicking. She got the hint—hold it in if you don't want the old man to get a heart attack. I held my breath during the entire concert and made it through unscathed.

This turned out to be one of many times my wife and I had to improvise to get my daughter through the second grade. You'll have to improvise a lot during your term as parent of a second grader, too. Schoolwork becomes more difficult than in the first grade. Old lessons must be reinforced and new concepts learned.

In this chapter I'll share with you some ways teachers have shown us to avoid potential disasters to make sure our second grader makes the grade.

Second-Grade Words

The novelty of school begins to wear thin in the second grade. Schoolwork is very similar to that of the first grade, but more challenging. Your child's vocabulary grows with more complex words than those learned last year. She also learns about multisyllable words and compound words and is introduced to prefixes and suffixes.

Your job is to make sure she doesn't lose her enthusiasm for learning and isn't frustrated by the difficulty of the new schoolwork. Don't underestimate the difficulty of your assignment either. I compare it to the guy who twirls plates at the end of a stick. You have to keep last year's lessons fresh in your child's mind while introducing new topics.

There is a trick I learned from teachers that made my job as a second-grade parent easy. Make the skills learned in the first grade an active part of her daily life. You and I and our children tend to consider learning less burdensome if we consistently apply our knowledge.

Remember when you first learned to count money? The topic was abstract and dull because you couldn't relate to the concept of money. However, once you received an allowance, you soon became a whiz with money calculations.

Your objective this year is to make your child's vocabulary words become part of her everyday life. I've included a sample list of second-grade vocabulary words (table 6-1) for reference; however, her second-grade teacher can provide you with the complete list of words she is responsible for learning.

Try not to segregate first- and second-grade vocabulary words when working with your child. I made that mistake and almost started World War III with my daughter's teacher. I concentrated on reinforcing her new vocabulary and let the first-grade lessons slip away. Somehow my daughter told the teacher she didn't need to use her first-grade vocabulary—Daddy said so.

After an hour lecture on the telephone about the importance of blending old and new vocabulary words, I conceded my error and promised to make amends. The teacher was correct. We need to reinforce all our child's vocabulary words by using as many of those words as possible around the house.

I found another point made during my phone lecture also valuable. My daughter's teacher suggested I challenge my daughter to give me a definition of the words she used in conversation. Until then, my pop quizzes—no pun intended—concentrated on correct pronunciation and spelling and correct use of words in a sentence. I assumed my daughter knew the meaning of the word.

Asking your child to explain the meaning of words she uses helps reinforce her knowledge of the definition. It may sound absurd to quiz her on the word **ball**. However, the mental procedures she uses to respond to your challenge are the same ones used in later years when the meaning of some words can become confusing.

The quiz also forces her to restate the same idea using other words. You probably remember this exercise from your elementary school days. The teacher asked you to define a word without breaking the cardinal rule of a definition—not to use the word you're defining in the definition.

P R O C E D U R E :
How to improve your child's vocabulary

1. Have your child update the flash cards used in the first grade with second-grade vocabulary words. Remember, you don't need to purchase flash cards. Index cards will do fine.
2. Mix up the first- and second-grade flash cards. The flash cards represent her vocabulary, which is a combination of both grades' vocabulary lists.
3. Create a set of flash cards that contains phonetic spelling. Separate compound words with a hyphen and use hyphens to divide multisyllabic words into their syllables.
4. Ask your child to place both stacks of flash cards in alphabetical order by the first and second letters of the word.
5. Tell her to search the phonetically spelled stack whenever she

has difficulty pronouncing a word. She should find the phonetic spelling quickly since the stack is alphabetized.

6. Have her solve multistep problems on her own. For example, let her know she mispronounced a word, but don't correct her error. Instead, show her how to find the solution to her problem herself by looking through the phonetically spelled flash cards.

7. Quiz your child naturally. I'd listen to my daughter convey a thought in a sentence using her vocabulary words. I'd respond, saying, "I'm not sure what you mean by **jump**," or whatever word she used. My response was a camouflaged quiz, although it sounded like a response I would give to my wife if I didn't understand her.

8. Repeat many of the vocabulary exercises I suggested you use last year (see chapter 5), except this time use both the first- and second-grade vocabulary words.

9. Have your child add newly learned words to the flash-card stacks even if they are not part of the official second-grade vocabulary list. I tried this with my daughter when she started to play the recorder. She learned about the staff, notes, and other musical terminology. Whenever I discovered her using those words frequently in conversations around the house, I would say, "That sounds like a great word for the flash cards." She'd then learn how to spell the word and would create both sets of flash cards, and we used the words as part of our daily vocabulary exercises.

TABLE 6-1
SECOND GRADER'S VOCABULARY

A
always, around

B
beats, because, bed, been, before, best, bicycle, big, book, both, buy

C
call, cold, cracks

D
dance, does, don't, dream, drum

F
fast, five, floor, fly, found

G
goes, gotten, grave, green

H
happy, heart, hide, honk, hot, hug

I
its

J
jump

L
large, laugh, leap, lose, love

M
made, many

O
off, or

P
pretend, pull

R
read, right, run

S
sad, shine, sing, sit, sleep, slide, snap, spin, star, straight, swing

T
tell, their, these, those, tricycle

U
upon, us, use

V
very

W

wash, which, whistle, why, win, wish, work, would, write

Y

your

Prefixes and Suffixes

My daughter rushed through the rooms screaming as I walked in the door from work.

"Daddy! Daddy! Guess what I'm going to start learning Monday?"

My briefcase quickly dropped below my belt as I awaited a plunge. It was like being a quarterback. You know you're in for a blow and you can't do anything about it. This time she stopped inches before contact. My guess is she had a little mother-and-daughter talk after the last episode.

Now don't get me wrong. I don't mind such a welcome. Just that I wish she would be a tad higher above my belt. She was forever blitzing my entrance to give me late-breaking news from the second-grade class. However, she would forget to stop before butting me in a very tender spot. Though I must give her credit for being persistent—my bending over in pain didn't seem to dampen the excitement as she spurted the news.

"We're going to learn Latin and Greek in school!"

What on earth is the teacher thinking? Latin and Greek? How about Spanish or another language more practical? I did what any overly concerned dad would do and called the school.

The phone rang off the hook. I slammed down the phone, criticizing the principal for not being in his office at 7 P.M. I fumed the rest of the night. I couldn't wait to give the school a piece of my mind.

You could call this school rage, which is just as dangerous to school employees as road rage is to you and me. I contained myself the next morning as I complained to the principal.

"I think you're mistaken. Latin and Greek haven't been taught for nearly half a century."

The conversation continued with me telling the principal she'd better keep better tabs on the second-grade teacher because he's teaching Latin and Greek starting Monday.

Well, this was another mess I had gotten myself into. I was wrong. Let's just say I overreacted more than a bit and forgot a cardinal rule about being a parent. Never assume your child is telling you the whole truth. Don't get me wrong. I'm not saying my daughter was lying. She wasn't. She simply left out a few important facts. Like the Latin and Greek they'd be learning were in the form of prefixes and suffixes.

My wife was a whiz with prefixes and suffixes and taught me that you and I don't need to know too much to do a good job coaching. A *prefix* is a group of letters appearing at the beginning of the word that tells something about the word. Likewise, a *suffix* is a group of letters at the end of a word that does the same. Collectively, they are called *affixes*.

The trick to teaching your child prefixes and suffixes is to pretend they are a secret code. Kids love to learn secret ways of doing things, so you grab and keep their attention immediately when you start talking about this super secret decoder chart that only second graders learn to use (tables 6-2 and 6-3). My wife went out of her way to dress up these charts to make them look spylike.

After a few weeks of practice, our daughter committed them to memory. During those weeks we made a family effort to help her learn prefixes and suffixes. Here is the strategy we used.

PROCEDURE:
How to teach your child prefixes and suffixes

1. Tell her to search a magazine to find words that use this secret code. This helps her to recognize prefixes and suffixes. Make sure she shows you those words so you can verify she selected the correct words. Also, scan the page to see if she missed any words.

2. Ask her to guess at the meaning of the words even if the words aren't in her vocabulary. She'll learn to explore words that haven't been formally introduced to her in class to gain practical experience using prefixes and suffixes.

3. Divide words that use prefixes and suffixes into components such as a prefix or suffix and a root. The *root* is the part of the

word that describes the object affected by the prefix or suffix, such as **cycle** (wheel) in **bicycle** (two wheels).

4. Speak in prefixes and suffixes around the house. I did this with our daughter. It was like talking in secret code. I'd ask my daughter to get me cookies from the kitchen. She'd ask how many. I responded with "bi."

TABLE **6-2**
HANDY PREFIXES

Prefix	Meaning	Sample
a	at, in, on	away
ab	away from	abscond
ad	to or forward	admit
after	afterward	afternoon
auto	self	automobile
bi	two	biplane
bio	life	biology
de	away from	deport
dis	apart or opposite of	disregard
il	not	illegal
im	not	immaterial
in	in or into	inside
in	not	incapable
ir	not	irregular
micro	small	microcosm
mid	midway	midday
mis	not correct	misspoken

out	outside, beyond	outstanding
over	above	overlord
pre	before	premed
re	again or back	reenter
sub	below	subway
tele	far off	telescope
thermo	heat	thermometer
tri	three	triangle
un	not	unknown
under	below	underwear

TABLE **6-3**
HANDY SUFFIXES

Suffix	Meaning	Sample
ary	relating to	aviary
er	one who; add to a verb and you have the person who did it	teacher
hood	state of	neighborhood
ian	one who	librarian
ic	like, having to do with	sonic
ive	of or relating to	detective
less	without, lacking	errorless
ly	like, when, how	sadly
ment	act of	ailment
meter	measurement	thermometer
phone	sound	telephone
some	inclined to	lonesome

Abbreviations

I wish I took pictures of computer-science students when I begin speaking computer jargon to them because this would be the right spot in the book to show you their memorable expressions.

"We'll be learning about the CPU, MHz, DOS, DASD . . ."

Panic sets in. They have no idea what I'm talking about, and they immediately wonder how they are going to pass the exams. Technical jargon is loaded with ways to shorten words to a mere few letters. The same holds true for everyday English.

I never stopped to think about the number of abbreviations we use in signs, correspondence, and books. And thanks to the military and government agencies like the National Aeronautics and Space Administration, special abbreviations called acronyms have entered our conversations. An *acronym* is an abbreviation for a term whose initial letters form a word, like MADD for Mothers Against Drunk Driving.

Abbreviations and acronyms are introduced to your child in the second grade. Many teachers present these topics when they teach the class how to write correspondence. Table 6-4 contains a sampling of abbreviations your second grader will learn. Consult her teacher for a complete list that will be taught in class.

Besides learning how to properly abbreviate a word, she'll learn the rules for when and when not to abbreviate. If you're like me, you're probably a little rusty on some of these rules, so let me share with you my notes.

PROCEDURE:
When to use abbreviations

1. Abbreviations are not used in very formal writing, such as an invitation to a wedding. The full word must be written in such situations.
2. Abbreviations are not used in informal writing, such as a note to family members, like *Dear Mom*.
3. Abbreviations are used in general writing to show respect for

the person, such as *Dear Mrs. Jones* where Mrs. Jones is the principal of the school.

4. Only well-known abbreviations should be used. Your child's teacher will provide you with a list of acceptable abbreviations.

5. Use abbreviations consistently in the document. Don't switch between *Dr.* and *Doctor*.

6. Some abbreviations are used for clarification purposes only, such as *Jr.* and *Sr.* They should be used only when there is reference to a first name, like *Mr. John Smith, Jr.*, and not *Mr. Smith, Jr.*

TABLE 6-4
COMMON SECOND-GRADE ABBREVIATIONS

Abbreviation	Meaning
Dr.	Doctor, drive
Mr.	A man
Mrs.	A married woman
Ms.	A woman
Prof.	Professor
Gen.	General
Rev.	Reverend
Gov.	Governor
Hon.	Honorable
Sr.	The father of a son who has the same name as he does
Jr.	The son having the same name as the father
St.	Street, saint
Ave.	Avenue
Rd.	Road

Reading

Reading becomes an integral part of a second grader's life, especially when they are introduced to various kinds of reading material. Don't be surprised like I was when your child comes home talking about tall tales, fables, and other formal names of stories in her reading books.

I was a bit confused to say the least when my daughter was able to categorize stories into various groups. These categories slipped my mind, which is a parent's way of politely saying I didn't know what she was talking about.

Everything she read in the first grade was called a story. This year the style and content of the stories allows her to group them together into poems, fables, folktales, myths, tall tales, comedies, limericks, and legends.

Don't go scratching your head trying to remember these definitions. Chances are pretty good your definitions won't coincide with those provided by her second-grade teacher. So I'll give you a quick review to keep you out of trouble.

A *story* is a group of sentences that tells a tale. When the tale is true, then the story is called *nonfiction*, and it's called *fiction* when the tale isn't true. Many of her stories are fiction, except when she reads about social studies and science.

Fiction has its own set of categories, such as a fable. A *fable* is a story that uses animals instead of people. Animals walk, talk, and have humanlike qualities. Another kind of fiction is myths. A *myth* is a story that provides a mystical explanation to mysterious things such as the sun and wind.

My daughter's favorite stories were ones told by storytellers. She liked these because they reminded her of family gatherings when the old folks would reveal family secrets. Some of these were stretching the truth more than a bit. These are called *tall tales* in the second grade. Others were bits of family history that probably lost most of the truth, but were fun to retell. My daughter rightfully categorized these as *folktales*.

And then there were stories about her Great Uncle George, a highly trained German craftsman who could do anything with metal. He had the equivalent of several engineering degrees in the States, and during World War II he created a revolutionary design for a torpedo for the navy.

My daughter was quick to pigeonhole this as a legend. Most *legends* aren't true, but their exaggerations give us hope for ourselves. George was the only family member who had any skill that could remotely equate with an engineering degree. His torpedo was a model he created in a metal shop but was never considered worthwhile by the navy.

On the lighter side, your child will learn about comedies, poems, and limericks. A *comedy* is a story that makes the reader laugh. A *poem* is a story where each line called a *verse* falls into a rhythmic pattern with all or some of the other lines, which is called *rhyming*. Sometimes second graders call poems *rhymes*. When a poem is humorous and consists of five lines it is called a *limerick*. Most limericks begin with "There was a . . ." or "There once was . . ."

Probably the most confusing reading my child encountered was simple, one-sentence sayings. A *saying* doesn't make much literal sense, but has a rewarding underlying meaning.

Here's a way to help your child look for hidden meanings. Ask her teacher for a list of sayings that will be used during the school year, then find a family story that helps to relate the meaning to your child. For example, I tell the story of my time on the town's volunteer ambulance corps to illustrate the meaning behind the saying "better late than never." It is better to drive a little slower than to speed, get into an accident, and never get to the emergency at all.

Second-Grade Math

Math is like a magic trick. Problems appear impossible to solve until someone shows you the steps, then you feel like a fool because the problem wasn't difficult at all to solve. Our perception of math is built from experiences in the first, second, and third grades. It is at this stage of education that many children develop a positive or negative attitude toward math.

Math is abstract. However, through exercises discussed in chapter 5, you can make math meaningful. Your child needs the confidence to succeed in solving a math problem and must believe she *can* solve it before she attempts the solution. The only way to develop such a belief is to be successful solving other math problems. Your job as coach is to make sure your child maintains a can-do attitude.

I'm the first to admit that no one ever got all the answers correct on all the math tests. Everyone makes mistakes. However, through perseverance, encouragement from you, and a little magic, those mistakes can lead to success.

A second-grade teacher told me her magic trick. She never moved on to the next math topic until all the class mastered the current topic. I thought this was more an ideal than an objective that could be accomplished with the average class of second graders. However, she relied on a bit of classroom magic to pull it off.

She kept close tabs on the problems the whole class mastered, then created a test that contained only those problems. The results? Nearly the entire class received an A on the test. All of them were mentally ready to tackle the next math topic and the problems the class hadn't mastered.

This method accomplished two important objectives. First, it maintained each child's self-esteem without lowering standards. It also practically eliminated negative peer pressure for those children who were perceived as unable to keep up with the class.

Perception plays a critical role in the way your child judges herself and how she judges others. If she perceives herself as a failure, she tends to become a failure. An indicator of failure is low grades on a series of tests. All of us fall into the trap of presuming poor grades imply the child isn't smart. Yet, we never question the accuracy of the test.

Here are a few ways you can keep success brewing in your child.

PROCEDURE:
How to encourage your child to have a positive attitude toward math

1. Don't allow mental blocks to develop that prevent her from solving math problems. I call this math anxiety.
2. Break each math lesson into steps, then concentrate on showing her how to perform each step. Focus on getting help for your child for steps she hasn't mastered.
3. Ask the teacher to help you coach your child through math lessons. Teachers are experts in restating the lesson many different ways in the hope that your child will understand one of those explanations.

> **4.** Don't let your child end a homework session in failure. Always let her finish up with a few problems you know she can solve.

Number Exercises

Practice, practice, practice is the way they say you get to play at Carnegie Hall. Actually, you only need the money to rent the hall. However, practice is the only way for your second grader to become comfortable with math.

You'll soon learn that second-grade math reinforces lessons learned in the first grade, then uses those lessons as building blocks for slightly more complex math lessons. For example, first graders are expected to count from 1 to 100. Second graders continue this progression by learning to count from 1 to 1,000. Last year they learned numbers are organized into a set order of 1, 2, 3, 4, etc. This year they learn about skipping numbers and the concept of odd and even numbers.

You can help your second grader keep in shape for math exercises by incorporating math into home activities. For example, ask your child to count from 1 to 100 by twos. You remember how this works: 2, 4, 6, 8, etc. Next, alternate with counting by threes: 3, 6, 9, 12, etc. Then follow up by asking her to count by odd, then even numbers. These exercises give your child different views of how numbers relate to each other.

Another fun exercise my daughters loved is to guess the number between two other numbers. Begin a sequence of numbers as illustrated in figures 6-1, 6-2, 6-3, and 6-4. Leave out one number in the series and ask your child to determine the missing number. She must analyze the number pattern correctly to find the missing number. The patterns, as you probably recognize, are the same patterns used to count by ones, twos, threes, and odd numbers.

1, 2, 3, __ , 5, 6, 7

FIGURE **6-1.** WHAT NUMBER BELONGS IN THIS SEQUENCE?

2, 4, __ , 8, 10, 12

FIGURE **6-2.** WHAT NUMBER BELONGS IN THIS SEQUENCE?

3, 6, __ , 12, 15, 18

FIGURE 6-3. WHAT NUMBER BELONGS IN THIS SEQUENCE?

1, 3, __ , 7, 9, 11

FIGURE 6-4. WHAT NUMBER BELONGS IN THIS SEQUENCE?

Numbers can be printed as digits or printed by name. It is important that she master both ways. My daughter's second-grade teacher showed me an exercise that helps six- and seven-year-olds learn to print the word form of numbers.

Many second graders become overwhelmed when told they must learn to print number words from 1 through 100. It seems like a lot of words to memorize. In this exercise, numbers are divided into three groups: 1 through 9; 10 through 19; and 20, 30, 40, 50, 60, 70, 80, 90, 100.

First, ask your child to print the number word for each group. Next, create a word number table as shown in table 6-5 with the words. Have your child print *twenty* in the first column and *one* through *nine* in the second. After completing this task, she'll discover that number words between twenty and thirty are the same as one through nine. Most of us retain knowledge we discovered through our own experiences. This exercise takes advantage of this phenomenon by setting up the situation so your child can discover the pattern of numbers herself. Have her complete the word number table up to one hundred.

TABLE 6-5
WORD NUMBER TABLE

twenty	one	thirty	one	forty	one
	two		two		two
	three		three		three
	four		four		four
	five		five		five
	six		six		six
	seven		seven		seven
	eight		eight		eight
	nine		nine		nine

The mother of all math exercises for second graders is to analyze an equation to determine the missing number. The equations in this exercise require your child to have a firm grasp of single-digit addition and subtraction, which should have been mastered in the first grade.

In the example shown in figure 6-5, she is asked to find the missing number. This is a two-step problem. The first step requires her to perform subtraction $(9 - 2)$, which results in 7. The second step is to determine what number added to 6 results in a sum of 7. The answer, of course, is 1.

Create similar exercises for your child. Be sure to use all single-digit numbers. Help her get started with the first few equations, then let her solve the rest without assistance. I found this exercise to be a great confidence builder as long as I took the time to allow my daughter to learn how to solve the problem.

$$6 + \underline{\quad} = 9 - 2$$

FIGURE 6-5. FIND THE MISSING NUMBER.

Addition and Subtraction with Thousands

Numbers used in your child's addition and subtraction problems become larger than numbers used in the first grade. First graders typically perform simple addition and subtraction using no more than two digits without carrying over values. This year your child performs the same manipulations using hundreds and thousands.

You and I know the process is the same whether small or large numbers are calculated. However, the additional digits can create a mental barrier with some second graders. They tend to panic without trying to analyze the problem. Yet when you break the problem down into simple steps, most are quick to catch on.

The critical concept for your child to learn is the thousands place value. Last year she was introduced to ones, tens, and hundreds place values. This year the thousands place value is added to her math vocabulary. The best way to help her to learn the thousands place value is to have her create another place-value table just like the one she built last year (table 6-6).

Ask her to count from 0 to 1,000 using the place-value table. Start by counting from 0 to 9 in the ones column, then replace the 0 in the tens column with the number 1 to signify she completed counting all the numbers in the ones column once. Continue this process until she places a 1 in the thousands column. She should catch on quickly after she practices this exercise a few times.

TABLE 6-6

THE PLACE-VALUE TABLE

Thousands	Hundreds	Tens	Ones
1	0	0	0
			1
			2
			3
			4
			5
			6
			7
			8
			9

Create a few simple addition and subtraction problems using thousands. Make sure you vary the numbers as shown in figures 6-6 and 6-7. Break down each problem into steps. There are four steps when she adds or subtracts thousands. Adding or subtracting each column is a step.

My wife has an excellent way of showing these steps. She takes two pieces of paper and covers all but the column my daughter is calculating. The paper is then moved to succeeding columns. When the last column is calculated, the paper is removed to reveal the solution to the problem.

1,132	1,123	2,435	3,241
+ 2,256	+ 142	+ 53	+ 5
3,388	1,265	2,488	3,246

512	23	5
+ 2,256	+ 1,142	+5,333
2,768	1,165	5,338

FIGURE 6-6. ADDING THOUSANDS WITH NO CARRYING

2,368	1,153	2,485	3,249
− 1,256	− 142	− 53	− 5
1,112	1,011	2,432	3,244

FIGURE 6-7. SUBTRACTING THOUSANDS WITH NO CARRYING

Two-Digit Addition and Subtraction with Carryover

A word of warning before discussing tips on how to coach your child through carryover addition. Don't allow her to attempt this topic unless she has a firm grip on place values and multidigit addition and subtraction. If she doesn't understand these concepts, then she doesn't have the necessary building blocks on which to learn carryovers.

With that said, let's explore ways you can help your child understand how to carry over values from one place value to another in an addition problem. Carryovers are called *regrouping*, where each place value is considered a group. The ones place value is the first group. When the sum of the ones column is more than 9, the sum must be regrouped into the second column, which is the tens group.

I was a bit confused about the regrouping since this was not the term I learned in school. We called regrouping "borrowing." I then made the mistake of trying to explain carryovers the way I was taught. Avoid making this mistake. You'll only confuse your child needlessly. Stick with the way her teacher presents regrouping.

The best way I found to explain regrouping is by example. Create a two-digit addition problem where the sum of the first column requires regrouping. Ask your child to add the first column and place the sum to the side of the problem as illustrated in figure 6-8. This gives her the opportunity to isolate the addition from the regrouping.

Next, have her place the sum of the first column into position in the problem and place the regrouped number at the top of the second column as shown in figure 6-9. This helps her to visualize the value being regrouped.

Second-grade teachers I've spoken with recommend creating exercises that require the regrouping of 1 from the ones column because six- and seven-year-olds have little problem adding 1 to other numbers. This exercise helps them focus on learning regrouping rather than worrying about adding numbers together. You can introduce other regrouping values once she masters the regrouping concept.

$$\begin{array}{r} 34 \\ +56 \\ \hline 10 \end{array}$$

FIGURE 6-8. REGROUPING DOUBLE-DIGIT ADDITION

$$\begin{array}{r} 1 \\ 34 \\ +56 \\ \hline 0 \end{array}$$

FIGURE 6-9. RESTATING THE ADDITION PROBLEM AFTER REGROUPING TAKES PLACE

Regrouping also applies to subtraction, except the value of the tens column is regrouped to the ones column. Set up a simple, two-digit subtraction problem that requires regrouping (figure 6-10), then ask your child to subtract values in the ones column. In this example, it is obvious that she can't subtract 6 from 0, so she'll need to take 1 from the tens column and regroup it to the ones column by placing the 1 alongside the 0.

I had my daughter create a separate subtraction problem for the ones column so she could see she'll be subtracting 6 from 10 after regrouping values. Regrouping requires her to also subtract 1 from the tens column (figure 6-11).

$$\begin{array}{r} 30 \\ -\ 6 \\ \hline \end{array} \qquad \begin{array}{r} 10 \\ -\ 6 \\ \hline 4 \end{array}$$

FIGURE 6-10. REGROUPING DOUBLE-DIGIT SUBTRACTION

$$\begin{array}{r} 30 \\ -16 \\ \hline 4 \end{array}$$

FIGURE 6-11. RESTATING THE SUBTRACTION PROBLEM AFTER REGROUPING TAKES PLACE

Checking Answers

Did you check your answers to addition or subtraction problems when you were in the second grade? Be honest. If you're like me, you probably rushed through solving the problems and maybe gave your work a quick glance before handing it in to the teacher.

How do you convince your child to slow down and check her work? Make checking answers to a math problem a required step to solving the problem. This sounds so obvious, but few parents and teachers ever enforce this step.

Require your child to check answers to addition and subtraction problems as the last step in her math homework. First, she'll need to understand the relationship between addition and subtraction, so show her an example of an addition and subtraction problem using similar numbers (figure 6-12).

Adding the difference of a subtraction problem (5) to the value subtracted (1) will produce the first number in the subtraction problem (6). This is the way she can check that the subtraction problem is correct.

Likewise, subtraction is used to check answers of an addition problem (figure 6-13). Here the sum of the addition problem (6) is reduced by either number in the addition problem (5 or 1) to produce the remaining addition number (1 or 5).

You can show her how to check answers, but your real job is to get her to do it. Try to make checking answers a game. When my daughter finishes her math homework, I look puzzled as if I didn't understand how she arrived at the answers. It is her job to be the teacher and show me that her answers are correct.

Problem: $6 - 1 = 5$

Check Answer: $6 = 1 + 5$

FIGURE **6-12.** ADDITION CAN BE USED TO CHECK THE ANSWER OF A SUBTRACTION PROBLEM.

Problem: $5 + 1 = 6$

Check Answer: $5 = 6 - 1$

Check Answer: $1 = 6 - 5$

FIGURE **6-13.** SUBTRACTION CAN BE USED TO CHECK THE ANSWER OF AN ADDITION PROBLEM.

Multiplication and Division

It is easy to become frustrated trying to coach your second grader to perform multiplication. I found myself solving the problem for my daughter instead of showing her the steps to solve the problem. My frustration centered around my inability to explain multiplication.

Teachers I've spoken to recommend using a simple addition expression (figure 6-14) to illustrate multiplication. Count the number of times 3 is added in the addition problem and write the answer to the right of the equal sign in the next expression. This is called the *multiplier*. Place the multiplication symbol next to the multiplier, followed by the number being multiplied, called the *multiplicand*. The result of multiplication is called the *product*. Those terms should bring back fond memories.

$$15 = 3 + 3 + 3 + 3 + 3$$
$$15 = 5 \times 3$$

FIGURE 6-14. A SIMPLE ADDITION PROBLEM USED TO EXPLAIN MULTIPLICATION

Second graders can easily pick up on the concept of multiplication as long as they keep the relationship between addition and multiplication in mind. Before my daughter attempted to solve a multiplication problem, I asked her to first create a similar addition problem. This exercise helped to reinforce the relationship.

We stopped this practice once she became comfortable with the concept of multiplication. I then turned my attention to showing her the special rules of multiplication.

1. The answer is always the same regardless of the order of the multiplier and multiplicand (e.g., 5×3 is the same as 3×5).
2. The multiplicand is the answer when a multiplicand is multiplied by a multiplier of one (e.g., $5 = 1 \times 5$).
3. Zero is always the answer when a multiplicand is multiplied by a multiplier of zero (e.g., $0 = 0 \times 5$).

The best way to learn rules is to apply them when solving a problem. So we had a game in our house where I'd create five single-digit multiplication problems.

Figure 6-15 shows one of our games. I set up a pattern in which 2 is the multiplier, or the first number in the expression. Next, I slipped in an expression that breaks the pattern. In this example, I asked her to multiply 2 by 0. The object of the game is for my daughter to answer all the problems and tell me which expression follows one of the special rules of multiplication.

$$2 \times 5 =$$
$$2 \times 3 =$$
$$2 \times 0 =$$
$$2 \times 4 =$$
$$2 \times 7 =$$

FIGURE 6-15. MULTIPLICATION GAME USED TO REINFORCE LEARNING MULTIPLICATION RULES

Answers to multiplication problems should be checked for accuracy as the final step of the problem. There are two ways to check answers: addition and division. Multiplication is taught before division in many school districts, so show your child the addition method of checking her answers. This method is illustrated in figure 6-14. The multiplication problem $15 = 5 \times 3$ is the same as the addition problem $15 = 3 + 3 + 3 + 3 + 3$.

Use division to check answers to multiplication problems once she learns simple division (see figure 6-16). Dividing the product (10) by the multiplier (2) will result in the multiplicand (5). Likewise, dividing the product (10) by the multiplicand (5) will result in the multiplier (2).

Problem: $2 \times 5 = 10$
Check Answer: $10 \div 5 = 2$
Check Answer: $10 \div 2 = 5$

FIGURE 6-16. CHECKING A MULTIPLICATION ANSWER USING DIVISION

Memorizing multiplication tables should bring back memories. Some school districts dropped this as a requirement. I strongly urge you to make sure your child knows her multiplication tables even if this is not a requirement.

Second graders are expected to memorize the one, two, three, four, and five times tables up to twelve. Unfortunately, there is no easy way to memorize except for nightly drills. Memorizing isn't what most second graders consider fun. There just seems to be too much to learn. Here's how I overcame this problem. I divided each table into six sets of two examples each, as shown in figure 6-17. Each night I asked my daughter to memorize one set. We continued this exercise until all six sets were learned.

1	2	3	4	5	6
$2 \times 1 = 2$	$2 \times 3 = 6$	$2 \times 5 = 10$	$2 \times 7 = 14$	$2 \times 9 = 18$	$2 \times 11 = 22$
$2 \times 2 = 4$	$2 \times 4 = 8$	$2 \times 6 = 12$	$2 \times 8 = 16$	$2 \times 10 = 20$	$2 \times 12 = 24$

FIGURE 6-17.
BREAKING MULTIPLICATION TABLES INTO DIGESTIBLE BITES

Division is introduced by showing how numbers can be divided in half. I showed my daughter how to divide in half by using an even number of items. I'd place ten candies on the table in a long row, then asked her to count half of them. I'd then push those aside to show that the row of ten candies was divided equally into two groups of five.

We tried the same exercise with other items until she had a firm understanding that division is separating a set of items into smaller sets. Stop, if you're able to get this concept across. Don't convert the items into numbers and avoid using the division symbol. You'll have plenty of opportunity to coach her through division next school year.

Measures

My home projects wouldn't impress anyone on *This Old House*, and you'll find most of them lying around the basement. Take my kitchen cabinet drawer for example. The original drawer had a wood front panel and a plastic body that eventually broke, leaving us with a hunk of wood and a gaping hole in the cabinet.

No problem. This is a simple project. I watched Norm make just such a drawer on *The New Yankee Workshop*. My wife had her doubts, but I insisted because it was a good way to teach our daughter about measuring.

Well, let's just say it's easy for Norm to build a drawer. For me the drawer turned out nearly perfect except it was a tad oversize, but the project did show my daughter what happens if you don't measure correctly.

Your child is introduced to the concept of measuring in the second grade. She'll learn that rulers and tape measures are divided into inches and feet and used to measure the length of objects. Likewise scales are used to measure the weight of objects in pounds.

PROCEDURE:
How to explain measuring to your child

1. Ask your child to measure common objects around the house, such as paper, pencils, boxes of food, doors, and chairs. Make sure she writes down the measurement using the proper abbreviations for inches and feet.
2. Have her compare those measurements and tell you which objects are larger than the other objects.
3. Point out that all objects are not exactly an inch and may need to be rounded to the nearest measure. Ask her teacher if rounding is taught this school year before you introduce her to the concept.
4. Use your bathroom scale to weigh objects she finds around the house.
5. Ask her to decide which objects are heavier than other objects.
6. Challenge your child to guess the weight of objects, then have her weigh them. This exercise introduces her to the concept of estimating.
7. Give your child this quiz: What weighs more, a pound of potatoes or a pound of feathers? Many second graders give the wrong answer, because they don't understand the concept of weight.

Arabic and Roman Numerals

My daughter is amazed at how her grandfather can tell time using his watch. She'd stare at the watch trying to determine the time. It's not that my daughter can't tell time. This watch has a different kind of face. All the numbers are in Roman numerals instead of the numbers she sees on the clock in the kitchen. Roman numerals are unquestionably a throwback to centuries ago when the Roman Empire was central to Western society.

Be prepared to be asked the question that has stumped many second-grade parents. Why must I learn Roman numerals? My suggestion is to avoid a history lesson beyond saying that at one time Roman numerals were used just like numbers we use today. Any additional historical explanation loses relevance.

Explain that Roman numerals are still used today on the faces of some clocks and watches, in copyright notices at the end of films and television shows, and as page numbers in the first few pages of books. At that point, open a book and let her find the pages numbered in Roman numerals, and then look at the end of a television show or movie to find the copyright date.

Once she understands Roman numerals are still used today, she's ready to learn how to read and print them. Second graders need to count only up to 12 in Roman numerals.

Table 6-7 is a handy tool to use when you help your second grader with Roman numerals. Numbers in the first column are called *Arabic numerals* and were adopted over the years from numbering symbols used in Arabia. The second column is the equivalent Roman numeral.

There is a trick to reading Roman numerals. The I represents the value 1; the V, the value 5; and the X, the value 10. Notice the value 6 is VI, or 5 plus 1. The value 7 is VII, or 5 plus 1 plus 1. The same pattern holds true for 11, which is XI, or 10 plus 1. The pattern is broken slightly with 4 and 9. Four is IV and 9 is IX. IV is like saying 5 minus 1, and IX is like saying 10 minus 1.

Your child needs to learn three Roman numerals (I, V, and X), then apply the simple rule of adding values when the ones are on the right side of the number and subtracting when they are on the left side.

TABLE **6-7**
ARABIC AND ROMAN NUMERAL TABLE

Arabic	Roman	Arabic	Roman
1	I	7	VII
2	II	8	VIII
3	III	9	IX
4	IV	10	X
5	V	11	XI
6	VI	12	XII

Geometry—Lines and Line Segments

Time for that dreaded topic—geometry. Second-grade geometry involves a little more than learning new shapes. Your child will learn to recognize cones and cylinders. She will also be introduced to concepts you probably learned in high school geometry. These are lines and line segments. Let's brush up on these.

A *line* goes on forever in two directions. I found this difficult for my child to understand, because every line she drew had a beginning and an end. Rather than get into an argument or spend hours explaining *forever*, I took pencil, paper, and a ruler and drew a line that went off both sides of the page. I used arrowheads to indicate that the line continued off the page (figure 6-18). This seemed to resolve the issue.

A *line segment* is a piece of the line and is identified by two points. Those *points* are identified by capital letters **A** and **B**. You probably understand this concept, but your job is to *explain* a line segment to your second grader. Don't underestimate the complexity of this job.

Relate the term *line segment* to division, where the line is the whole thing and the line segment is a piece of the thing.

I used a little discovery learning to reinforce this concept, which should work for you. However, you'll need to guide your child through the process. Ask your child how to make a line segment out of a line. With some careful prodding, she'll decide to divide the line by placing two dots on it.

Next, ask her how she knows which is the beginning and end of the line segment. Expect to spend a half hour or so talking about different ways to accomplish this task. Let her do most of the talking. Jump in when she runs dry of ideas.

Eventually she'll give each end of the line segment a name. Expect to devote another half hour deciding on a name. Steer her into naming them **A** and **B**, then place the letters on the line segment. This technique worked well for my daughter because *she* made the decisions.

There is a special way to refer to a line segment (figure 6-18) without drawing a line. Letters identifying the ends of the line segment are displayed with the line above them to indicate a line segment.

Write a simple assignment as illustrated in figure 6-19. Ask your child to use a ruler and draw a line segment one inch long. This will prove to her that she has mastered lines and line segments.

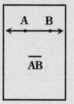

FIGURE **6-18.** A LINE AND LINE SEGMENT

$$\overline{AB} = 1 \text{ inch}$$

FIGURE **6-19.** DRAW THIS LINE SEGMENT.

Geometry—Symmetry

Second graders learn to explore the shapes of things; to recognize sizes as large and small; to understand the difference between interior and exterior; and to begin understanding the concept of proportionality.

Your child should have little problem understanding shapes. However, she might have trouble with the topic of symmetry. *Symmetry* occurs when parts of a shape are in proportion to the other parts.

My wife best described this to my daughter by comparing Pierce Brosnan to her Uncle George. This gave her an accurate picture of when shapes are not symmetric. We then held our breaths every time Uncle George came over for a visit, in fear she would describe symmetry for him. It never happened.

A safer way to explain symmetry is with two pieces of paper, a pencil, and a ruler. Draw a line down the center of the page of one piece of paper, then fold the paper in half along the line. Each side of the line is the same size as the other. Each side is symmetrical because they are the same shape and size (figure 6-20). The line down the center of the paper is called the *line of symmetry*.

Repeat the same exercise except draw the line across the bottom of the second piece of paper. Be sure the line appears below the center point of the page. Fold the paper at the line. Each side of the line is a different shape and size (figure 6-21). Each side isn't symmetrical and the line isn't a line of symmetry.

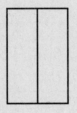

FIGURE 6-20. DRAW A LINE TO CREATE TWO SYMMETRICAL SIDES OF THE PAPER.

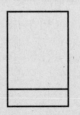

FIGURE 6-21. DRAW A LINE TO CREATE TWO NONSYMMETRICAL SIDES OF THE PAPER.

Second-Grade Word Problems

Word problems are a kid's nightmare, because they are forced to think, reason, and use all their knowledge to derive the correct answer to the problem. Your second grader is required to identify information needed to solve the problem; identify the type of operation to be performed; and properly translate the problem into an arithmetic problem.

Last year's word problems contained more pictures than words. The pictures were used as a tool to help your child understand the problem. Second grade is a little harder. Pictures are used sparingly, and when they are used they are less of a tool than in the first grade.

I also noticed the topics of the word problems involved calculating money, which reinforces skills developed in other math lessons. This approach makes the word problem more meaningful and gives your child the skills she can use every day.

I'll give you fair warning. You'll need to be patient and creative when coaching your second grader through word problems. Word problems are more challenging than other math topics. My wife and I got through this trying time by using two techniques: showing our daughter how to analyze the problem, and reenacting the problem.

Our technique is to break the words into three categories: needed to solve problem, not needed to solve problem, and unsure if needed to solve problem. I showed you how to use this technique in chapter 5.

Reenacting the word problem is a fun way to make the problem come to life. We use provisions found in the kitchen and money from my wife's purse to solve the problem. For example, the problem in figure 6-22 can easily be played out in your home.

My wife placed a few dollars and coins on the table, then asked my daughter to tell her how much she needed to go shopping. I tried to encourage my daughter to set up the addition problem on paper rather than count the money, because she won't have money to count when taking a test in school. We finished the exercise by asking her to count the money she'll require, then go to the food closet and take the merchandise.

PROBLEM:
Tom wants a box of cereal for $1.59 and a box of cookies for $1.25. How much money must Tom bring to the store?

FIGURE 6-22. REENACT WORD PROBLEMS TO MAKE THEM REAL TO YOUR CHILD.

Biology

Coming home late one evening, I was greeted by the shock of my life.
I walked into the kitchen. There my daughter had her biology book
opened.

"The teacher wants you to tell me where I came from."

Where you came from? Sex education in the second grade? I never
expected a second grader to ask this question. So I did what any quick-
thinking father would do.

"Ask your mother."

"Mom is busy. I want you to tell me."

This isn't fair. I thought my wife would have this heart-to-heart talk
with her when she reached her preteens. Why is the teacher bringing
this topic up in the second grade? I don't need this trouble now.

"Not now. Let me have supper first."

She paused.

"I got an idea. You can tell me while you're eating!"

How on earth was I going to break this news to a seven-year-old? I
started slowly, hoping my wife would save me, but to no avail. I smelled
a conspiracy afoot. I spent the next fifteen minutes squirming, talking
generally about babies and animals.

"That's not what Sam's mom told her."

"What did Sam's mom say?"

"She said Sam came from Germany."

Like many parents, I think in the extremes. Second-grade biology
isn't sex education. It is your child's introduction to learning about
her body.

Lessons are focused on general concepts rather than the details you
remember from high school health class. Coaching your child through
second-grade biology isn't all that tough if you keep your explanations
simple and avoid scientific terminology. The most important factor to
know is the relationship tree (figure 6-23), which shows how cells are
assembled to make the body work.

    Cells
        Tissues
            Organs
            Heart   **Systems**
            Lungs   Respiratory
            Stomach Digestive
                       Nervous

FIGURE 6-23. THE RELATIONSHIP TREE SHOWING THE RELATIONSHIP OF CELLS TO PARTS OF THE BODY

Your child is also introduced to the life cycle, where she learns that living things are born, grow, reproduce, and die. The hows are left for another grade.

She'll learn about the food groups—meat and fish, dairy foods, fruits and vegetables, and cereals and grains—and how each group contains vitamins and minerals that help her body grow. Table 6-8 was helpful with my daughter's homework.

Biology homework presents a unique opportunity to discuss with your child a topic I believe only parents can teach—which is death. It is in the second grade when your child is formally presented with mortality, something none of us really wants to face.

Typically, her teacher approaches the topic in a scientific way. Animals rather than people are used as subjects, and death is spoken of in the biological sense. Nothing is mentioned about the philosophical concept of life after death. This is the perfect opportunity to enhance classroom lessons with your family's religious beliefs.

Aside from the religious aspect of death, this is also the occasion to talk about the topic in relation to older members of the family who have recently passed away or who are terminally ill. I was surprised to learn how well six- and seven-year-olds are capable of dealing with the loss of a family member if the subject is presented in a way they can understand. Your child's teacher and school counselors can give you advice on how to hold such a conversation with your child.

TABLE 6-8
VITAMINS AND MINERALS NEEDED FOR A BALANCED DIET

Vitamin/Mineral	Source	Used By
Vitamin A	Carrots	Skin, hair, and eyes
Vitamin C	Citrus fruits	Cells for growth and protection
Vitamin D	Milk	Bones and teeth
Calcium	Milk	Bones
Potassium	Table salt	Nerves
Iron	Spinach	Blood
Sodium	Table salt	Nerves

7.

Making the Grade in the Third Grade

- Parts of Speech
- Sentences
- Third-Grade Math
- Multiplication
- Division
- Fractions
- Estimating Values
- Mental Math
- Money Math
- Calendar and Time Math
- Measurement
- Geometry
- Word Problems

C ome on. Come on. You're almost there."
Another squeaker.
"Ah!"
We were all quietly rooting for at least one perfect musical phrase to come from our third grader's room as we sat watching television.

She'd spent weeks practicing at school and in her room for the holiday concert.

Then came the moment of truth, the proud moment when she asked to give my wife and me a preview of her concert. We gave her the nod and she rushed in with music, stand, and instrument in hand. She tapped her foot, played three notes, and continued tapping for another fifteen seconds. Next, a solid note for ten seconds. This went on for a while. We had no idea what song she was playing, but applauded every time she paused, only to receive a dirty look.

"I'm not finished!"

Finally, silence. We waited patiently. Neither of us wanted to break into applause at the wrong time again. She eventually cued us and we clapped, praising her performance as if she had appeared on MTV. Deep in our hearts we couldn't wait until the concert was over. Our patience was wearing thin, bombarded each night with her rehearsals.

Third-grade parents need a lot of patience with their child, because schoolwork becomes extremely challenging this school year. Some teachers believe the third grade is the make-or-break year for most children. Success this year could mean achievement throughout your child's academic life. An unsuccessful year could mean rough times ahead in school unless remedial help is provided. All the basic building blocks for a general education should be firmly in place when she finishes the third grade. It is this foundation on which the rest of her learning is built.

A number of school districts around the country treat the first, second, and third grades as a single block of time within which your child is expected to master fundamental skills. School officials who follow such a theory don't become concerned when kids fail to master first-grade skills or second-grade skills, because they feel all those skills will be learned by the end of the third grade.

Many third-grade teachers disagree and warn not to fall into this trap. Your child doesn't have time in the third grade to learn first- and second-grade skills. There is simply too much material and too little time for most eight- and nine-year-olds to absorb the extra burden. They recommend that you make sure each lesson is learned in the proper school year even if it requires help during the summer so missed lessons are recaptured before the new school year begins.

You'll notice less emphasis is placed on increasing your child's vocabulary through word lists. Vocabulary is built from words learned by reading biographies and autobiographies, speeches, and fiction and nonfiction stories. Ask the teacher to provide you with the vocabulary words your child will learn this year. You can reinforce these words by using them around the house.

Although schoolwork becomes more intense, you'll notice many lessons are more of the same kind of material you saw in the first and second grades, only the work is more challenging. In this chapter I'll be showing you techniques to use to help your child with new lessons.

Parts of Speech

I had everything under control. First- and second-grade homework was a breeze. I could answer nearly any question my daughter asked. Those that stumped me, I managed to bluff until I conferred with her teacher.

However, I was in the dark when she asked about articles, adjectives, pronouns, and conjunctions. Sure, I've heard of them, but don't ask me to find them in a sentence. To stave off embarrassment I cracked open a few books and brushed up on the topic. What I found I'm sure will help you save face with your child.

Nouns, verbs, adjectives, adverbs, pronouns, conjunctions, prepositions, interjections, and articles are called the *parts of speech*. Some school districts don't include articles in this list. Your child's teacher can supply you with the list he'll be teaching.

Be prepared for the question most third graders ask their parents: Why must I learn this stuff? This is a fair question for her to ask, especially when she already demonstrates the proper use of grammar in a conversation. Grammar used in conversation is a little different from written grammar. Avoid any further explanation and focus her attention on learning the parts of speech.

Your third grader already learned two parts of speech in the first grade. These are nouns and verbs. The other parts of speech embellish the sentence, making it easy for someone to read a group of sentences.

Adjectives are words that tell something about a noun, how the noun feels, sounds, tastes, or looks. For example, **big** is the adjective in figure 7-1, because **big** tells how the **ball** looks. More than one adjective can be used in a sentence to describe the same noun; however, a comma must separate them as shown in figure 7-2. **Big** and **round** are both adjectives and must be separated by a comma.

Your child must be able to identify the adjectives in sentences on tests and on homework assignments.

PROCEDURE:
How to find adjectives in a sentence

1. Find the nouns in the sentence. Some nouns have adjectives, and others don't.
2. Look at the word to the left of the noun. Does it tell anything about the noun? If so, then this is an adjective.
3. If an adjective is found, then look to the left of the adjective. Is there a comma? If so, does the word to the left of the comma also describe the noun? If so, this, too, is an adjective.

The **big** ball bounced.

FIGURE 7-1. *BIG* IS AN ADJECTIVE AND DESCRIBES THE NOUN *BALL*.

The **big, round** ball bounced.

FIGURE 7-2. *BIG* AND *ROUND* ARE ADJECTIVES AND DESCRIBE THE NOUN *BALL*.

Adverbs are words that describe a verb and commonly refer to the time or degree in which the verb performs the action. In figure 7-3, the verb is **drive** and the adverb is **slowly**, which tells the reader how the **car** drives.

My daughter had trouble picking out adverbs, because adverbs can be located practically anywhere in the sentence, as is shown in figure 7-4. The adverb can be to the right of the verb, to the left of the verb, or somewhere else in the sentence. The position of the adverb often affects the emphasis of the sentence.

The clue that helped my third grader pick out adverbs is the **ly** at the end of the adverb. Many, but not all, adverbs end with **ly**. Another way for your child to identify an adverb is to ask herself the question, How does the action take place? For example, how fast does the car drive?

The car drove **slowly**.

FIGURE 7-3. ADVERBS TELL SOMETHING ABOUT THE VERB *DROVE***.**

The car drove **slowly**.
The car **slowly** drove.
Slowly the car drove.

FIGURE 7-4. ADVERBS CAN BE IN VARIOUS POSITIONS IN A SENTENCE.

Pronouns are words that take the place of a noun in a sentence. Your child knows them better as **he**, **she**, **it**, and **they**. A pronoun is used so you don't have to repeat the noun.

Figure 7-5 illustrates a poor use of a pronoun. **He** describes who caught the **ball**. However, the pronoun doesn't replace a noun since there are no other sentences in this example. Figure 7-6 fixes this problem by including a sentence using a noun to identify the person **Bob**. The pronoun **he** in the second sentence refers to **Bob**.

Kids fall into the same habit as you and I do by using pronouns in conversations without first using the noun. This is wrong, although we usually overlook the error because we know to whom our child is referring. However, this is one of our biggest mistakes.

Our children will speak correctly and more clearly if you and I take the time to correct them when they are young. I tried this and it worked. Whenever my daughter started a conversation with *he, she, it,* or *they,* I'd ask, "Who is he?" She responded with a dirty look and became a little frustrated, but eventually caught herself before making the same error again.

He caught the ball.

FIGURE 7-5. A POOR USE OF A PRONOUN IN A SENTENCE

Bob ran fast. **He** caught the ball.

FIGURE 7-6. HERE'S A BETTER USE OF A PRONOUN IN A SENTENCE. *HE* IS USED IN PLACE OF REPEATING THE WORD *BOB*.

Conjunctions are words that link together two ideas or make you choose one of those ideas. You recognize them as **and**, **or**, and **but**, which are three of the most common. Others include **so**, **how**, and **because**. Figure 7-7 illustrates several ways conjunctions are used in a sentence.

Sometimes a comma is used to separate the conjunction from the first idea in the sentence; this is often the case with the conjunction **so**. The comma helps your child identify a conjunction in a sentence, although she'll quickly recognize the words **and**, **or**, and **but**.

The ball bounced high, **and** Bob caught the ball.
Either Bob **or** Mark could have caught the ball.
The bell rang, **but** the class left.

FIGURE 7-7. CONJUNCTIONS COMBINE TWO THOUGHTS INTO ONE SENTENCE.

Prepositions are words that tell how one thing is related to another thing. We know them as **in**, **into**, **on**, **upon**, **underneath**, **under**, **over**, **to**, **from**, **away from**, **after**, **before**, **with**, **along with**, **of**, **by**, and **about**. Ask your child's teacher to provide you with the complete list of prepositions that he'll teach this school year. You can use that list to help your child identify prepositions in sentences.

Prepositions always refer to words that come after the preposition in the sentence. Figure 7-8 contains one preposition, which is **underneath**. The preposition tells how **books** relate to **her bed**. **Underneath** refers to **her bed**.

Words that are referred to by a preposition and the preposition itself are called a *prepositional phrase*. **Underneath her bed** is the prepositional phrase in figure 7-8.

Mary kept her books **underneath her bed**.

FIGURE 7-8. PREPOSITIONAL PHRASE

Interjections are words that are thrown into a sentence to emphasize a feeling, such as **Wow! Great! Right on!** They are easy for your child to pick out of a sentence, because interjections stand out and typically end with an exclamation mark.

Articles are **a**, **an**, and **the**, which are placed before a noun in a sentence to refer to a specific or general thing. An article that refers to a specific thing, such as "the car," is called a *definite article*. An article that refers to an unspecific thing, such as "a car," is called an *indefinite article*.

Your third grader shouldn't have any difficulty identifying articles in a sentence, but she might be confused about when to use **an** or **a** with a noun. My daughter stumbled over this (see figure 7-9) until her teacher gave her these clues.

- Use **an** if the noun begins with a vowel sound.
- Use **a** if the noun begins with a consonant sound.

Wrong
An car travels fast.
I have a idea.

Correct
A car travels fast.
I have an idea.

FIGURE 7-9. ARTICLES MUST AGREE WITH THE NOUN.

Sentences

Sentences are filled with challenging concepts for your child to learn— such as parts of a sentence and tense. Make a strong effort to help your child master these concepts. If you succeed, then these lessons will be with her for life. If you fail, then she'll be spending time catching up with the class and falling behind in her other lessons.

Let's bring you up to speed on the topic with a quick review. A *sentence* is composed of two pieces: a subject and a predicate. The *subject* of the sentence is the person, place, or thing that is the topic of the sentence. Your third grader can easily find the subject of any sentence with a little practice.

A *predicate* is the verb that tells about the actions of the subject. Predicates are divided into two groups: simple predicates and complete predicates.

A *simple predicate* is the single, best verb that describes the action of the subject. A *complete predicate* is all the words that tell about the action. Take a look at figure 7-10. **Ball** is obviously the subject of the sentence. **Flew** is the simple predicate, because it is the word that describes what the ball is doing. **Flew off the wall** is the complete predicate.

Give your child spontaneous quizzes asking her to point out the subjects, the simple predicates, and complete predicates in newspaper or magazine articles you're reading. Do it often and she'll quickly become an expert.

The ball **flew off the wall**.

FIGURE **7-10.** THE COMPLETE PREDICATE

Tense refers to the time in which the idea of the sentence takes place. You'll remember this as present, past, and future. The key to recognizing the tense of a sentence is to first identify the auxiliary verb, which your child calls a *helping verb*.

A verb tells what is happening with the subject. An *auxiliary verb* tells when the action takes place. The action could occur today (present tense), yesterday (past tense), or tomorrow (future tense). This is the best way my child understood tense. Figure 7-11 shows sentences that convey the same idea, but each changes the time when the action takes place.

I was a member.
I am a member.
I will be a member.

FIGURE **7-11.** PAST, PRESENT, AND FUTURE TENSES

Third-Grade Math

I was astonished to see all the new math skills my daughter was required to learn in the third grade. Third graders learn division; addition, subtraction, and multiplication of large numbers; and mental math.

Your child expands skills she already knows, such as counting and place values. This school year she'll count by hundreds, memorize multiplication tables up to 9×12, and learn the ten thousands and hundred thousands place values. My daughter didn't find these difficult, since they were more of what she had already learned in the second grade.

Last year, your child was introduced to simple, one-step expressions such as the one in figure 7-12. This year, she'll learn multistep expressions, which aren't easy to solve. For example, what is the answer to the expression in figure 7-13? Is the answer 28 or 13? It all depends on whether the addition is performed before or after the multiplication: $5 + 2 = 7$, then $7 \times 4 = 28$; and $2 \times 4 = 8$, then $8 + 5 = 13$.

Parentheses are used in a multistep expression to tell which step is performed first, as shown in figure 7-14. In this example, numbers are added, then the sum is multiplied by 4.

You shouldn't have difficulty helping your child with many of the math topics she'll learn in the third grade, since most of them are intuitive. However, there are some topics easier to do yourself than to explain to your child. I asked many third-grade teachers to give me some tips on how to help my daughter with those difficult third-grade math lessons. I share their responses with you throughout the remainder of this chapter.

$$5 + 2 =$$

FIGURE **7-12.** A ONE-STEP EXPRESSION

$$5 + 2 \times 4 =$$

FIGURE **7-13.** A MULTISTEP EXPRESSION

$$(5 + 2) \times 4 =$$

FIGURE **7-14.** STEPS INSIDE PARENTHESES ARE PERFORMED FIRST IN A MULTISTEP EXPRESSION.

Multiplication

Your child learns to multiply by hundreds and thousands, which at times requires carryovers. Some third graders find this confusing and become easily overwhelmed with the complexity of the new work.

Your job is to help her focus on the method used to solve multiplication problems involving large numbers. Break down the problem into steps your child learned how to perform in the first and second grades.

Begin with problems that use a simple factor to multiply a large number composed mostly of zeros, such as 5 × 10, 5 × 100, and 5 × 1,000. These calculations allow your child to concentrate on multiplying the entire number rather than multiplying a single column.

For example, my daughter seemed to have difficulty memorizing the 8 and 9 times tables. She would freeze whenever she had to multiply 9 × 789 and 9 × 7899. The obstacle was 9 × 9, not multiplying by hundreds and thousands.

However, multiplying numbers with zeros, such as 10, 100, and 1,000, removed this psychological barrier and gave me the opportunity to teach her a trick that makes multiplication a little easier to calculate.

When she multiplies 5 × 10, she only needs to multiply 5 × 1, then bring down the zero. The same is true when multiplying 5 × 100 and 5 × 1,000. Figure 7-15 illustrates this technique. She doesn't have to multiply 5 × 0 because the product is always zero. This trick comes in handy when she learns to perform mental multiplication later in the school year.

	Bring down		Bring down		Bring down
5 × 1	the zero.	5 × 1	the zeros.	5 × 1	the zeros.

$$
\begin{array}{cc}
10 & 10 \rule{0pt}{0pt} \\
\times 5 & \times 5 \\
\hline
5 & 50
\end{array}
\qquad
\begin{array}{cc}
100 & 100 \\
\times 5 & \times 5 \\
\hline
5 & 500
\end{array}
\qquad
\begin{array}{cc}
1{,}000 & 1{,}000 \\
\times 5 & \times 5 \\
\hline
5 & 5{,}000
\end{array}
$$

FIGURE 7-15. MULTIPLYING BY TENS, HUNDREDS, AND THOUSANDS IS THE SAME AS SINGLE-DIGIT MULTIPLICATION.

My daughter had trouble comprehending carryovers when solving multiplication problems. Carryover is called *regrouping*, which was introduced last year when performing addition and subtraction. She was able to master carryovers last year with a little practice. However, the method used to carry over values in multiplication is different from what she learned.

Carryovers are noted by multiplying each digit by the factor, then placing the product on a separate line. Each product is indented to reflect the value position of the number being multiplied. If this sounds confusing to you, just think of how the concept appears to your third grader.

Here's what I did to avoid the confusion. I avoided any explanation about regrouping in multiplication. The third-grade teacher is better trained for this than you and I are. Instead of explaining, I showed my daughter the steps in multiplication, using the example shown in figure 7-16. Each digit in the number is multiplied separately by the factor and placed in the appropriate position beneath the line, then the products are added together to complete the multiplication.

$$
\begin{array}{r}
344 \\
\times\ 5 \\
\hline
20 \\
20 \\
+15 \\
\hline
1,720
\end{array}
$$

FIGURE 7-16. MULTIPLYING THREE-DIGIT NUMBERS

Division

Trouble was brewing one night when I came home from work. Sobbing was coming from the kitchen as my wife left the room and gave me one of the now's-not-the-time-to-ask looks. Sitting at the table was my daughter, pencil in hand, books sprawled all over, trying to hold back tears.

"What happened?"

"Nothing," she sniffed.

I learned a long time ago to keep my mouth shut in times like these. No matter what I say, it will be taken the wrong way by either my wife or daughter. Of course, I never take my own advice, so based upon the books laid out on the table, I gathered she was doing division homework.

"Learning division?"

That was enough to break the cease-fire. My daughter rambled on in near hysterics, saying division is impossible to learn. Then my wife chimed in that my daughter wouldn't listen when she tried to explain division to her.

Division is tough for an eight-year-old to grasp, so when the situation calmed down, I took a crack at explaining it to my daughter and became just as frustrated as my wife. Back to school I went to find out how third-grade teachers break down mental barriers and teach division. Here's what I learned.

Kids need to picture the concept of division in their minds before learning the steps necessary to solve a division problem. *Division* transforms one group into more than one group.

Draw a group of four boxes as I've done in figure 7-17. Break the group into two groups of two boxes. Regrouping is division, where you divided a group of four into two groups of two. Don't proceed further until she has a firm understanding of this concept. Repeat this exercise several times using different-size groups until it sinks in.

Before moving on, ask her to regroup boxes herself. This will prove to both of you that she understands the concept of division.

4   2

FIGURE **7-17.** DRAW A PICTURE SHOWING HOW A WHOLE THING IS DIVIDED INTO TWO THINGS.

The next step is to relate the picture to the division expression. This is where you introduce the division sign. Take one of the drawings used to illustrate the concept and create an expression that says the same thing as the picture. Figure 7-18 is the expression for figure 7-17.

It is important that you properly identify the numbers in the expression. The first number is 4 and called the *dividend*; the first 2 is the *divisor*, and the second 2 is the *quotient*.

Here's a better way to explain the expression. The number to the left of the division sign (4), which is usually the largest number, tells how many are in the first group. The number to the right of the division sign (2) tells how many smaller groups the first group must be broken into.

And the number to the right of the equal sign (2) tells how many are in each of the smaller groups.

$$4 \div 2 = 2$$

FIGURE 7-18. THE DIVISION EXPRESSION FOR FIGURE 7-17

Show your child the expanded way to state the division problem after she proves to you she can relate the expression to the picture of the dividing blocks. Don't rush to introduce the expanded form, because each new concept further complicates the process of learning division. Your objective is to reduce the complexity by gradually introducing new topics after previous topics are secured in your child's mind.

Figure 7-19 illustrates the expanded form of the expression in figure 7-18. I found this diagram a good tool to use when showing my daughter the mechanics of solving a division problem.

The diagram provides a lot of information. First, it sets up the division problem in the expanded form and shows where to place the numbers. The diagram also properly labels components of division and introduces the concept of a remainder.

Don't go into too much detail about remainders at this point, because she'll perform division without remainders. I simply say remainders are leftovers after you've solved the division problem.

The diagram also serves as a road map to solving the problem. The dividend is regrouped according to the divisor, and the result is placed in the quotient. The quotient is then multiplied by the divisor and placed beneath the dividend, then subtracted from the dividend to determine if there is a remainder.

Quotient ⟶ 2   R0 ◀— Remainder
Divisor ⟶ 2 ⟌ 4   ◀— Dividend
                − 4   ◀— 2 × 2
                  0   ◀— Remainder

FIGURE 7-19. THE SIMPLE DIVISION DIAGRAM

It is at this point when you can show that division is the opposite of multiplication. Avoid going into too much of an explanation. I showed my daughter the example in figure 7-20, then went no further until I showed her how to use multiplication to check her answers to the division problem.

A third-grade teacher once told me that eight-year-olds are eager to do things, rather than listen to theory. Learning the mechanics of solving a division problem becomes your child's focus. She prefers to learn how to do something than why it must be done.

So, don't beat your head against the wall if your child doesn't grasp the regrouping explanation of division. Instead, focus her attention on the mechanics of solving a division problem, which she'll need to master to pass tests in school.

$$4 \div 2 = 2$$
$$4 = 2 \times 2$$

FIGURE 7-20. SHOW THAT DIVISION IS THE OPPOSITE OF MULTIPLICATION.

After your child has solved a few simple division problems on her own, take her to the next step by showing the rules of division. There are only four (figure 7-21):

1. Zero divided by any number always has a quotient of zero.
2. Zero cannot be a divisor.
3. A number divided by itself except for zero has a quotient of one.
4. A number divided by one equals that number.

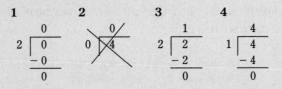

FIGURE 7-21. EXAMPLES OF RULES FOR DIVISION

Many school districts cram nearly all the topics in division into this school year, so don't be surprised if the teacher shortens the amount of time allocated for your child to properly learn division. It's your job to slow things down and to make sure she comprehends each topic before moving on to more difficult ones.

Traditionally, the next topic presented is division that results in two- and three-digit quotients without any remainder. This process requires your child to modify the mechanics learned to solve division problems with single-digit quotients.

Figure 7-22 shows a division problem with a double-digit quotient. I found the best way to explain the process to my daughter was to focus each step on a single group of numbers in the problem. Here are the steps I followed using figure 7-22 as the example.

1. Divide 6 by 5, which results in 1.
2. Place the result 1 in the quotient over the 6 in the dividend.
3. Multiply 1 in the quotient by the divisor 5, the result of which is 5.
4. Place the result 5 below the 6 in the dividend.
5. Subtract 5 from 6 in the dividend. The result is 1.
6. Place the result 1 below the 5.
7. Divide 1 in the dividend by 5, the divisor. You can't.
8. Bring down the zero.
9. Divide 10 by 5. The result is 2.
10. Place the result 2 in the quotient over the 0 in the dividend.
11. Multiply 2 in the quotient by the divisor 5. The result is 10.
12. Place the result 10 below the 10.
13. Subtract 10 from 10. The result is 0. There is no remainder. The problem is solved.

Dividing three numbers is basically the same operation as shown in figure 7-19. The main difference is the placement of the numbers over and under the proper columns. This is where many third graders make their biggest mistake.

My daughter was always in a rush to work through the steps and solve the problem. Placing numbers neatly in the proper columns wasn't her top priority. Some numbers quickly became misaligned, causing her to make mistakes subtracting and obviously arriving at the incorrect answer.

Fortunately for her, my daughter's teacher carefully reviewed each division problem to determine where she made mistakes. Partial credit was given for performing the correct operation even if the calculation was incorrect.

Break this bad habit now. Few teachers beyond the third grade examine division problems carefully. If the answer is wrong, then the entire problem is wrong regardless of whether the answer was caused by sloppiness.

It was a tough job for my wife and me to enforce the neatness rule with my daughter. We eventually purchased a pad of graph paper filled with squares, which served as guidelines for my daughter. Each box was large enough for her to write one number.

$$
\begin{array}{r}
12 \quad \text{R0} \\
5 \overline{\smash{\big)}\ 60} \\
-\ 5 \\
\hline
10 \\
-\ 10 \\
\hline
0
\end{array}
$$

FIGURE **7-22**. QUOTIENTS CAN HAVE TWO DIGITS.

$$
\begin{array}{r}
231 \quad \text{R0} \\
2 \overline{\smash{\big)}\ 462} \\
-\ 4 \\
\hline
06 \\
-\ 6 \\
\hline
02 \\
-\ 2 \\
\hline
0
\end{array}
$$

FIGURE **7-23**. SOME QUOTIENTS HAVE THREE DIGITS.

Your child knows the term *remainder* means *leftover*. It's time for you to explain what is really meant by a remainder. I found the easiest way to avoid confusion and arguments is to return to the blocks used when I first introduced her to division (figure 7-17). However, I modified the number of blocks so the regrouping produced a remainder.

I created a group of five boxes. Then I told my daughter to break up the group into two even subgroups. She was puzzled because there wasn't a way to create two equal groups out of five. Once she realized this dilemma, I asked her how many even groups she could create. She answered two. I asked her what happened to the fifth box. She said it was left over.

And there you have it. She understood the concept of the remainder. I must say it took us a couple of nights to achieve this understanding, so don't expect immediate results when you try this with your child. Figure 7-24 contains the diagram I used.

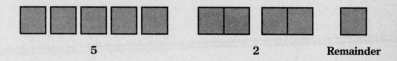

5   2   **Remainder**

FIGURE **7-24.** BREAK UP THE GROUP OF FIVE INTO TWO EVEN GROUPS.

When your child is comfortable with the concept of a remainder, create a division example such as in figure 7-25. Be sure your example uses simple numbers that result in a remainder. Use the times tables your child has memorized as a guide for selecting the numbers for the problem.

For example, I was sure my daughter knew $3 \times 6 = 18$, so I used 19 as the dividend. When she attempted to solve the problem, I prodded her by asking, "What number times 3 is almost 19?" I could see her reciting her three times table in her head. She said 6 and placed it in the quotient. This also introduced her to mental math, which we'll talk about a little later in this chapter.

My daughter proceeded to work through the problem. All was going well until she subtracted 18 from 19, then tried to divide the result by 3. She was stumped. I didn't leave her pondering too long because that would lead only to unwarranted frustration. I simply blurted out that she couldn't divide 1 into three groups. The 1 is the remainder to the problem.

I repeated the exercise using different numbers every night until she could perform division with remainders in her sleep. I slowly increased the complexity of the numbers and eventually ended with problems that had three-digit quotients and two-digit remainders.

$$
\begin{array}{r}
6 \quad \text{R1} \\
3 \overline{\smash{)}19} \\
-18 \\
\hline
1
\end{array}
$$

FIGURE **7-25.** DIVIDING WITH REMAINDERS

Build your child's self-confidence by challenging her answer to a division problem. I do this all the time with my kids.

"Are you trying to tell me that 462 divided by 2 is 231? You mean there's no remainder?"

This is enough to raise self-doubt in anyone's mind, especially when I couple my challenge with one of those disappointed looks only a father can give. I started using this technique when my daughter was in the second grade, so by the third grade she knew the routine. The old man is trying to trick her.

She realized I wouldn't stop until she proved her answer by using multiplication as shown in figure 7-26. You'll notice the quotient is multiplied by the divisor. The product of the multiplication problem is equal to the dividend if the division problem was solved correctly.

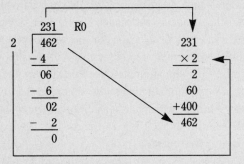

FIGURE **7-26.** MULTIPLICATION IS USED TO CHECK THE ANSWER TO A DIVISION PROBLEM.

Fractions

Last school year your child was introduced to fractions. She was shown how a whole of something, such as a pie, can be broken up into pieces. Cutting the pie into two pieces created two halves, each half a fraction of the whole pie.

Fractions are covered in more depth in the third grade, where numbers are used to describe a fractional part of a whole thing. Kids learn best when they can visualize the problem in pictures, so explain fractions by showing a picture of a whole thing.

I used boxes with my daughter, which worked fine. As shown in figure 7-27, I drew three boxes stacked on top of each other to illustrate the whole group of boxes. I then represented this with numbers as a fraction.

The bottom number in the fraction tells how many things are in the whole. This is called the *denominator*. The top number tells how many equal parts the whole is broken into. This is called the *numerator*.

In the first example in figure 7-27, the denominator is 3 indicating there are 3 boxes that compose the whole thing. The numerator is also 3, because all the boxes are being referenced. This fraction represents the whole thing.

In the second example, I colored the first box to indicate the piece of the whole I want to use in the fraction. Therefore, I had to change the numerator to 1. Only one piece of the whole is being represented by the fraction.

Take your time explaining fractions. Let the concept seep in before leaving the topic. My wife and I created several kinds of problems for my daughter to practice, such as in figure 7-27, then asked her to write the corresponding fraction. We'd reverse the problem and show her a fraction, then ask her to draw the picture.

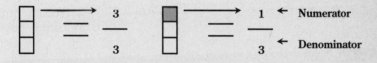

FIGURE 7-27. A FRACTION IDENTIFIES THE NUMBER OF ITEMS SELECTED FROM A GROUP OF ITEMS.

Once your child learns the fundamentals of fractions, her teacher is likely to show how fractions can have different numerators and denominators, yet still refer to the same amount. These are called *equivalent fractions*.

Equivalent fractions are difficult for many third graders to understand, because they can't believe fractions with different numbers refer to the same amounts. Difficulty occurs because two concepts are at work: breaking up a whole into the same proportional piece such as half, quarter, and third; and identifying those pieces as a fraction.

Here's how to explain equivalent fractions to your child. Draw a picture similar to the one in figure 7-28. These are equivalent fractions. The denominator in the first example is 2, which states two boxes make up the whole thing. The numerator is 1, which states the fraction represents one box.

The second example states the whole is made up of four boxes and the fraction refers to two boxes. Two boxes are half of all the boxes in the second example. Therefore, both fractions refer to half the number of the whole thing.

$$\frac{1}{2} \qquad\qquad \frac{2}{4}$$

FIGURE 7-28. BOTH FRACTIONS REFER TO HALF OF ALL THE BOXES.

Estimating Values

One of the many responsibilities school board members have is to approve a budget for the school year. This isn't an easy task. You're inundated with a thick loose-leaf book of numbers that would choke an IRS agent. And you have a few hours over the course of about eight weeks to understand those numbers.

This didn't bother some board members since they could glance at the book and point out miscalculations in the budget without using a calculator, because they estimated values.

They ignored the finer details and concentrated on large-dollar items that appeared in each year's budget. Those amounts were mentally compared with previous years' amounts to determine if the trend was maintained. For example, the cost of textbooks normally increased by about $10,000 a year. If the proposed increase was $20,000, then an error in the calculation was suspected.

I taught this skill to my daughter so she could quickly check answers to her math problems. You can do the same with your child. Here's how it works. Say you need to check the answer to the addition problem in figure 7-29.

- Round 34,299 to the ten thousands, with is 34,000.
- Do the same with 52,132, which results in 52,000.
- Add 34 and 52, which is 86.
- Add the zeros to the end of the sum (86,000). Is the answer to the addition problem about 86,000? If so, then the answer is likely to be correct.

$$
\begin{array}{r}
34{,}299 \\
+\ 52{,}132 \\
\hline
86{,}431 \\
\end{array}
\qquad
\begin{array}{r}
34{,}000 \\
+\ 52{,}000 \\
\hline
86{,}000 \\
\end{array}
$$

FIGURE 7-29. ESTIMATE THE ANSWER TO AN ADDITION PROBLEM BY ROUNDING.

I used numbers my daughter would find on her math problems when I showed her how to estimate. She could relate to those numbers better than to the example I used in figure 7-29. The hardest concept for her to embrace was that an estimate is not exactly the same as the answer to the problem.

Confusion came when she compared estimating with other methods of checking her answers. An estimate gives an "about" value. That is, the estimate is about the value of the correct answer, which is close enough to identify obvious errors. The other methods of checking answers give exact values.

Mental Math

We had a school board member who did more than estimate to find errors. She calculated numbers in her head.

How did she do that? She used one of two methods, depending on which was more expedient at the time. She'd either regroup numbers or round numbers.

Say you're asked to calculate the sum of the digits shown in step 1 of figure 7-30. At first the list looks imposing. However, you can reorganize the numbers into groups that add up to 10 as in step 2. Count the number of groups, then multiply the result by 10.

In this example there are two groups whose sum is 10. When multiplied by 2, the result is 20. Notice all the numbers can't be paired to produce a sum of 10. Those numbers that can't be regrouped are added to the result as shown in step 3.

This sounds a bit complicated to understand, and my daughter wasn't quick to catch on until I allowed her to solve part of the problem on paper and the other part in her head. Here's another way to approach mental math.

PROCEDURE:
How to explain mental math to your child

1. Write an addition problem as shown in figure 7-30. Make the regrouped numbers small addition problems.
2. Tell your child to cross out the numbers she already grouped. This lets her visualize the numbers that still need to be addressed.
3. Ask her to count the number of groups, then multiply them by 10. Place the product in a third addition problem.
4. Place all the numbers that weren't regrouped into the third addition problem, then add together the numbers.
5. Ask her not to write down steps she can perform in her head. Gradually the entire problem will be solved without the need to write any step of the problem.

1	2		3
6	6	8	20
8	+ 4	+ 2	+ 5
4	10	10	25
5			
+ 2			

FIGURE 7-30. REGROUPING NUMBERS THAT, ADDED
TOGETHER, RESULT IN 10

The rounding method also requires your child to simplify the addition problem, this time by rounding each number to tens, hundreds, or thousands depending on the size of the number. My daughter found this technique particularly useful when adding two-digit numbers. Here's how the rounding method works.

PROCEDURE:
How to round numbers

1. Round up each number in the addition problem. Notice the numbers in the first step of figure 7-31 are rounded in the second step to 50 and 30 respectively.
2. Determine the difference between the rounded number and the original number in the addition problem.
3. Add the differences together as shown in step 3.
4. Add the rounded numbers (step 2).
5. Subtract the sum of the differences from the sum of the rounded numbers (step 4) to arrive at the answer to the original addition problem.

The rounding method is also complicated to explain. Encourage your child to use paper and pencil and make notes as you show her how to use this method. With much practice she'll be doing it in her head.

A word of caution! Learning mental math isn't very important when you consider all the other skills she needs to master. Emphasis must be on achieving the correct answer to a math problem, rather than learning to solve problems in her head.

1	2	3	4
46	50	4	80
+ 27	+ 30	+ 3	− 7
	80	7	73

FIGURE **7-31.** THE ROUNDING METHOD OF MENTAL MATH

Money Math

The math takes on a different meaning when addition and subtraction problems involve money. Third graders are expected to know how to count money, to know how much money they have left after paying for a purchase, and how to make change.

Like most third graders, my daughter knew currency and recognized coins and bills up to $20. She could also relate coins to each other and to bills. A nickel is the same as five pennies, a quarter is the same as twenty-five pennies, and so on.

This relationship served as a basis for money addition and subtraction. Pennies are in the ones place value; dimes are in the tens place value; a dollar is in the hundreds place value because a dollar is equal to one hundred pennies.

The only new concept she needed to learn was the decimal place. I simply told her the decimal place is always positioned between the hundreds and tens place values whenever she added or subtracted money. I avoided any talk about the decimal system since that topic is covered in the fourth grade.

Once my daughter understood that setting up an addition or subtraction problem with money is the same as setting up any addition or subtraction problem, she was able to solve money math problems.

Making change is also a new concept your third grader needs to learn. This isn't difficult to master as long as you teach her the grocer's trick.

Say she buys a box of cookies that costs $1.10 and she gives the grocer $2.00. The grocer begins counting the change from the cost of the item ($1.10). He'd keep $1.10 in his head, then add money to it from the cash register until he reached $2.00.

My wife and I set up a kitchen store so my daughter could practice making change. We used the knives-and-forks tray as the cash register drawer. My wife supplied the money, and family members had to take turns buying from the kitchen store every time they wanted a snack.

Calendar and Time Math

Another practical application of your child's arithmetic lessons is the calculation of elapsed time. Third graders determine elapsed time both in minutes and in days.

Calculating elapsed time can be a tricky operation because time can be measured in a combination of minutes and hours. Figure 7-32 contains a typical problem you'll find on a homework assignment.

Before attempting to calculate an answer, the problem must be set up as shown in figure 7-32. This example looks like a typical subtraction problem to your child, except a colon separates the hours from the minutes.

My daughter assumed the colon was like a comma in a thousands number (1,000), which helps you read the number, but this is incorrect. The colon separates two unit measurements—hours and minutes—which can be difficult for a third grader to understand because all her arithmetic problems use the same unit of measurement. She learned units of measurement in the second grade, but never grasped the relationships among these units until lessons in the third grade.

The best way for me to explain hours and minutes was to take the kitchen clock off the wall and ask my daughter to count the number of hash marks on the clock. Each mark represented a minute. After counting, my daughter realized she had made one sweep around the clock, which she knew to be equal to an hour. This proved to her that sixty minutes is the same as one hour.

Ask your child's teacher which is the best method for you to use to explain elapsed time. I prefer going into more detail this school year, because it is easier for my daughter to understand the concept of elapsed time by learning the relationship between hours and minutes.

How many minutes elapsed between 2:15 and 2:30?

$$
\begin{array}{r}
2{:}30 \\
-\ 2{:}15 \\
\hline
{:}15
\end{array}
$$

FIGURE 7-32. SETTING UP AN ELAPSED-TIME PROBLEM

Calendar calculations are easier for your third grader to solve than time problems because calendar problems are typically solved by using the calendar as a tool. Figure 7-33 is a typical calendar problem you'll find on your child's homework.

Here's how she can solve the problem. Turn to the proper month on the calendar and find the date specified in the problem, then count the number of days on the calendar to arrive at the answer. Typically, third graders won't be asked to determine elapsed dates that extend beyond a month.

If today is January 1, what date is seven days from today?

FIGURE 7-33. A TYPICAL CALENDAR PROBLEM

Measurement

Your child has probably driven you nuts measuring things around the house with a ruler. At least my third grader did after learning the concept of measuring. She'd remove the ruler from our kitchen junk drawer and work her way through the rooms taking measurements. My wife and I didn't mind until the holidays when the family came over.

"Grandpa, I want to measure you."

The old man was taken by surprise, but he'd do anything for his pretty granddaughter.

"Wait. What are you doing?"

He panicked as she raised the twelve-inch plastic ruler to his face.

"I'm measuring noses!" she said.

By this time he couldn't refuse, so Pops gently guided the ruler toward the base of his nose and prayed no one was watching. Let's simply say the story made the family history books.

Like all the skills your third grader learns, measuring things is the only way for her to practice her new skill. This is especially true with fingers, feet, toes, and, of course, noses, because those parts of our bodies are rarely even in length. Their size typically falls between inches on the ruler.

When things don't measure exactly an inch, your child must round the measurement. If the object is less than a half inch, then the measurement is rounded down, otherwise the measurement is rounded up.

Another problem your child will likely encounter is using a ruler to measure things that aren't straight. Sometimes it is difficult to use a ruler to measure, and this requires your child to estimate the measurement using fingers.

PROCEDURE:
How to estimate a measurement using two fingers

1. Place her thumb and first finger at opposite ends of an inch mark on a ruler.
2. Keep the fingers the same distance apart as she walks to the object she is going to measure.
3. Place the first finger on the corner of the object.
4. Remember the number one in her head and the position of her thumb.
5. Move the first finger to the position of the thumb on the object.
6. Remember the number two, since this is the second time she placed both fingers on the object.
7. Repeat the same process until she is at the end of the object.
8. The number of times she places her fingers on the object approximates the length of the object in inches.

Your third grader will learn to convert one unit of measurement to another, such as finding the number of feet in a yard and the number of inches in a foot.

Converting from one unit of measure to another involves multiplication and division. Here are two rules to remember whenever she is stuck on a conversion problem:

- Use multiplication to convert a larger unit into a smaller unit (figure 7-34).
- Use division to convert a smaller unit into a larger unit (figure 7-35).

I built myself a conversion table to help my daughter remember the equivalent measurements (table 7-1). You'll find this handy when your child tackles conversion problems.

Don't be surprised if she's asked to convert units of measurement in the metric system. I found a few of those questions on my daughter's homework assignment. I've included the conversion factors for the metric system on the table.

The side of a box is 3 feet. How many inches is this?
Remember: 12 inches = 1 foot

$$12 \text{ inches} \times 3 \text{ feet} = 36 \text{ inches}$$

FIGURE 7-34. CONVERTING A LARGER UNIT INTO A SMALLER UNIT

The side of a box is 36 inches. How many feet is this?
Remember: 12 inches = 1 foot

$$36 \text{ inches} \div 12 \text{ inches} = 3 \text{ feet}$$

FIGURE 7-35. CONVERTING A SMALLER UNIT INTO A LARGER UNIT

TABLE 7-1
CONVERSION TABLE

U.S. Customary Measurements		Metric Measurements	
1 foot (ft.)	= 12 inches (in.)	1 meter (m)	= 100 centimeters (cm)
1 yard (yd.)	= 3 feet (ft.)	1 kilometer (k)	= 1,000 meters (m)
1 yard (yd.)	= 36 inches (in.)		
1 pound (lb.)	= 16 (oz.)	1 kilogram (kg)	= 1,000 grams (g)
1 tablespoon (tbs.)	= 3 teaspoons (tsp.)	1 liter (1)	= 1,000 milliliters (ml)
2 tablespoons (tbs.)	= 1 fluid ounce (oz.)		
16 tablespoons (tbs.)	= 1 cup (c.)		
1 cup (c.)	= 8 fluid ounces (oz.)		
1 pint (pt.)	= 16 fluid ounces (oz.)		
1 pint (pt.)	= 2 cups (c.)		
1 quart (qt.)	= 2 pints (pt.)		
1 quart (qt.)	= 4 cups (c.)		
1 gallon (gal.)	= 4 quarts (qt.)		
1 gallon (gal.)	= 8 pints (pt.)		

Geometry

You probably relived nightmares from geometry class the first time you discovered geometry on your child's homework. Geometry describes the shapes of things using some math terms you and I have long forgotten. Here's what you need to know to help your child with third-grade geometry:

- A *line* flows in two directions and does not have a beginning or an end (see chapter 6).
- A *line segment* is defined as the portion of a line between two points on the line. We commonly call a line segment a line.
- The *name of a line segment* is the combination of labels used to identify the points of the line segment, such as **AB**.
- A *shape* is composed of several line segments. For example, there are four line segments in a rectangle (figure 7-36) or a square.
- A *vertex* is the point on the shape where two line segments meet.
- The *name of a vertex* is the single letter used to identify the point where the ends of the line segments meet. In figure 7-36, line segment **AB** and line segment **AD** meet in the upper left corner of the rectangle. That end of both these line segments is called **A**. Therefore, the vertex is called **A**.
- An *angle* is the distance between line segments that compose a vertex.
- A *right angle* occurs when the angle forms a square corner, such as the rectangle in figure 7-36.
- The *perimeter of a shape* is the distance around the shape. You calculate the perimeter by adding together all the sides.
- The *area of a shape* is the measurement of the space within the perimeter. The best way to explain this to your child is to use squares as shown in figure 7-37. The area is determined by the number of squares that can be placed within the perimeter of the shape. Let's say each square is an inch. There are sixty squares in figure 7-37. Multiply the number of squares by the size of each square **(60** × 1 inch = 60 square inches) to determine the area of the shape. The area 60 square inches is abbreviated as 60 in². Once your child understands this concept, then show her the

formula for calculating the area of a shape, which is **length ×
width**. In Figure 7-37, the length is 10 inches and the width is 6
inches. The area is **10 inches × 6 inches = 60 in².**

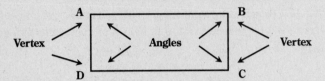

FIGURE 7-36. WAYS TO DESCRIBE A POLYGON

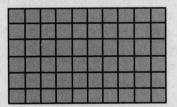

FIGURE 7-37. MEASURING THE AREA OF A SHAPE USING SQUARES

Third graders are introduced to a new figure called a solid. A *solid* is
a shape that has three dimensions, as seen in figure 7-38. Each side of
a solid is called a *face*, and is composed of line segments. The place
where two edges come together is called an *edge*, just like the edge of a
cliff.

This is about all you need to know to help your child through homework involving solids. Most school districts don't require third graders
to learn how to measure a solid.

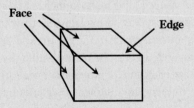

FIGURE 7-38. A SOLID IS A SHAPE WITH THREE DIMENSIONS.

Another geometrical concept I found on my daughter's homework is congruency. You might recall this term being associated with congruent angles from your high school geometry class. Don't go scratching your head trying to remember the definition of a congruent angle. I've done the scratching for both of us.

Congruent means the same shape and size. Angles that are the same shape and size are called *congruent angles*, however your third grader learns the term *congruent* in relation to shapes, not angles.

Figure 7-39 is the diagram I use to illustrate the difference between congruent objects and incongruent objects. You may want to draw a similar diagram when explaining this concept to your child so she'll associate this picture with the terms in her mind.

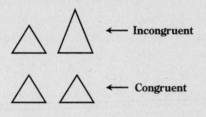

FIGURE 7-39. CONGRUENT AND INCONGRUENT OBJECTS

Word Problems

Expect your third grader to face a battery of word problems. She'll have to decide when to add, subtract, multiply, and divide. Sometimes she'll be required to use two operations to solve a single word problem.

Some third graders can be overwhelmed by word problems, because most of the math problems they solve are spoon-fed. That is, the problem is already set up in a familiar format by you, by the teacher, or in their math book.

Word problems make your child think. She'll need to use everything she has learned to come up with the correct answer, including good reading and comprehension skills, good analytical skills, and good math skills.

Figure 7-40 shows a typical problem you'll find on your child's homework. Here's how to approach the problem. Identify clue words that indicate what math she'll need to solve the problem. **Dozen** is the first clue, which should trigger your child to remember a dozen is twelve. The next clue is **give all of them to the class**, which means all twelve must be disposed of in the problem. **Six students in the class** is another piece of the puzzle, as is **how many each will receive**, which indicates division.

Once the analytical step is completed, set up the problem. In this example, she'll know division is required. Make sure she properly identifies the dividend and the divisor and places them in the proper position in the expression.

The dividend is the whole thing, which is the 12 pencils. The divisor is the number of students who are to receive part of the whole thing, 6 students. Figure 7-41 shows the setup of the problem in figure 7-40. Your child should be able to perform the mathematical operation without help.

The teacher has a **dozen** pencils and needs to **give all of them to the class**. There are **six students in the class**. **How many** pencils will **each student receive**?

FIGURE 7-40. A SINGLE-STEP DIVISION PROBLEM

$$6 \overline{\smash{)}\ 12}^{\ 2}$$

FIGURE 7-41. SETTING UP THE PROBLEM IN FIGURE 7-40

Time word problems make even some adults stop and think. Take the problem in figure 7-42 as an example. The clue words are **begin at 1:30, before reading, 20 minutes long**, and **begin math lesson**.

Before reading indicates subtraction. Your child may need help to recognize that reading begins 20 minutes after math starts. Use the kitchen clock to help her think through the process. Once she firmly understands the problem, she should be able to set up the math in the proper form, and then solve the problem (figure 7-43).

Reading is to **begin at 1:30.** The math lesson is taught immediately **before reading** and is **20 minutes long.** What time must the teacher **begin the math lesson?**

FIGURE **7-12.** A TIME PROBLEM

$$
\begin{array}{r}
1:30 \\
- \ :20 \\
\hline
1:10
\end{array}
$$

FIGURE **7-43.** SETTING UP THE PROBLEM IN FIGURE **7-42**

A multistep word problem such as the one illustrated in figures 7-44 and 7-45 will challenge your child's analytical skills. I discovered that nearly all my child's word problems emphasized thinking rather than testing her arithmetic skills: 10 percent of the time is spent calculating the problem, while 90 percent is devoted to identifying clues and setting up the problem.

The problem in figure 7-44 is more difficult than the other problems because there is no clear distinction between the two operations required to solve the problem. Nothing tells your child where the first operation ends and the second begins.

PROCEDURE:
How to help your child solve a confusing word problem

1. Ask her, "What are you asked to solve?" In this example, the final answer is **the change the grocer gives Mike.**
2. Ask her, "How much money did Mike give the grocer?" The answer is given in the problem, which is **90 cents.**
3. Ask her, "How much did the items cost?" A bell should ring in her mind when she realizes addition and multiplication are required to answer this question. She'll add all the items, then multiply it by 10 cents, and arrive at 60 cents.
4. Ask her, "How much change did the grocer give Mike?" She'll need to subtract 60 cents from 90 cents to arrive at 30 cents change.

Don't expect your third grader to catch on quickly to solving multi-step word problems. The only way eight- and nine-year-olds master this skill is through repetition. Your child must constantly practice, and you must show her how to think through the problem.

Mike buys 3 apples, 2 bananas, and 1 pear. Each costs 10 cents. Mike gives the grocer 90 cents. How much change must the grocer give Mike?

FIGURE 7-44. A MULTISTEP MONEY PROBLEM

1	2	3
3	10	.90
2	× 6	− .60
+ 1	60	.30
6		

FIGURE 7-45. SETTING UP THE PROBLEM IN FIGURE 7-44

8.

Making the Grade in the Fourth Grade

- Reading
- Language
- Polishing Your Child's Writing
- More Grammar
- Fourth-Grade Math
- Division
- Fractions
- Decimals
- Geometry—Rays and Angles
- Geometry—Polygons
- Formulas—Area, Perimeter, Volume
- Time Math

I was excited to give up my weekends and evenings to see my nine-year-old cheer at junior football games, in cheering competitions, and all those other occasions novice parents look forward to attending.

Somehow my spirits dampened about three weeks into the first football season when I realized I'd become the de facto chauffeur for the cheering squad.

It began 8 A.M. every Saturday when the house filled with nine- and ten-year-old girls downing a breakfast truck drivers I know couldn't handle. My daughter volunteered for the first two Saturdays, but by the third Saturday, kids just showed up at our doorstep uninvited.

We spent two hours driving them to the game, followed by another two hours sitting on concrete bleachers in all kinds of weather. I couldn't believe it. Our food budget was ruined. Game days were longer than we anticipated. And there I was sitting at the game, holding an umbrella in one hand and a camcorder in the other while being bombarded with cold, hard-hitting rain from all directions.

I thought by the time my daughter reached the fourth grade my life would become easier. My wife and I assumed this school year would be much like the other three. Little did we realize we were mistaken.

After-school activities became more demanding, as did our role in our child's schoolwork. Simple reading, writing, and arithmetic were no longer simple. I found myself having to hit the books to keep pace with my daughter's grammar, fractions, decimals, geometry, and formulas lessons.

Expect to have a similar experience with your fourth grader. Throughout this chapter I'll explore fourth-grade homework topics that are likely to puzzle you. Brush up on these lessons and you'll be in a fine position to help your child make the grade this school year.

Reading

Reading in the fourth grade is like boot camp preparing your child for adult-length reading assignments. Until now, lessons have concentrated on building reading and comprehension skills using short stories and excerpts from recognized works.

Your child has learned to pick out components of stories, such as the introduction, plot, and main characters, and can differentiate between fiction and nonfiction. And you've probably noticed her reading assignments cover a breadth of topics and styles of writing.

You'll see much of the same kind of reading assignments this year as in previous years, although you'll notice the length of the stories is gradually increasing to build up her endurance to read full-length works.

This is a critical year for your child, because this is the year when some children turn off to reading. Teachers aren't sure why this occurs. However, some feel it has something to do with overly aggressive reading assignments.

They compare conditioning your child for longer reading assignments to long-distance running. A person who is poorly trained will quickly become discouraged when asked to run five miles. He may drudge through the first mile, then give up. He lacks the endurance and desire to successfully complete the assignment. And he is likely to make a marginal effort at future attempts. Yet the same person who has gradually built up to a five-mile run won't hesitate to enter a five-mile race.

Is your child prepared to read adult-length reading materials? There is no easy way to answer this question. Test the waters with your child by encouraging her to read longer stories. Pull back if she stumbles, then return to shorter assignments until her endurance level increases.

Teach your child to pace herself when reading a long story. Kids seem to always want to finish whatever they're doing in one sitting. This is possible when reading short stories. However, fatigue can set in when reading adult-length material. She could easily lose interest in the story and never complete it.

My wife came up with a good method for encouraging my daughter to take time reading. She would force my daughter to break down the reading assignment into logical segments. My daughter was asked to read the first paragraph on a page, then tell my wife what she thought was happening in the story.

The pace increased by repeating the same process, only the next time my daughter read a complete page. The final step was to have her pause whenever the action in the story changed, then tell us about the story and foretell what action was to come.

Two important objectives were accomplished using this technique. First, my fourth grader learned to recognize segments of a story. She also recognized natural breaks in the story where she could stop reading and take a breather. I call this a commercial break without the commercial.

It is important for your child to realize that a natural break in a story is a good place to stop, put down the book, and do something else for a while before continuing with the story. These breaks are a good way for your child to pace herself through an adult-length reading assignment.

The only practical way for her to become hooked on reading is to be self-motivated to read. She must want to read because she's interested in the topic, not because the story is required reading.

Your job is to cultivate her self-motivation to explore a variety of reading topics even if the story doesn't seem appealing. This is a difficult task, to say the least. Not every reading assignment is going to interest her. School officials make an effort to select material that should be of interest to most of the class, but there is no guarantee everyone will find all the stories of interest.

A conflict always arises in the fourth grade. You want her to read stories because the stories are interesting, yet she'll be required to read stories of no interest to her. This is a dilemma. My wife came up with a way to make this situation less painful for our child. This technique may work for you.

Preview each reading assignment and find something in the story that complements your child's interest. For example, a story about the Middle Ages can be boring until you introduce the story as knights battling to defend the castle or the princess looking to win the knight.

My wife was always able to find something in every story that she could relate to my daughter. My wife's introductions were like movie previews. All the best scenes are shown in a sixty-second clip enticing you to sit through the full two-hour movie.

Think back to when you were in school and given a reading assignment. If you're like me, your main focus was to know enough about the story to answer the teacher's questions. Instead of reading, you probably scanned the text for facts that could be used as the basis for questions.

Make sure your child doesn't fall into this trap. Reading for pleasure is her first objective and will prepare her for the teacher's questions. Don't ask her to analyze the story. Instead, have her tell you what she read. Let her recite the story in her own words.

Reading assignments also provide an opportunity for her to increase her vocabulary. Preview your child's reading assignment and pick out unfamiliar words before she begins reading.

Ask her the meaning of each new word after she completes the assignment. She'll be able to derive the meaning from the other words in the paragraph. If her definition is incorrect, have her write down the word, then copy the definition from a children's dictionary.

You'll also notice she'll be required to write book reports. Book reports are more than a mechanism for the fourth-grade teacher to determine whether or not your child read the assignment. Book reports provide an avenue for your child to express herself, a way of sharing her experience with someone else. Unfortunately, most kids see book reports as another homework assignment.

It is up to you to change your child's attitude. Use her natural tendencies to retell stories. My wife anticipated problems with book reports, so she enlisted Grandma's help. The subject of reading strategically came up in a conversation Grandma had with my daughter. Grandma thought the stories my daughter was reading sounded very interesting and were something she'd like to read herself, if she had time to read. She asked if my daughter would do her a favor by writing her a letter telling about each story she read in school.

The letters were the same as a book report. However, changing the name from "book report" to "a letter to Grandma" took on a whole new meaning and made writing the report meaningful to my daughter.

When it came time to write a book report, my wife suggested my daughter copy the letters written to Grandma and submit it as the book report. She jumped at the chance, thinking this was a shortcut for doing the homework assignment.

Language

Nine- and ten-year-olds are experiencing the challenges of growing up. They're no longer the little kids in the school and still far from being the big kids. Schoolwork becomes harder, the teacher's expectations are demanding, and new assumptions are made about the skills they mastered in previous school years.

These assumptions can cause difficulty for some fourth graders. Teachers spend little time reviewing basic skills and instead plunge into new material. Youngsters who haven't mastered first-, second-, and third-grade lessons are in for a shock.

A major area of concern is language skill. Your child should have a decent vocabulary and have mastered the language structure when she begins the fourth grade. Those skills become the foundation for fourth-grade language lessons, which are primarily centered around writing.

Writing is the major element in this year's language curriculum. This gives your child the opportunity to use her knowledge of the language and her vocabulary to create her own stories.

My daughter was given all kinds of writing assignments. She was asked to write short stories, poetry, newspaper stories, and short plays, some of which the kids performed in the classroom. However, the most intriguing writing assignment I found was when she was asked to write a journal.

Initially, I considered this a trivial assignment. But I quickly discovered I was mistaken. According to fourth-grade teachers I've spoken to, a journal is a vehicle for nine- and ten-year-olds to express their feelings.

In the hustle and bustle of getting everything done, we sometimes forget that our children have feelings and emotions they may not express to anyone. A journal gives your child a private place to tell what she feels without the fear of being criticized for her thoughts.

Teachers who read journals told me fourth graders reveal a lot about themselves and about their families. They tell their journal pleasant experiences, some nonsensical goings-on with their friends, and situations that trouble them.

Don't overreact if your child is assigned to write a journal. I nearly panicked when the teacher discussed the journals during parents' night. I could only imagine the stories my daughter was writing about our family, and the teacher was reading them, and as a school board member, I was one of the teacher's bosses.

We were told only the student and the teacher read the journal, and if we pressed hard, we, too, would get a peek inside the covers without our daughter knowing. However, fourth-grade teachers read journals through the eyes of a nine- or ten-year-old.

Kids don't always see things correctly. Come to think of it, neither do we. I tend to see a pattern of clues, then jump to the worst conclusion I can imagine, and I'm wrong all the time. Journals, which provide a mechanism for the teacher to monitor your child's thoughts, also provide certain patterns and clue words that can raise a caution flag and cause the teacher to intervene to get things back on the right track.

Polishing Your Child's Writing

Your child is expected to do more than express feelings in her writing assignments. The teacher expects her writing to be fully developed as if the story is to appear in a publication. This objective goes directly against what many fourth graders have in mind. They want to write the story once and never read it again.

Think back to writing assignments you received when you were in school. Did you really rewrite them many times and polish your prose so you would be proud of your work? Probably not. Your child is likely to have the same approach to writing.

The problem seems to stem from the attention span of a nine- or ten-year-old. Most find writing the same story over again boring. Don't fight a losing battle. Screaming and threats won't give her any more patience to complete the assignment properly.

Instead, break the writing assignments into segments, each segment being achievable within the attention span of your child.

PROCEDURE:
How to divide a writing assignment into segments

1. Ask her to think of things that she'd like to write about relating to the theme of the assignment. Have her write them down on paper or on the computer, then stop and do something else.
2. Ask her to organize the ideas in segment 1 to develop an outline for the assignment. Again stop and do something else. This completes segment 2.
3. Ask her to write the first draft following the outline she developed in segment 2. Each point in the outline should be a paragraph. She should read the complete text aloud when she finishes writing, then find something else to do for a few hours.
4. Ask her to read the first draft, then change words, sentences, or paragraphs to make the draft read more easily. She should read the complete text aloud when she finishes editing. Stop when she finishes.

> **5.** You read the final draft and point out obvious errors. Pay careful attention to spelling errors and errors in grammar. Don't be overly critical, yet make sure you catch mistakes she shouldn't be making in the fourth grade.

More Grammar

Grammar continues as a topic for study in the fourth grade. The teacher reinforces the parts of speech learned in the third grade and introduces the concept of regular and irregular verbs. Some school districts may cover this material in the third grade, so check with your child's teacher to learn exactly the areas of grammar that are to be taught this school year.

A *regular verb* is like any verb your child learned except it refers to the past tense by placing the letter **d** or letters **ed** at the end of the word. Table 8-1 contains examples of regular verbs.

An *irregular verb* is a verb that refers to the past tense by using a different word. Table 8-2 shows examples of irregular verbs. Be sure to ask your child's teacher for a complete list of regular and irregular verbs she'll be teaching your child, so you'll have a guide when helping with her homework.

Sometimes fourth graders improperly use the past tense of verbs. You have probably heard kids say, "He threwed me the ball." I cringe whenever I hear such a sentence.

You and I pick out the incorrect past tense of a verb when our kids speak because we are used to hearing the verb spoken correctly. Your child may not have had this opportunity, so it is your job to train her ear to the sound of correctly spoken sentences.

My wife and I came up with an informal game we played with our daughter. Each of us used regular and irregular verbs correctly around the house for about a week. The following week I'd use the incorrect past tense of the verbs. Right away my daughter stopped and corrected me. Her ears had been attuned to regular and irregular verbs.

My daughter's fourth-grade teacher provided another handy technique. Whenever your child takes a test on regular or irregular verbs, ask her to read the sentence aloud in her mind. If the past tense of the verb doesn't sound right, then chances are good the past tense form of the word is incorrect.

TABLE **8-1**
EXAMPLES OF REGULAR VERBS

Present Tense	Past Tense
open	opened
close	closed
type	typed
kick	kicked
call	called

TABLE **8-2**
EXAMPLES OF IRREGULAR VERBS

Present Tense	Past Tense
run	ran
throw	threw
speak	spoke
come	came
drink	drank

Fourth-Grade Math

You'll find fourth-grade math to be much the same as in the third grade except the teacher goes into more depth, which can place your child in a very precarious situation if she hasn't mastered lessons from last year.

My daughter's fourth-grade teacher didn't spend much time reviewing. She gave the class a series of tests to determine their current knowledge of first-, second-, and third-grade math, then picked up where their knowledge left off.

Notice I didn't say all the students. This means some kids didn't have the foundation to learn new math topics. This spelled trouble. They didn't have a learning problem nor were they given remedial help.

They simply fell through the cracks. They couldn't keep up with the class and yet were not so far behind to be enrolled in special programs.

Be alert for signs your child is falling into this gap. Help her by following the tips in the previous chapters to assure she's prepared for fourth-grade math. If time runs out, then find her a tutor.

In the fourth grade, she'll learn how to divide and multiply using large numbers. Fractions become a working tool this year and are used to express remainders in division. She'll also be taught how to create equivalent fractions and be pushed to learn more about geometry. Don't fret. I'll give you tips to make you sound like a whiz in front of your child.

Division

In the third grade, your child learned to perform division where the divisor was always less than the leftmost digit in the dividend, as shown in figure 8-1. However, division problems take a different turn in the fourth grade. Some division problems will have a divisor greater than the leftmost digit in the dividend. For example, divide 2,055 by 5 (see figure 8-2). Last year your child learned the first step in solving this problem is to divide 2 by 5, but this can't be done.

The new rule she'll learn this year is to divide the two leftmost digits of the dividend by the divisor whenever the leftmost digit can't be divided by the divisor. In figure 8-2, 20 is divided by 5. Once your child learns this rule, she'll solve the rest of the problem using methods learned in the third grade.

I found it easy to explain the new rule to my daughter using the terms *leftmost digit* and *two leftmost digits* because these numbers are easy for my nine-year-old to identify in the dividend. However, your child's teacher may use more precise terminology called place values.

Each column in a number is identified as a place value. Beginning with the rightmost column, the place values are ones, tens, hundreds, thousands, ten thousands, hundred thousands, millions, and so on.

In figure 8-2, your child first divides the thousands place value (2) by the divisor, and if she can't, then tries to divide the thousands and hundreds place values (20) together.

Use whatever terminology you feel makes the concept clear to your child. I always use the simplest terms, then once my daughter firmly grasps the concept, I introduce the proper terminology.

$$
\begin{array}{r}
231 \quad \text{R0} \\
2 \overline{\smash{)}462} \\
-\,4 \\
\hline
06 \\
-\,6 \\
\hline
02 \\
-\,2 \\
\hline
0
\end{array}
$$

FIGURE 8-1. THE DIVISOR IS LESS THAN THE LEFTMOST DIGIT IN THE DIVIDEND.

$$
\begin{array}{r}
411 \quad \text{R0} \\
5 \overline{\smash{)}2{,}055} \\
-20 \\
\hline
05 \\
-\,5 \\
\hline
05 \\
-\,5 \\
\hline
0
\end{array}
$$

FIGURE 8-2. DIVISION OF LARGE NUMBERS

Your child also learns to divide by numbers larger than a single digit, such as in the division problem shown in figure 8-3. The divisor is 15 and the dividend is 2,055. This problem introduces a new degree of complexity to division and can be an obstacle to some fourth graders.

Avoid two-digit divisor problems until your child is comfortable solving division problems having a single-digit divisor. Without this foundation, she won't be prepared to handle more difficult division problems. Don't let her develop a "can't do" attitude. Stop her from undertaking new material before she is prepared to learn the new lesson.

I was fortunate because my daughter could solve simple division problems without any difficulties. My wife worked with her during the summer to beef up her skills. However, I was confused about how to explain division with a double-digit divisor to her. A few teachers suggested I talk my daughter through the first few steps of the problem (figure 8-3) until she noticed the pattern, at which point she could take over.

PROCEDURE:
How to talk your child through a division problem with a double-digit divisor

1. "How many times can you divide 15 into 2?" (Figure 8-3.) Don't pause longer than a breath if she hesitates. Instead, you give the answer, "It can't be done." Elaborate if you must, but don't get bogged down in too many details, otherwise you'll be diverted from the lesson.
2. Explain that she must use the two leftmost numbers in the dividend because 15 can't be divided into 2.
3. "How many times can you divide 15 into 20?" The same delay rule applies. Don't wait. Offer the answer first. "Fifteen can be divided into 20 once."
4. Show that you multiply 1 in the quotient by the divisor 15 to arrive at the product 15, which is entered at the appropriate place in the division form.
5. "What do you get when you subtract 15 from 20?" This is an easy subtraction problem that most fourth graders can answer in their heads.

$$
\begin{array}{r}
137 \quad \text{R0} \\
15 \enclose{longdiv}{2{,}055} \\
-\ 15 \quad\;\; \\
\hline
55 \quad\;\; \\
-\ 45 \quad\;\; \\
\hline
105 \quad \\
-\ 105 \quad \\
\hline
0 \quad
\end{array}
$$

FIGURE **8-3.** DIVIDING USING A TWO-DIGIT DIVISOR

Fourth graders are pushed to perform arithmetic in their heads. This is called *mental math*. The objective is to tune their minds to work through answers to simple mathematical operations without using pencil and paper.

Your child was introduced to mental addition, subtraction, and multiplication in the second and third grades. This year she learns to perform mental division using a single-digit divisor. Mental division problems (see figure 8-4) are different from the expanded form of division (figure 8-3).

Notice in the first example, the divisor can easily be divided into each digit in the dividend. While the dividend 428 is a big number, the division operation breaks down the dividend into three very simple division problems that can be easily performed in your child's head.

The other example also seems overwhelming at first since the dividend 1,624 is also a large number and the divisor cannot be divided into the leftmost digit in the dividend. This threw my daughter a curve the first time she saw this problem.

However, my daughter had already learned to use the two leftmost numbers in the dividend if she couldn't divide the divisor into the first leftmost number. I reminded her of this rule, then the division problem became simple to solve because she knew $8 \times 2 = 16$ and the rest of the dividend consisted of two simple, single-digit division problems where there were no remainders.

$$428 \div 2 =$$
$$1,624 \div 2 =$$

FIGURE 8-4. TYPICAL MENTAL DIVISION PROBLEMS

Fractions

In the second grade, your child learned the concept of fractions when she saw the whole of something being broken up into pieces. The third-grade teacher taught her how to represent those pieces in numbers known as *fractions*. This year she learns to manipulate fractional numbers.

Many school districts introduce fraction math with the concept of factors. A *factor* is a number that divides evenly into another number, such as 4 divided by 2 where 2 is a factor. The reason for teaching factors is to prepare her for reducing fractions using the greatest common factor. A *common factor* is a factor that is found in two numbers. The *greatest common factor* is the largest number that can be used as a factor.

You can help your child learn to identify common factors by making the connection between multiplication tables and factors. Here's a typical question your fourth grader will find on a homework assignment: What are the common factors of 8 and 16?

At first glance she'll probably panic. My daughter did because she wasn't sure how to approach solving the problem.

PROCEDURE:
How to help your child solve factor problems

1. Make sure she understands the definition of the term *common factor*. A common factor is like a divisor in a division problem, and the numbers (8 and 16) in the problem are the dividends.
2. Restate the problem by asking, What number can be divided into both numbers (8 and 16) in the problem evenly?
3. Remind her that division is the opposite of multiplication, then ask her to look at the times tables to find products equal to the numbers (8 and 16) in the problem. These are likely candidates to be factors. Figure 8-5 shows the correct answers. Notice there can be more than one correct answer because in this example several numbers can be used as a common factor.
4. Write all the factors to a problem and identify the greatest common factor. Looking at the first example in figure 8-5, you can see the quotients can be factored further. The same is true in the second example. However, the third example can't be factored since there isn't a number that can be divided evenly into 1 and 2. So 8 is the greatest common factor.

$$1 \qquad 8 \div 2 = 4$$
$$16 \div 2 = 8$$

$$2 \qquad 8 \div 4 = 2$$
$$\underline{16 \div 4 = 4}$$

$$3 \qquad 8 \div 8 = 1$$
$$\underline{16 \div 8 = 2}$$

FIGURE 8-5. THE COMMON FACTORS OF 8 AND 16

Once the class learns factoring, your child's fourth-grade teacher is likely to revisit equivalent fractions, a topic introduced in the third grade. *Equivalent fractions* are two fractions that represent the same relationship between the whole and the fractional parts of the whole. Figure 8-6 shows two fractions that are equivalent fractions because both refer to half of the whole. In the first example, 1 is half of 2 boxes. In the second example, 2 is half of 4 boxes.

$$\frac{1}{2} \qquad\qquad \frac{2}{4}$$

FIGURE 8-6. BOTH FRACTIONS REFER TO HALF OF ALL THE BOXES.

Your child will be shown how to create an equivalent fraction by multiplying or dividing the numerator and denominator of a fraction by the same number.

Say you want to create a fraction equivalent to $1/2$. You can multiply 1 (the numerator) by 2 and the 2 (the denominator) by 2, which results in the equivalent fraction shown in figure 8-7.

It is important that you relate the multiplication to real objects. Be sure to reinforce the concept that the denominator tells how many are in the whole and the numerator tells the number of pieces of the whole represented by the fraction.

When an equivalent fraction is created using multiplication, your child increases the number of objects in the whole and in the pieces of the whole. The example in figure 8-7 shows how to create the equivalent fraction shown in figure 8-6.

Dividing the denominator and numerator by the same number also changes the number of objects in the whole and in the pieces of the whole. In this case, your child decreases the number of objects, as is illustrated in figure 8-8.

Dividing the denominator and numerator by the same number is also the method used to reduce a fraction to its lowest terms. This means an equivalent fraction cannot be created using division once the fraction is reduced by its greatest common factor.

$$\frac{1}{2} \times \frac{2}{2} = \frac{2}{4}$$

FIGURE 8-7. MULTIPLY A FRACTION TO CREATE AN EQUIVALENT FRACTION.

$$\frac{2}{4} \div \frac{2}{2} = \frac{1}{2}$$

FIGURE 8-8. DIVIDE A FRACTION TO CREATE AN EQUIVALENT FRACTION.

Fractions can be added or subtracted to form new fractions. My daughter had a difficult time comprehending this concept since she viewed the entire fraction as an entity rather than separating the numerator and denominator in her mind.

The example in figure 8-9 illustrates her problem. She couldn't visualize what was meant by these fractions. She recognized that the denominators of both fractions were the same and the numerators were different. However, she didn't associate the fractions with objects until I showed her the drawing in figure 8-10.

Figure 8-10 shows these fractions as boxes. The first drawing has 1 box of the 4 boxes shaded. The second drawing has 2 boxes of the 4 boxes shaded. When they are added together we end up with three shaded boxes. The shaded boxes represent the numerator of the fraction while the total number of boxes represent the denominator of the fraction. This is an important concept for your child to grasp, as it becomes the foundation for learning how to create common denominators, which she'll learn in the fifth grade.

The same concept helps her to understand how to subtract fractions.

Figure 8-11 illustrates a typical problem she'll find on her homework. Figure 8-12 illustrates the problem as boxes where the shaded boxes represent the numerator of the fractions.

$$\frac{1}{4} + \frac{2}{4} =$$

FIGURE 8-9. ADDING FRACTIONS

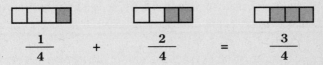

$$\frac{1}{4} \quad + \quad \frac{2}{4} \quad = \quad \frac{3}{4}$$

FIGURE 8-10. RELATING ADDING FRACTIONS TO OBJECTS

$$\frac{3}{4} - \frac{1}{4} = \frac{2}{4}$$

FIGURE 8-11. SUBTRACTING FRACTIONS

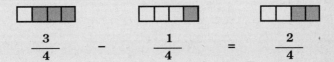

$$\frac{3}{4} \quad - \quad \frac{1}{4} \quad = \quad \frac{2}{4}$$

FIGURE 8-12. RELATING SUBTRACTING FRACTIONS TO OBJECTS

Next, your child is introduced to unusual fractions called improper fractions. An *improper fraction* is a fraction where the numerator is equal to or larger than the denominator. Figure 8-13 contains examples of improper fractions.

This was another difficult concept for my daughter to understand. She knew the numerator represented the number of pieces in the denominator. Now the numerator had more pieces than there were in the whole (denominator).

Figure 8-14 relates an improper fraction to objects. In this example, there are more shaded boxes than there are in one whole. In other words, there is at least a whole object in the numerator.

This is a perfect lead-in to mixed numbers. A *mixed number* is a number that contains both a whole number and a fraction. A mixed number is created from an improper fraction by dividing the denominator into the numerator as illustrated in figure 8-15. The line between the numerator and denominator is like a division symbol. The numerator is the dividend and the denominator is the divisor.

Notice in this example the numerator (11) isn't divided equally by the denominator (2). There is a remainder (1). A *remainder* means less than a whole, and anything less than a whole is a fraction. Your child learns that remainders are fractions of the divisor and so remainders can be written as a fraction.

The remainder becomes the numerator of the fraction and the divisor becomes the denominator. This is also illustrated in figure 8-15.

$$\frac{6}{4}, \frac{3}{2}, \frac{10}{3}, \frac{6}{6}, \frac{8}{5}, \frac{7}{4}$$

FIGURE **8-13.** A SAMPLING OF IMPROPER FRACTIONS

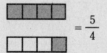

FIGURE **8-14.** RELATING IMPROPER FRACTIONS TO OBJECTS

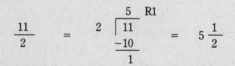

FIGURE **8-15.** DIVISION IS USED TO CREATE A MIXED NUMBER FROM AN IMPROPER FRACTION.

Decimals

Many school districts introduce decimals in the fourth grade as a follow-up to fractions, because a decimal is another way to write a fraction. However, the lack of a physical resemblance between a fraction and a decimal is bound to confuse your child.

Here's the method I used to overcome this obstacle. I explained to my daughter that a decimal point separates the whole numbers from less-than-whole numbers. Numbers to the left of the decimal point are whole numbers while numbers to the right of the decimal point are less-than-whole numbers, similar to a remainder in division. I drew a picture (figure 8-16) to show her what I was talking about.

Decimal Point

$$37.456$$

←———— Whole Numbers   Less than a Whole Number ————→

FIGURE 8-16. THE DECIMAL POINT SEPARATES WHOLE NUMBERS FROM LESS-THAN-WHOLE NUMBERS.

Fourth graders learn simple decimal equivalents, typically 0.1, 0.01, and 0.001. A *decimal equivalent* is the decimal form of a fraction. The fractional equivalents of these decimals are $\frac{1}{10}$, $\frac{1}{100}$, $\frac{1}{1,000}$.

Some decimals are written with extra zeros, such as 0.10. These zeros are not necessary, but make the numbers easy to read. Zeros after the last decimal number don't change the value of the number. Likewise a zero on the left side of the decimal point when there is no whole number will not change the value of the number, but will alert you to the decimal point.

The easiest way to draw the connection between fractions and decimals is by their names. The numbers 0.1 and $\frac{1}{10}$ are called one-tenth. Likewise, 0.01 and $\frac{1}{100}$ are called one-hundredth, and 0.001 and $\frac{1}{1,000}$ are called one-thousandth.

Make sure your child uses the **ths** at the end of each name. My daughter kept confusing *tens* with *tenths*, *hundreds* with *hundredths*, and *thousands* with *thousandths*. The best way to clarify these terms is to follow this simple rule: If the number is to the right of the decimal point, then use the **ths**, otherwise leave off the **ths**. Table 8-3 is a good way to drive home the difference in the place values between whole numbers and decimal numbers.

TABLE 8-3

PLACE VALUES FOR WHOLE NUMBERS AND DECIMAL NUMBERS

Hundreds	Tens	Ones	Decimal Point	Tenths	Hundredths	Thousandths
1	1	1	.	1	1	1

Your child will be expected to convert a fraction to a decimal value. If she's like my daughter, she'll develop a mental block. There is no obvious way to relate numbers in a fraction to a decimal equivalent. Break through this mental block by having your child follow a simple two-step procedure for converting a fraction to a decimal. Let's say your child needs to convert $37/100$ into a decimal.

P R O C E D U R E :
How to teach your child to convert a fraction to a decimal

1. Place a decimal point on a piece of paper.
2. Place the numerator (37) to the right of the decimal point to form the decimal equivalent. This is illustrated in figure 8-17.

Converting a decimal to a fraction is just as easy.

P R O C E D U R E :
How to teach your child to convert a decimal to a fraction

1. Place the numbers on the right side of the decimal point in the numerator of the fraction.
2. Determine the place value of the decimal. In this example, the decimal is thirty-seven hundredths, so the place value is hundredths.
3. Write the place value as the denominator of the fraction. (See figure 8-18.)

A word of caution. The method used to convert fractions to decimals and decimals to fractions works fine for the simple fractions taught in the fourth grade. However, she'll probably be shown in the fifth or sixth grade how to use a formula to convert more complex fractions.

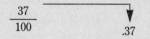

FIGURE **8-17**. CONVERTING A FRACTION TO A DECIMAL

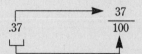

FIGURE **8-18**. CONVERTING A DECIMAL TO A FRACTION

Decimal values can be added, subtracted, multiplied, and divided. Most fourth graders, however, are taught only to add and subtract decimal values because the math is the same as adding and subtracting whole numbers.

Columns of numbers and the decimal point must be aligned properly, otherwise your child can easily calculate the wrong numbers. A trick my daughter learned should help your child keep decimal values aligned properly. Always fill empty spaces in a problem with zeros. This is illustrated in figure 8-19 where zeros are used to the left and right of the decimal point.

$$
\begin{array}{rr}
0.532 & 8.732 \\
+\ 8.200 & -\ 8.200 \\
\hline
8.732 & 0.532
\end{array}
$$

FIGURE **8-19**. FILL EMPTY SPACES IN COLUMNS WITH ZEROS.

Geometry—Rays and Angles

Fourth-grade geometry is all about defining parts of lines and shapes. These definitions are tricky to understand since a subtle alteration in a shape can take on a whole different meaning. I needed a crash course in geometric terms before I could help my daughter with her geometry homework. Here's what I relearned. You'll find this information handy when working with your child on her homework.

All shapes are created from one or more line segments. You and I think shapes are made up of lines. This is technically incorrect. A *line* flows endlessly in two directions. A *line segment* also flows in two directions, but has a beginning and an end called *points on the line*.

Some shapes are composed of rays. A *ray* is similar to a line segment in that there is a beginning point, but it has no end. A ray goes on forever in one direction (figure 8-20). Each point on a line segment and ray is identified by a letter. The ray in figure 8-20 contains two points **A** and **B**. The combination of the letters becomes the *name of the ray* **(AB)**.

Two rays are joined together to form an angle. An *angle* is a combination of two rays where each ray shares the same beginning point. The shared point forms the *vertex* of the angle (like a corner). The *name of the angle* is the combination of the points on the rays **(ABC)** where the name of the shared point is always the middle letter (figure 8-21). The name of an angle is sometimes abbreviated using the angle sign ∠**ABC**.

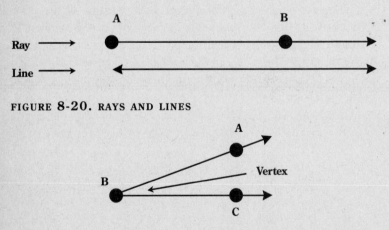

FIGURE **8-20.** RAYS AND LINES

FIGURE **8-21.** AN ANGLE IS COMPOSED OF TWO RAYS THAT SHARE A COMMON POINT.

Fourth graders learn that various kinds of angles can be formed by arranging the rays. The first angle your child learns is the right angle. A *right angle* is formed when one ray points straight up and the other ray points to the right, as shown in figure 8-22. This is a very important angle to recognize. Other angles are defined by making reference to a right angle.

Two other angles she'll learn are acute angles and obtuse angles. An *acute angle* is formed when the vertical ray is tilted toward the horizontal ray when compared with a right angle. In contrast, an *obtuse angle* is formed when the vertical ray is tilted away from the horizontal ray. These angles are shown in figure 8-22.

The easiest way for your child to identify the correct angle is to associate the picture with the name of the angle. I told my daughter to simply look at the ray that points up. If the ray is pointing straight up, then it is a right angle. If the ray is to the left, then it is an obtuse angle. If the ray is to the right, then it is an acute angle.

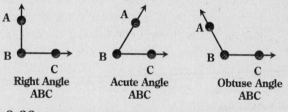

FIGURE 8-22. TYPES OF ANGLES

Geometry—Polygons

Your child learns that a shape that has many sides is called a *polygon*. Think of a polygon as a general term that describes shapes like squares and rectangles, which your child learned about in the third grade.

In the fourth grade, polygons are divided into two groups, which are triangles and quadrilaterals. A *triangle* is a shape that has three sides. Each side connects with another side to form an angle. The point at which two sides meet is called a vertex.

There are two special kinds of triangles learned about in the fourth grade. These are equilateral triangles and right triangles (see figure 8-23). The length of the sides of an *equilateral triangle* are equal, while one angle of a *right triangle* is a right angle. Equilateral triangles and right triangles are named using letters the same way your child named angles.

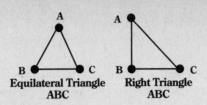

Equilateral Triangle ABC   **Right Triangle ABC**

FIGURE 8-23. TWO KINDS OF TRIANGLES

Quadrilaterals are shapes that have four sides. They include squares and rectangles. Your child will use quadrilaterals to learn three concepts—opposite sides, diagonals, and parallel sides.

Opposite sides of a quadrilateral are the sides that aren't connected to form a vertex. I explained this to my daughter by saying the two sides that don't touch each other are opposite sides. Sides **AB** and **CD** in the first example in figure 8-24 are opposite sides, as are sides **AD** and **BC**.

Diagonals are lines, sometimes imaginary, that connect opposite vertices. A diagonal can be drawn from **A** to **C** in the first example of figure 8-24. Another can be drawn from **B** to **D** in the same example.

Two sides of a quadrilateral are *parallel* if the lines in which they are contained are parallel. Two lines are parallel if they never meet. Remember, lines go on forever.

Two new quadrilaterals your child will be introduced to this year are trapezoids and parallelograms (figure 8-24).

A *trapezoid* contains only one pair of parallel sides. The parallel sides are never the same length. The other pair of opposite sides are not parallel to each other, and they may or may not be the same length. Sides **AB** and **CD** are the parallel sides of the trapezoid in figure 8-24.

In contrast, the opposite sides of a *parallelogram* are parallel to each other and are the same length. In the parallelogram in figure 8-24, sides **AB** and **CD** are parallel to each other and are the same length. Sides **AD** and **BC** are also parallel to each other and are the same length.

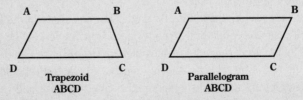

Trapezoid ABCD   **Parallelogram ABCD**

FIGURE 8-24. TWO TYPES OF QUADRILATERALS

Formulas—Area, Perimeter, Volume

Don't be surprised if your child comes home and asks you to explain a formula or two she found on her homework assignment. And don't be like me and try to duck answering because you don't remember much about formulas.

A *formula* is shorthand for an equation that defines a relationship among things. Probably the most used formula is for miles per hour, which is stated as **Miles Per Hour = Total Miles Traveled / Elapsed Hours**. Simply substitute values for the words and perform the math to arrive at miles per hour.

Fourth graders understand formulas as long as words are used in place of values. Trouble begins when letters replace words, like **MPH = M/H**. How can you divide M by H?

Here's how to explain formulas to your child. Write the formula twice, once with the words and the other time using letters. Figure 8-25 illustrates this technique, using the formula for calculating the area of a rectangle. Plug in values on the third line, then calculate the expression. She'll be able to see the relationship among the words, the letters, and the values.

The formula for calculating the area of a rectangle is one of three formulas she learns in the fourth grade. The *area* is the space within the sides of the rectangle and is measured in a square value. The rectangle in figure 8-26 is measured in inches, and the area is measured in square inches, which is abbreviated as in^2. I used this drawing to show my daughter that each square is an inch long and an inch wide, and it takes fifty of those squares to fill the rectangle. This helped her to visualize exactly what an area looks like.

Formula:	Area	=	Length	×	Width
	A	=	L	×	W
Solution:	$50\,in^2$	=	10 in.	×	5 in.

FIGURE 8-25. HOW TO CALCULATE THE AREA OF A RECTANGLE

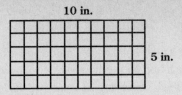

FIGURE **8-26.** THE AREA OF A RECTANGLE

A formula is composed of two known factors and one unknown factor. The length and width in figure 8-26 are the known factors while the area is the unknown factor. Your child performs arithmetic using the known factors to find the unknown factor.

Any factor in a formula can be an unknown factor and can be found by changing the formula slightly. Figure 8-27 and figure 8-28 are good examples to use when explaining this concept to your child.

The unknown factor in figure 8-27 is the width of the rectangle, which is found by dividing the area by the length of the rectangle. The unknown factor in figure 8-28 is the length of the rectangle. The length can be found by dividing the area by the width of the rectangle.

Formula:	Width	=	Area	/	Length
	W	=	A	/	L
Solution:	5 in.	=	50 in²	/	10 in.

FIGURE **8-27.** HOW TO CALCULATE THE WIDTH OF A
RECTANGLE

Formula:	Length	=	Area	/	Width
	L	=	A	/	W
Solution:	10 in.	=	50 in²	/	5 in.

FIGURE **8-28.** HOW TO CALCULATE THE LENGTH OF A
RECTANGLE

Fourth graders are also expected to know how to measure the perimeter of a rectangle. The *perimeter* is the combined length of all sides (figure 8-29) and is calculated using the formula in figure 8-30.

Looking at this problem, my daughter asked, "Why are the length and width added together within parentheses? Why is the sum multiplied by two?"

I focused her attention on how to use the formula rather than why the formula works the way it does, because the objective is to learn how to solve a problem on a test. The whys can be left for a less pressing time.

However, here are the answers for the perimeter formula. Your child learned in the third grade to calculate numbers within the parentheses first. In figure 8-30, the length and the width of the rectangle are added together. However, the sum represents only half the sides of the rectangle. Multiplying the sum by two accounts for all sides of the rectangle.

10 in.

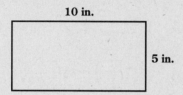

5 in.

FIGURE 8-29. DETERMINING THE PERIMETER

Formula:	Perimeter	=	2	×	(Length	+	Width)
	P	=	2	×	(L	+	W)
Solution:	30 in.	=	2	×	(10 in.	+	5 in.)

FIGURE 8-30. HOW TO CALCULATE THE PERIMETER OF A RECTANGLE

The third formula your child is responsible for learning is used to determine the volume of an object. *Volume* is the measurement of the space occupied by the object. You can best explain this concept by showing her the drawing in figure 8-31, which shows a group of blocks called cubes.

A *cube* is similar to a square where all measurements are the same, except a *square* has two dimensions (length and width) and a cube has three dimensions (length, width, and height).

Figure 8-32 shows the formula used to calculate the volume. Volume is measured in a cubic value, because it represents the product of three dimensions. Inches are used in this example, therefore the volume is cubic inches, which is abbreviated as in³. Regardless of the unit of measure, the result is always in cubic measurement.

Many fourth graders have problems visualizing volume and cubes. Here's an approach that helps to clarify the issue. Ask your child to count the number of cubes in the drawing. The total number of cubes is equal to the volume calculated using the formula.

Try counting yourself and you'll discover a problem. Only thirteen cubes are shown. Three cubes are hidden from view. Those are on the bottom right row. My daughter didn't believe they existed, so I built the object using her blocks, then let her count each block to prove the count was correct.

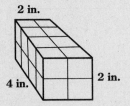

FIGURE 8-31. DETERMINING THE VOLUME OF A SHAPE

Formula:	Volume	=	Length	×	Width	×	Height
	V	=	L	×	W	×	H
Solution:	16 in³	=	4 in.	×	2 in.	×	2 in.

FIGURE 8-32. HOW TO CALCULATE THE VOLUME OF A CUBE

Time Math

Your child has been learning about time since the first grade. This school year, she'll use her addition and subtraction skills to calculate time.

Figure 8-33 shows typical addition and subtraction problems that you'll find on her homework. They look like any addition and subtraction problem except for the colon (:). Last year she learned the colon is used to separate hours and minutes. Therefore, 1:30 is the same as 1 hour and 30 minutes. In the first example, 15 minutes are subtracted from 1 hour and 30 minutes. The second example adds 15 minutes to 1 hour and 30 minutes.

These examples shouldn't cause problems, because she knows how to add and subtract and neither problem requires regrouping. She only needs to know how to properly place the colon in the results.

$$
\begin{array}{r}
1{:}30 \\
-\ {:}15 \\
\hline
1{:}15
\end{array}
\qquad
\begin{array}{r}
1{:}30 \\
+\ {:}15 \\
\hline
1{\cdot}45
\end{array}
$$

FIGURE **8-33.** SUBTRACTING AND ADDING TIME WITHOUT REGROUPING

Many fourth graders have difficulty solving the examples in figure 8-34 and figure 8-35, because both problems require regrouping numbers in a different way than they learned in the third grade. Regrouping a time calculation requires your child to convert units of measurement.

The example in figure 8-34 adds 20 minutes to 1 hour and 50 minutes (step 1). The sum of the minutes (step 2) is 70 minutes. However, 70 minutes is more than an hour, so minutes must be regrouped to hours by dividing 60 minutes into 70 minutes (step 3). She already knows 60 minutes is equal to one hour. The division results in 1 hour and a remainder of 10, which is 10 minutes. After regrouping, the problem is reformed (step 4), then the arithmetic is performed.

Figure 8-35 illustrates the steps required to regroup a subtraction problem. Notice the problem requires 75 minutes to be subtracted from 50 minutes (step 1). This can't be done unless regrouping occurs. Since 75 minutes is more than an hour, you can convert 75 minutes to 1 hour and 15 minutes by dividing 75 minutes by 60 minutes (step 2). The regrouped values can be used to reform the problem (step 3), which is easy for her to solve.

1	2	3		4
$\begin{array}{r} 1{:}50 \\ +\ {:}20 \\ \hline \end{array}$	$\begin{array}{r} {:}50 \\ +\ {:}20 \\ \hline {:}70 \end{array}$	$\begin{array}{r} 1 \\ 60\ \overline{)\ 70} \\ -60 \\ \hline 10 \end{array}$	R10 = 1:10	$\begin{array}{r} 1{:}00 \\ +1{:}10 \\ \hline 2{:}10 \end{array}$

FIGURE **8-34.** ADDING TIME WITH REGROUPING

```
   1                    2                               3
     1:50                    1  R15 = 1:15                 1:50
   − :75              60 | 75                            −1:15
                        −60                                :45
                      ─────
                         15
```

FIGURE 8-35. SUBTRACTING TIME WITH REGROUPING

9.

Making the Grade in the Fifth Grade

- Reading
- Language
- Fifth-Grade Math
- Finding Unknown Values
- Multiplication
- Division
- Fractions
- Fractions—Adding, Subtracting, and Multiplying
- Going from a Fraction to a Decimal
- Mixed Numbers—Adding and Subtracting
- Percents
- Geometry—Measuring Angles
- Geometry—Measuring Circles
- Geometry—Measuring Area

I t was settled. After months of racking our brains my wife and I came up with the perfect gift for a ten-year-old, a gift guaranteed to wow our daughter Christmas morning. Our fifth grader was about to become the proud owner of her first adult bike.

Sounds like a great idea, doesn't it? Well, it turned out to be the experience of a lifetime. Buying a bike today has changed since the day I rode my Schwinn out of the local bike shop.

The first sign of trouble came when I visited the toy store in the mall. Sticker shock. I had no idea bikes were so expensive and so complicated to buy. There are five-speeds, ten-speeds, mountain bikes, beach bikes, street bikes. I even found a few designer bikes in the mix. Whatever happened to the plain simple bike they used to make when we were growing up?

Then I discovered my daughter had to be measured for the bike. I'd never heard of such a thing, but the sales clerk was unwavering. My guess is the company was sued for liability when they sold a big bike to a small kid.

How was I expected to bring her into the store to be measured if I wanted to keep the bike a surprise? After a few weeks of fighting a losing battle with the store manager, I made up some excuse to bring her into the bike department to browse. Of course, she headed toward the designer bikes while I stood in the low-price section.

Did you know bikes are sold unassembled? I had a fit when the sales clerk told me this. All I could imagine was trying to assemble the bike from a box of parts on Christmas Eve. I have little luck putting anything together, let alone building a bike under the pressure of a deadline.

But the sales clerk was quick to say the store staff would assemble the bike for me—for a price. There I stood, my daughter eyeing the Rolls-Royce of bicycles and the sales clerk raising the ante. I had no choice but to pay.

"How do you plan to get the bike home?" the sales clerk asked.

"What do you mean?" Then it hit me. The assembled bike would never fit into my car, and the store didn't offer a delivery service.

I gave the sales clerk the look that said "hit me again." And she did by suggesting I could rent a van or she just happened to know of a delivery service that would be more than willing to help me out—for a price. I could have bought a cheap motor scooter for the price I ended up paying for my daughter's bike.

Late on Christmas Eve we stood the bike on its kickstand smack in the middle of the living room alongside chairs filled with other presents. Christmas morning arrived.

With camera rolling, my wife and I took up positions so we wouldn't miss her expression when she saw the bike. She came into the room blurry-eyed and headed right for the chairs filled with presents. Not a word about the bike. Ten minutes went by and she was still unwrapping.

Now it's not every day we have a twenty-eight-inch two-wheeler sitting in the living room. The bike wasn't even wrapped. You had to be blind not to see it, because my wife decorated the bike with a big red bow. Finally, with a little prodding from her mother, she noticed.

"A bike!"

She ran over to it, then went back to playing with her Barbies.

Fortunately, the rest of the fifth grade wasn't as trying as buying a bike that received less-than-overwhelming reviews Christmas morning. You'll find fifth grade to be more challenging for your child and you than all the previous school years combined.

Fifth-grade teachers normally assume students are proficient in basic skills. This can be a dangerous assumption if your child doesn't live up to expectations. In preparation for the school year, I asked my daughter's fifth-grade teacher to tell me what skills she expected my daughter to have mastered. I then used the coaching techniques discussed in previous chapters to bring my daughter up to speed. This is a good technique you can also use with your child. And when she's up to speed, you can use similar hints and tips for fifth-grade work in this chapter.

Reading

By now there is practically nothing your child can't read. She has developed a good working vocabulary and can comprehend most reading material. This is the time in her life when she begins to make personal reading choices. My wife and I discovered this fact when our daughter declared a section of the newspaper hers. She also adopted a few magazines targeted for her age group.

As a parent of a fifth grader, you'll be expected to continue your efforts to encourage reading by reading in front of your child. Teachers have told me the more kids see their parents read, the better the chance they'll become readers, too.

Although our fifth grader had reached a good level of comprehension, there were still some forms of writing that confused her. Fortunately, the fifth-grade reading curriculum in our school district quickly steered my daughter back on course.

Your fifth grader might have similar gaps in her comprehension, so I'll share with you my experience and give you some tips I used to fill those gaps. My daughter's problems started when she read that the main character in a story was going to kill a cat.

Our family is fond of animals. You can imagine how disturbed my daughter was reading this passage. Her crying turned to anger, and she was bent on voicing her opinions to the teacher, the principal, and the school board. She felt such a book shouldn't be used in school.

I was a bit disturbed, too, and I found myself in a very delicate situation. I was one of the school board members who had approved the book. None of us saw anything wrong with the publication. At least, nothing that would disturb an eleven-year-old.

Fortunately, I read the story before my daughter had the opportunity to make her accusations public. The cat in the story got into a little mischief. The main character in a fit of frustration blurted, "I'm going to kill you!" as he chased the cat out of the room.

Of course, the author of the book assumed kids would know the passage was meant figuratively and not literally as my daughter thought. To avoid embarrassing situations in the future, my wife quickly gave her a lesson in how to recognize when someone is writing figuratively.

The other problem involved the misunderstanding of literature terminology. Fifth graders learn the technical terms for styles used in stories and poems, such as personification, metaphor, simile, alliteration, and onomatopoeia.

You probably remember these terms from your school days, but if you're like me you probably remember little else about them. Here's a refresher to get you back up to speed before you coach your child through her homework.

Personification is a style of writing in which the author gives inanimate objects or animals humanlike qualities such as speech. I used the movie *Toy Story* as an example, so my daughter fully understands the definition.

A metaphor and a simile are figures of speech. We've all said at one time, "Fast as a speeding bullet," or, "She's a doll." Both of these are figures of speech. A *simile* draws a comparison using either **like** or **as** in the sentence. A *metaphor* does not use these words, but still makes a comparison.

Alliteration and onomatopoeia are found throughout your child's poetry readings this school year. Both terms refer to the sounds of words in the poem. *Alliteration* occurs when words in a sentence start with either the same sound or the same letter. You see alliteration used in "Peter Piper picked a peck of pickled peppers," where most of the words begin with the same letter and the same sound.

Onomatopoeia has nothing to do with using the bathroom facilities, although fifth graders usually think otherwise when hearing the term for the first time. *Onomatopoeia* is the term used to describe words that sound like the object or action they describe. Your child will easily recognize these. They are words like *buzz* and *hiss*.

Language

I was prepared when the school year began. Over the summer I cracked open a few grammar books myself to brush up on the concepts my daughter would be learning in school. I was tired of coming home each night and being asked questions about grammar that I couldn't answer off the top of my head.

To my surprise, there were only a few new concepts for my daughter to learn. Most of her homework assignments tested her knowledge of grammar learned in the second, third, and fourth grades.

I've discovered some school districts use the fifth grade as a catch-up year for grammar. This year your child has the opportunity to brush up on missed grammar lessons from previous school years.

Don't expect these lessons to be retaught to the class. Instead, the fifth-grade teacher typically helps students who have problems in an area of grammar while classmates tackle a class assignment. You can also help by asking the teacher to identify areas in grammar where your child needs work, then using the appropriate chapter of this book to help coach her to a mastery level.

New grammar lessons center around objects of a sentence and the agreement of objects. Fifth-grade grammar begins with learning how to identify objects in a sentence.

There are two kinds of objects. These are direct objects and indirect objects. A *direct object* is a noun or pronoun directly affected by the verb of the sentence. The word **ball** in figure 9-1 is the direct object of the sentence because the verb **threw** directly relates to the action of the **ball**.

Jack threw the *ball*.

FIGURE **9-1**. THE DIRECT OBJECT OF A SENTENCE

An *indirect object* is the noun or pronoun that receives the action from the direct object. Figure 9-2 highlights the indirect object of the sentence. In this example, **ball** is the object of the sentence, **threw** is the verb, and **Jill** is the indirect object.

Jack threw *Jill* the ball.

FIGURE **9-2**. THE INDIRECT OBJECT OF A SENTENCE

Your fifth grader also learns the proper use of personal pronouns. A *personal pronoun* is used in place of the name of a person or a thing to make a sentence easier to read than if you kept repeating the name of the person or thing over again.

Take a look at the first example in figure 9-3. Notice the number of times **Tom** is used in the example. Read this example aloud and listen to how strange the sentences sound. The second example reads more smoothly because two personal pronouns were substituted for the word **Tom**. They were **he** and **his**.

1) Tom bought a bike. Tom shared the bike with Tom's sister.
2) Tom bought a bike. *He* shared the bike with *his* sister.

FIGURE **9-3**. THE USE OF PERSONAL PRONOUNS MAKES SENTENCES EASIER TO READ.

The personal pronoun must be in agreement with the noun replaced by the personal pronoun in the sentence. This is called *agreement of case*. In most homework assignments, your child won't have difficulty choosing the proper personal pronoun, because the sentence sounds strange if the wrong personal pronoun is selected.

For example, "Me want to buy the car." This sentence sounds incorrect, because **me** is not the correct case. The correct case is **I**, and the sentence should read "I want to buy the car."

However, listening to the sentence doesn't always lead to choosing the correct personal pronoun. Instead of intuitively making the selection, your child should follow the standard procedure for picking the personal pronoun.

Personal pronouns are divided into three categories. These are called the nominative case, the objective case, and the possessive case. Table 9-1 lists the personal pronouns in each category. Choose the proper category, then look up the available personal pronouns in the table.

PROCEDURE:

How to select the correct personal pronoun for a sentence

1. Determine the case of the personal pronoun.
2. *Nominative case* personal pronouns are used to replace the subject of the sentence.
3. *Objective case* personal pronouns replace objects in the sentence. These include direct objects and indirect objects, along with the object of a preposition.
4. *Possessive case* personal pronouns are used when the noun shows ownership, such as in *Jane's house*.
5. Look up the case in table 9-1, then pick an appropriate personal pronoun.

The personal pronoun must also match the gender and the number of the noun it is replacing. This is called *agreement in gender* and *agreement in number*. *Gender* is divided into masculine, feminine, and neuter. For example, the sentence "Tom shares his bike with her sister" is incorrect because the gender of the personal pronoun **her** is feminine while the noun **Tom** is masculine. The correct sentence should read, "Tom shares his bike with his sister."

Agreement in number simply means the personal pronoun must be singular or plural based on the number of the noun it replaces. Here is a sentence showing the disagreement by number between the noun and the personal pronoun: "Tom shares his bike with our sister." Obviously, the personal pronoun **our** is plural while the noun **Tom** is singular. The correct sentence should read, "Tom shares his bike with his sister."

TABLE 9-1
PERSONAL PRONOUNS

Nominative Case Personal Pronouns	Objective Case Personal Pronouns	Possessive Case Personal Pronouns
I	me	my, mine
he	him	his
she	her	her, hers
we	us	our, ours
it	it	its
they	them	their, theirs
you	you	your, yours

Fifth-Grade Math

Expect math homework to get tougher this year compared with the previous four years of your child's education. I was surprised by the complexity and variety of the math fifth graders are required to learn.

By the end of the fourth grade your child has learned arithmetic. She knows how to add, subtract, multiply, and divide. In the fifth grade she'll contine to practice her arithmetic skills using large and small numbers. She'll be asked to solve problems involving the billions place value and perform arithmetic using decimal values to the thousandths place.

Fifth graders are also shown how to use arithmetic to solve problems familiar to adults, such as calculating the area of a shape and the volume of a rectangular prism. This comes in handy the next time you're shopping for a new carpet. Let your fifth grader handle the measurements. She is also expected to measure the angles learned in the fourth grade.

Your child is introduced to the proper terminology for concepts learned in previous years. For example, rules of arithmetic are called *properties* of the operation, such as properties of addition and properties of subtraction.

Her knowledge of equations is expanded when she is taught about variables and constants. A *variable* is a value in an equation that can be changed. Values that can't be changed in an equation are called *constants*. She'll see her first constant used when measuring the distance around the circumference of a circle.

There are two other math terms you'll hear your child talk about. These are sets and functions. A *set* is a group of related things. Each thing in a set is called a *member*.

Your child's fifth-grade class is a set of students, and all the boys in the class are a set of fifth-grade boys. In math, sets are used to identify a group of related values and are enclosed within braces: {}.

For example, {10, 11, 9, 10, 11, 10} is a set of ages of all the boys in my daughter's fifth-grade class. Many school districts don't expect fifth graders to use sets in a calculation. Instead, they simply introduce the concept, which will be used in later years.

A *function* is an operation performed on things. The best way to describe a function to your child is to look at the 2 times table, where every number is multiplied by 2. The use of functions in calculations won't be seen this school year.

I like to think of the fifth grade as the thinking year. Nearly all the basics have been learned, and now it is time to apply these skills to real-life situations. Arithmetic becomes challenging when simple addition, subtraction, multiplication, and division are performed with complex numbers such as fractions and decimal values. Word problems can't be solved intuitively anymore. Instead, your child must analyze words carefully, form an equation, then manipulate the equation until it can be solved.

This is a challenge. The remainder of this chapter gives you plenty of tips on how to be a good math coach to your child.

Finding Unknown Values

A man drives five miles down the road. Two of those miles are uphill. He travels at 35 mph downhill. How old is when he arrives at his destination?

Remember how you hated those homework problems? No one really cared about the answer. The problem was unclear, too complex, and had nothing to do with reality. If you conjured those excuses only to have them immediately dismissed by the teacher, you're not alone. So did I. Now you can imagine how I felt when I discovered a whole bunch of these problems on my daughter's homework. Be prepared. You'll be revisiting this nightmare when you look at your fifth grader's homework.

The best way to solve any word problem is to set up an equation that follows the logic of the problem.

Many fifth graders are unsure of the first step to take when solving a word problem. They hit a brick wall by reading a sentence, then assuming the problem is too difficult for them to solve.

Make sure your child's thinking doesn't come to a dead stop after reading a sentence or two of a problem. You can get her on the right track by reminding her to follow the standard procedure (see Procedure box), which begins by setting up an equation.

The carton is 5 times longer than the length of each box of toys stored in the carton. The carton is 30 inches long. What is the length of each box of toys?

FIGURE 9-4. TRANSLATE THIS WORD PROBLEM INTO AN EQUATION, THEN SOLVE FOR THE UNKNOWN VALUE.

Be prepared to help her determine which arithmetic operation is used in the equation. Don't answer this question for her. Instead coach her into thinking through the problem herself.

Ask if she sees any clue words in the problem. There are two clue words in figure 9-4. These are **times** and **each**. The word **times** refers to multiplication, and the word **each** refers to division. At first the clues seem to contradict each other, but they don't, as you'll see.

Ask her to write each piece of the equation as she reads the problem. She can use words from the problem as placeholders for the unknown value. I used **length of each box** to identify the unknown value in the equation in figure 9-5.

You'll notice the flow of the equation parallels the flow of the word problem. This helps her hone her skills in translating word problems into equations.

$$5 \times \text{length of each box} = 30 \text{ in.}$$

FIGURE 9-5. WRITE THE EQUATION TO READ LIKE THE WORD PROBLEM.

There's a problem with the equation in figure 9-5. Although the equation is set up to mimic the flow of the word problem, the equation is not in the proper form to be solved. She'll recognize that known values should be on one side of the equal sign and the unknown value on the opposite side. In this example, there is a known and unknown value on the same side of the equal sign.

Before calculating, she must restate the equation using the inverse operation. An *operation* is addition, subtraction, multiplication, and division. An *inverse operation* is the opposite of the current operation. Your fifth grader already learned that addition and subtraction are opposites and so are multiplication and division. She used the inverse operation to check answers to arithmetic problems in the third and fourth grades.

The equation in figure 9-5 is set up as a multiplication operation. However, there isn't enough information to solve the problem since you can't multiply an unknown value by 5. This is the clue that hints the equation must be rewritten as the inverse operation of multiplication—which is division.

Figure 9-6 is the inverse operation of the equation in figure 9-5. The rewritten equation is a familiar form that your fifth grader should solve without any difficulty.

$$\text{length of each box} = 30 \text{ in.} \div 5$$

FIGURE 9-6. REWRITE THE EQUATION USING THE INVERSE OPERATION IF NECESSARY TO SOLVE THE PROBLEM.

I noticed my daughter's fifth-grade word problems becoming increasingly difficult to translate into equations. The example I used in this section was one of the easier problems. Other problems involve several steps and the use of parentheses to identify those steps in the equation. You'll recall from last year that operations within parentheses in an equation are performed before operations outside the parentheses.

I also discovered there is no one procedure that can be used to solve all the word problems she'll see. Ask your child's teacher for help whenever you come across a word problem you can't translate into an equation. Keep in mind there is a procedure to follow. You just need to learn the procedure, and the teacher is the person who can teach you.

PROCEDURE:
Translating a word problem into an equation

1. Identify the values of the problem. These are called variables. For example in figure 9-6 the values 30, 5, and the unknown value (length of each box) are the variables.
2. Look for clue words in the word problem, such as **times** and **each** in the example used in this section. **Times** indicates multiplication and **each** indicates division.
3. Translate the words and values into an equation as you read the problem. The first clue word probably tells you the operation used in the equation.
4. Are all the known values on one side of the equal sign and is the unknown value on the other? If so, then solve the equation.
5. If all the known values aren't on the same side of the equal sign, rewrite the equation using the inverse operation, and then solve the equation.

Multiplication

Multiplication is easy for your child to perform as long as she has memorized the times tables in the third and fourth grades. Fifth graders who skipped over memorizing the times tables probably will have difficulty performing multiplication this school year.

This is especially true because multiplication becomes more complex with the introduction of decimals. Until now your child multiplied whole numbers. Decimal values present another twist in an already complicated operation.

My daughter went into a panic the first time she was asked to multiply a decimal by a whole number. Like most fifth graders she wasn't sure how to handle the decimal place, which seemed to overshadow the simplicity of the calculation.

Figure 9-7 shows the problem in question. She was asked to multiply 3.44 by 5. Unfortunately for her, the problem wasn't presented in the multiplication form shown here. Instead it was stated as $3.44 \times 5 = ?$

I could see why she was confused. She wasn't able to see the problem in the proper form. I asked her to set up the equation as if the decimal point wasn't there, but to include the decimal point as part of the number (see figure 9-7).

She felt more at ease as soon as the problem took on a familiar form. Her next job was to multiply as if the decimal value didn't exist. She breezed through this calculation thanks to the multiplication tables she had memorized.

The final step was for her to count the number of decimal places, then make sure the product had the same number of decimal places. There are two decimal places in figure 9-7 (3.44). Therefore, the product must have two decimal places counting from the right character (0).

PROCEDURE:
Multiplying decimals

1. Lay out the problem in the multiplication form (see figure 9-7).
2. Multiply as if the decimal point wasn't there.
3. Count the number of decimal places.
4. Make sure the product contains the same number of decimal places. Begin counting decimal places with the rightmost character in the product.

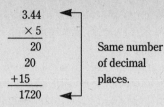

$$
\begin{array}{r}
3.44 \\
\times\,5 \\
\hline
20 \\
20 \\
+15 \\
\hline
17.20
\end{array}
$$

Same number
of decimal
places.

FIGURE **9-7**. MULTIPLYING A DECIMAL BY A WHOLE NUMBER

Your fifth grader will also be required to multiply a decimal value by another decimal value, such as **3.44 × 1.5**. Looking at this problem I could see how my daughter and some of her classmates could be baffled. The problem looks very complex.

Multiplying two decimal values is the same procedure as multiplying a decimal by a whole number. First set up the problem to restate it in the multiplication form, then multiply as if the decimal points weren't there.

The tricky part is when my daughter counted the number of decimal places. As shown in figure 9-8, there are three decimal places. Therefore, the product must include three decimal places.

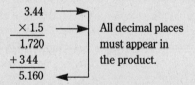

$$
\begin{array}{r}
3.44 \\
\times\,1.5 \\
\hline
1,720 \\
+344 \\
\hline
5.160
\end{array}
$$

All decimal places
must appear in
the product.

FIGURE **9-8**. ALL DECIMAL PLACES MUST APPEAR IN THE PRODUCT WHEN MULTIPLYING DECIMAL VALUES.

A new twist arose when the product didn't have enough decimal places (see figure 9-9). My daughter counted three decimal places in the problem. She knew she had to place three decimal places in the product. However, the product had only two digits.

The solution was simple. To the left of the product, insert the necessary zeros to fill out the required decimal places in the product. It is important that your child understands the zeros she inserts into the product change the value of the number. This is not like inserting zeros to the right of the last digit in a decimal value, which doesn't change the value of the decimal.

Your child learned last year that places to the right of the decimal represent smaller and smaller numbers. One digit to the right of the decimal is the tenths position. The second is the hundredths position. The third is the thousandths position.

The problem in figure 9-9 calls for three decimal places in the product. There are only two digits, so a zero must be inserted between the decimal and the product (25) to form the correct answer to the problem.

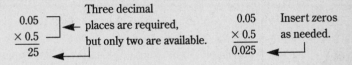

FIGURE **9-9.** INSERT ZEROS IN THE PRODUCT TO PROVIDE THE NECESSARY DECIMAL PLACES.

Division

Fifth-grade division homework consists of pretty much the same kind of problems you saw last year except larger and smaller numbers are used in the calculation. Your child has probably become proficient at dividing large numbers, just as my daughter did. However, dividing numbers of values less than one can be tricky to solve.

Your fifth grader already knows that a number less than one is written as either a fraction or a decimal. Many division problems you'll see this year will use the decimal form because fractional numbers are represented as decimals in real life, especially when dividing money.

Figure 9-10 is the kind of division problem I found on my daughter's homework. Here she's asked to divide the dividend 20.55 by 5. The only confusion my daughter had with the problem was where to place the decimal point in the answer.

I was able to clear up the issue by asking her to set up the problem like any division problem by placing the dividend and the divisor in the correct positions on the division form.

I asked her to place the decimal point in the quotient right over the decimal point in the dividend, and then solve the division problem as if the decimal point didn't exist. When trying this method with your child, be sure she carefully aligns digits in the quotient over corresponding digits in the dividend. If she misaligns the digits, she could easily lose sight of the decimal place in the quotient.

PROCEDURE:
Dividing a decimal number

1. Set up the divisor and the dividend in the division form (figure 9-10).
2. Place the decimal point in the quotient over the decimal point in the dividend.
3. Divide the dividend by the divisor as if the decimal didn't exist in the dividend.

```
        4.11  RO
  5 ) 20.55
     −20
      ‾‾‾
       05
     −  5
      ‾‾‾
       05
     −  5
      ‾‾‾
        0
```

FIGURE 9-10. PLACE THE DECIMAL POINT IN THE QUOTIENT ABOVE THE DECIMAL POINT IN THE DIVIDEND.

Most fifth-grade teachers introduce dividing decimal numbers using a dividend that contains both a whole and a decimal value, such as 20.55 in the previous example. This provides a transition between dividing whole numbers and dividing decimal numbers.

Dividing decimal numbers became more challenging when the teacher asked my daughter's class to divide a decimal value by a whole number, such as shown in figure 9-11. This posed a problem for my daughter. She couldn't fathom how 0.3 could be divided by 15.

I had to agree with her until I reviewed the process with my wife. The trick is to insert zeros into the problem. Instead of the dividend being 0.3 it became 0.30. The value of the dividend didn't change. Remember you can insert as many zeros as you need after the last digit following the decimal point, and the value always remains the same.

Adding the zero gave my daughter a different picture of the problem. Now the problem looked as if she was dividing 30 by 15, which she solved on other homework assignments.

Her next mental block came after she inserted the decimal point in the quotient and began dividing the numbers. She knew from her division lessons of last year that the 2 in the quotient had to be placed over the third digit in the dividend (0), but this left a space between the decimal and the 2 in the quotient. The solution? Insert a zero to fill up the space. This zero in the quotient is meaningful since it takes the tenths place value while the 2 takes the hundredths place value.

PROCEDURE:
How to insert zeros where necessary to perform division with decimal numbers

1. Insert any number of zeros after the last digit in the dividend as necessary to complete the division.
2. Insert zeros between the decimal point and the first digit in the quotient so no spaces exist between them.

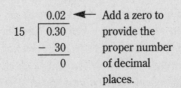

FIGURE **9-11.** INSERT ZEROS AS REQUIRED IN THE QUOTIENT.

In previous years, your child used a remainder whenever the divisor couldn't divide evenly into the dividend. Fifth graders don't use remainders. Instead they insert a decimal point and zeros after the whole number in the dividend, then keep dividing. You could say the remainder is the decimal value in the quotient. This helped my daughter understand why she no longer used remainders in the quotient.

Figure 9-12 was one of my daughter's first division problems that used a decimal value in place of a remainder. Notice I placed two zeros after the decimal in the dividend when only one zero was required to solve the problem. Although the other zero wasn't necessary, it also didn't change the value of the dividend.

$$
\begin{array}{r}
4.2 \\
5 \overline{\smash{)}21.00} \\
-20 \\
\hline
1\,0 \\
-\ 1\,0 \\
\hline
0
\end{array}
$$

FIGURE 9-12. INSERT DECIMALS, THEN CONTINUE TO DIVIDE TO ELIMINATE REMAINDERS.

Fractions

Since the second grade your child has been learning more and more about fractions. She has learned how fractions relate to real things and how fractions are compared with each other. All the fractions she worked with until now have the same denominator. This year she'll be comparing fractions that have different denominators.

My daughter calls fractions that share the same denominator *like fractions*, because they can be compared with each other. She calls fractions with different denominators *unlike fractions*. Unlike fractions cannot be compared to each other, nor can they be used in arithmetic calculations, as you'll see later in this chapter.

Our job as parents is to show our kids how to convert unlike fractions into like fractions. It's really not difficult. The objective is to create two equivalent fractions to take the place of the unlike fractions.

An *equivalent fraction* is a fraction that represents the same relationship as another fraction, only different numbers are used in the numerator and denominator. Your child learned how to create equivalent fractions last year.

When comparing unlike fractions, you must convert both fractions to equivalent fractions that have the same denominator. You'll recall from last year, the numerators and the denominators are multiplied by a common multiple to create equivalent fractions.

A *common multiple* is a value that can be evenly divided by the two denominators. How on earth is a ten- or eleven-year-old expected to find such a number? Better put, how are we going to find a common multiple? The answer lies in knowing the multiplication tables. Here's the approach my daughter used.

First she wrote down the times table for each denominator, then compared the tables to find products common to both tables. In one of her homework problems she needed to find common multiples of 4 and 6. She followed the procedure as shown in figure 9-13 and discovered 12 and 24 to be common multiples of 4 and 6.

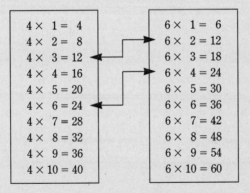

FIGURE **9-13.** FIND THE COMMON MULTIPLES BY WRITING THE TIMES TABLES OF EACH DENOMINATOR.

The next step is to choose 12 or 24 as the common denominator. Her teacher recommended using the lowest number, which is called the *least common multiple*. The least common multiple in this example is 12. Figure 9-14 illustrates this method.

P R O C E D U R E :
Finding the least common multiple

1. Create a multiplication table for each denominator in the unlike fractions.
2. Locate products that appear on both multiplication tables.
3. Choose the lowest common product as the denominator for the equivalent fractions.
4. Divide the common denominator by each of the denominators of the unlike fractions to find the multiplier.
5. Multiply the numerator and the denominator of each unlike fraction by their corresponding multiplier to create an equivalent fraction (see step 1 and step 2 in figure 9-14).
6. Step 3 in figure 9-14 contains the equivalent fractions.

---

1   **2**   **3**

$$\frac{1 \times 3}{4 \times 3} = \frac{3}{12} \qquad \frac{1 \times 2}{6 \times 2} = \frac{2}{12} \qquad \frac{3}{12} , \frac{2}{12}$$

FIGURE **9-14.** USING THE LEAST COMMON MULTIPLE

Another approach to finding a common multiple is to multiply the denominators of the unlike fractions. Following this method, you'd multiply **4 × 6 = 24**, which is a common multiple. Notice that the results match the method my daughter used except instead of finding several common multiples, this method results in one common multiple.

One problem with this method is the common multiple may not be the least common multiple, which is required to find the correct answer to the problem. However, this is a minor problem, because after creating the equivalent fractions, you can reduce the equivalent fractions to lower terms as long as both fractions have the same denominator. Figure 9-15 shows an example of this method.

PROCEDURE:

Finding the least common multiple by multiplying denominators

1. Multiply the denominators of the two unlike fractions to find a common denominator.
2. Divide the common denominator by each of the denominators of the unlike fractions to find the multiplier.
3. Multiply the numerator and the denominator of each unlike fraction by their corresponding multiplier to create an equivalent fraction (see step 1 and step 2 in figure 9-15).
4. Can the equivalent fractions be reduced (see step 3 in figure 9-15)?
5. Reduce the equivalent fraction to the lowest terms that allow the same denominator to exist in the equivalent fractions (see step 4 in figure 9-15).

1   **2**   **3**   **4**

$$\frac{1 \times 6}{4 \times 6} = \frac{6}{24} \qquad \frac{1 \times 4}{6 \times 4} = \frac{4}{24} \qquad \frac{6}{24} , \frac{4}{24} \qquad \frac{3}{12} , \frac{2}{12}$$

FIGURE 9-15. FINDING THE LEAST COMMON MULTIPLE BY MULTIPLYING DENOMINATORS

Fractions—Adding, Subtracting, and Multiplying

By now your fifth grader has a good understanding of what a fraction is. It is a way to express a part of a whole thing. Over the past couple of years, teachers have been gradually introducing the concepts of *whole*, *part*, and *fraction* to your child. This year is the payoff year. It is this year when she learns to treat fractions like numbers that can be added, subtracted, and multiplied.

My daughter was puzzled when this topic was discussed in class. She was familiar with performing arithmetic using whole numbers, but a fraction posed problems that seemed to baffle her. She couldn't conceive of how to use fractions in arithmetic.

It took me time to find a way to relate her knowledge of arithmetic to fractions. I had to go back to basics, and I reviewed the meaning of a fraction with my daughter before moving on to adding fractions. The *denominator* is the number of things that make up the whole. The *numerator* is the number of things in the piece of the whole.

Figure 9-16 contains the example I used with my daughter. The **4** is the number of things in the whole, and the **1** is the number of pieces of the whole represented by the fraction. When adding fractions, you add only the pieces of the whole. You add the number in the numerator of both fractions. The number in the denominator is simply carried over to the sum.

In figure 9-16 I add the numerator **1** to the numerator **3** to arrive at the sum, which is **4**. I carry over the denominator **4** as the denominator of the answer, because the number of pieces in the whole doesn't change. Notice the fraction has the same number in the numerator and in the denominator. Your child should recognize this as a fraction that represents 1.

$$\frac{1}{4} + \frac{3}{4} = \frac{4}{4}$$

FIGURE 9-16. ADDING FRACTIONS HAVING THE SAME DENOMINATOR

Give your fifth grader many of these simple addition problems to calculate so she becomes very proficient at adding fractions. Avoid rushing through this lesson, for if she doesn't have a firm grasp on addition, she is bound to have difficulty with the next lesson: adding fractions with different denominators.

Not all the problems she sees on homework assignments will have the same denominator. There will be many problems where the denominators of the fractions are different. This requires her to perform an intermediate step before adding the numerators.

Figure 9-17 is a problem I found on my fifth grader's homework. I went back to basics to explain the solution to my daughter. In step 1, the fraction represents 1 piece of 4 pieces. The whole is 4 pieces. In step 2, the fraction represents 1 piece of 6 pieces. The whole is 6 pieces.

Before we can add together these fractions, we must make each fraction have the same whole. That is, each fraction in the addition problem must have the same number in the denominator. We must convert each fraction into an equivalent fraction using a common denominator.

In step 1 and step 2, I multiplied the numerator and denominator of both fractions to create equivalent fractions. The new denominator is 12 in both fractions. At this point I can proceed with step 3, which is to add together the numerators of the fractions, then carry over the denominator to the answer.

$$1 \qquad\qquad 2 \qquad\qquad 3$$

$$\frac{1 \times 3}{4 \times 3} = \frac{3}{12} \qquad\qquad \frac{1 \times 2}{6 \times 2} = \frac{2}{12} \qquad\qquad \frac{3}{12} + \frac{2}{12} = \frac{5}{12}$$

FIGURE 9-17. ADDING FRACTIONS HAVING DIFFERENT DENOMINATORS

PROCEDURE:
Adding fractions

1. All fractions in the addition problem must have the same denominator.
2. Create equivalent fractions for both fractions in the problem if the denominators of the fractions differ. Make sure both equivalent fractions have the same denominator.
3. Add the numerators of the fractions, then carry over the denominator to the sum.

Subtracting fractions is similar to addition. The only difference is that the numerators are subtracted, then the denominator is carried over to the difference.

Figure 9-18 illustrates this technique. The denominators for both fractions are the same, therefore we are dealing with a whole consisting of 4 pieces. Subtracting 1 piece from 3 pieces leaves a numerator of 2 pieces with 4 as the denominator.

Notice the difference isn't reduced to its lowest terms. This is acceptable for most homework assignments. However, some teachers prefer the class to reduce the fraction. In this case, 2 is a common factor, which can be evenly divided in the numerator resulting in 1 and the denominator resulting in 2. One-half is the lowest terms for the problem in figure 9-18.

I always recommend to my daughter that she provide both answers and indicate which one is in the lowest terms. This gives her some insurance in case the teacher looks for the reduced fraction as the final answer to the problem.

$$\frac{3}{4} - \frac{1}{4} = \frac{2}{4}$$

FIGURE 9-18. SUBTRACTING FRACTIONS HAVING THE SAME DENOMINATOR

Fractions can be subtracted only if the denominators of the fractions are the same. If the denominators are not identical, then equivalent fractions must be created, as shown in figure 9-19, before the numerators can be subtracted.

1   2   3

$$\frac{1 \times 3}{4 \times 3} = \frac{3}{12} \qquad \frac{1 \times 2}{6 \times 2} = \frac{2}{12} \qquad \frac{3}{12} - \frac{2}{12} = \frac{1}{12}$$

FIGURE 9-19. SUBTRACTING FRACTIONS

PROCEDURE:
Subtracting fractions

1. All fractions in the subtraction problem must have the same denominator.
2. Create equivalent fractions for both fractions in the problem if the denominators of the fractions differ. Make sure both equivalent fractions have the same denominator.
3. Subtract the numerators of the fractions, then carry over the denominator to the sum.

Fifth graders also are asked to become masters of multiplying fractions. This, too, could become a mental block for your child as it was for my daughter. Multiplying fractions is unlike addition and subtraction. In the fifth grade, multiplication involves a fraction multiplied by a whole number.

Remind your child the objective is to multiply the number of pieces, not the whole. Therefore, the numerator, not the denominator, is multiplied by the whole-number multiplier.

Figure 9-20 shows a good example. Step 1 sets up the problem. Step 2 restates the problem in a way most ten- and eleven-year-olds can understand. The multiplier is clearly associated with the numerator. The product produces an improper fraction, which is reduced in step 3. Not every multiplication problem produces an improper fraction, therefore step 3 may not be required.

$$\textbf{1} \qquad\qquad \textbf{2} \qquad\qquad \textbf{3}$$

$$5 \times \frac{2}{5} \qquad\qquad \frac{5 \times 2}{5} = \frac{10}{5} \qquad\qquad \frac{10}{5} = 2$$

FIGURE 9-20. MULTIPLYING A FRACTION BY A WHOLE NUMBER

PROCEDURE:
Multiplying fractions

1. When fractions are multiplied by a whole number, only the numerator of the fraction is actually multiplied.
2. Place the whole number (multiplier) above the line in the fraction (step 2 in figure 9-20).
3. Multiply the whole number and the numerator of the fraction, then carry over the denominator to the product.

Going from a Fraction to a Decimal

I understand the homework problem. I'm pretty sure I know how to solve it, but I go blank on the steps required. This occurs all the time when I try helping my daughter with math. One of those occasions happened when my daughter asked me how to convert a fraction to a decimal equivalent. If you're a little rusty, too, here's how it is done.

There are actually two ways to convert a fraction to a decimal: the way I was taught and the way my daughter was taught. Both arrive at the same answer, but the teacher's method is the correct method to use on your child's homework.

My method is to remember that a fraction is really another way to write a division problem. The numerator is divided by the denominator. The fraction shown in figure 9-21 implies 1 is divided by 4. Notice you can't divide 1 by 4, so you need to insert a decimal point in the quotient and continue dividing. The result is the decimal equivalent of the fraction.

$$\frac{1}{4} \quad = \quad 4\overline{\smash{\big)}\,1.00} \quad = \quad 0.25$$

$$\begin{array}{r} 0.25 \\ 4\overline{\smash{\big)}1.00} \\ -\,8 \\ \hline 20 \\ -\,20 \\ \hline 0 \end{array}$$

FIGURE 9-21. WRITE A FRACTION AS A DECIMAL BY DIVIDING THE NUMERATOR BY THE DENOMINATOR.

My daughter's method converted the fraction to an equivalent fraction containing 10 as the denominator. Converting the equivalent fraction to a decimal is easy. Simply move the decimal point the corresponding number of places in the numerator based on the value of the denominator.

For example in figure 9-22 I converted the fraction to an equivalent fraction by multiplying the numerator and the denominator by 5. Next, I placed the decimal point in the tenths position, which is 0.5. I chose the tenths position because the denominator is ten.

I could create an equivalent fraction with 100 in the denominator or even 1,000 as long as I move the decimal point to the hundredths or thousandths position respectively.

So if the denominator of the equivalent fraction in figure 9-22 is 100 instead of 10, then the decimal equivalent is 0.05. Likewise, 1,000 in the denominator will result in an equivalent decimal value of 0.005.

$$\frac{1 \times 5}{2 \times 5} = \frac{5}{10} = 0.5$$

$$\frac{1 \times 5}{20 \times 5} = \frac{5}{100} = 0.05$$

$$\frac{1 \times 5}{200 \times 5} = \frac{5}{1,000} = 0.005$$

FIGURE 9-22. WRITE A FRACTION AS A DECIMAL BY CREATING AN EQUIVALENT FRACTION.

PROCEDURE:
Converting a fraction to a decimal value

1. Divide the numerator by the denominator.
                    Or
1. Create an equivalent fraction that has 10, 100, or 1,000 as the denominator.
2. The numerator is the decimal value.
3. Place the decimal point in the tenths, hundredths, or thousandths position corresponding to the value of the denominator.

Mixed Numbers—Adding and Subtracting

Last year your child learned about mixed numbers. A *mixed number* is a number that has a whole number and a fraction, such as those shown in figure 9-23. This year she'll be required to add and subtract mixed numbers. Mixed numbers are likely to confuse your child, because fifth graders don't visualize the problems correctly.

Here's how you solve a mixed-number problem. Break down the problem into small steps that are easy for your child to understand, then follow these procedures.

PROCEDURE:
Adding mixed numbers

1. If the fractional parts of the mixed numbers have the same denominator, then add the numerators of the fractions and place the sum in the form of a fraction below the line (figure 9-23 step 1).
2. Add the whole numbers and place the sum alongside the fraction (figure 9-23 step 2).

$$1 \qquad\qquad 2$$

$$6\frac{1}{4} \qquad\qquad 6\frac{1}{4}$$

$$+\,4\frac{2}{4} \qquad\qquad +\,4\frac{2}{4}$$

$$\frac{3}{4} \qquad\qquad 10\frac{3}{4}$$

FIGURE 9-23. ADDING MIXED NUMBERS

Sometimes the sum of the fraction is an improper fraction. That is, the numerator is larger than the denominator. When this occurs, the improper fraction must be converted to its lowest terms before continuing with the addition.

This is shown in figure 9-24, where I reduced the improper fraction to a mixed number in step 2. The fractional part of the mixed number is the sum of the fractions. The whole number of the mixed number must be added to the other whole numbers in the problem in step 3. Here is the procedure your fifth grader should follow.

PROCEDURE:
Adding improper fractions

1. Add the numerators.
2. If the sum creates an improper fraction, then reduce the fraction to its lowest terms, which will result in a mixed number (figure 9-24 step 2).
3. Add the whole numbers together (figure 9-24 step 3).

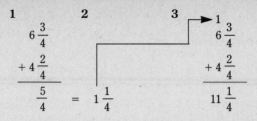

FIGURE 9-24. CONVERT IMPROPER FRACTIONS TO A MIXED
NUMBER, THEN ADD.

Your child must add mixed numbers where the fractional part of the
numbers have different denominators. Before the addition can take
place, the fractions must be converted to equivalent fractions. This also
must be done when subtracting mixed numbers with different denominators. Step 2 in figure 9-26 illustrates how to convert fractions to
equivalent fractions. Use the same method whether you're adding or
subtracting mixed numbers.

Subtracting mixed numbers is similar to adding mixed numbers in
that the arithmetic is performed on the numerators of the fractions. Figure 9-25 shows a typical mixed-number problem you'll find on your
child's homework.

As with addition, the first step is to solve the fractional part of the
problem. In this case, subtract the numerators of the fractions (figure
9-25 step 1). This is possible only if the denominators of both fractions
are the same number. If the denominators are different, then you must
convert the fractions to equivalent fractions (see figure 9-26). The last
step is to subtract the whole numbers.

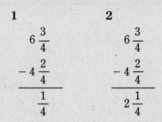

FIGURE 9-25. SUBTRACTING MIXED NUMBERS WITH A COMMON
DENOMINATOR

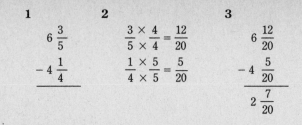

FIGURE 9-26. SUBTRACTING MIXED NUMBERS WITH DIFFERENT DENOMINATORS

Expect a twist on your child's homework such as the one in figure 9-27. Notice the top fraction is smaller than the bottom fraction. The problem asks your child to subtract 3 from 2, which can't be done.

Remember back a few years when your child learned to regroup numbers in subtraction. A similar rule applies here. The numerator of the top fraction must be regrouped. Regrouping is also known as borrowing a value and, in this case, the value is borrowed from the top whole number. Explaining this can be tricky since the method used to regroup is not intuitive and requires your child to perform a few steps before getting to the point when she can subtract the numerators.

First, she needs to subtract 1 from the whole number 6 and convert the 1 into a fraction by using the same value in the numerator as in the denominator. Next, add the converted 1 and the fraction (see figure 9-27 step 2). Notice this results in an improper number where the numerator is larger than the denominator. The final steps are to reduce the whole number 6 by 1, then perform the subtraction of the numerators and the whole numbers (see figure 9-27 step 3).

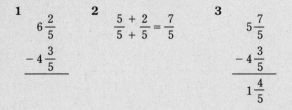

FIGURE 9-27. REGROUPING WHEN SUBTRACTING MIXED NUMBERS

PROCEDURE:
Subtracting mixed numbers

1. Subtract the numerators.
2. Regroup the numerator if necessary (step 1 in figure 9-27) by subtracting 1 from the whole number; convert the 1 to a fraction; and then add the fraction to the fraction in the problem (step 2 in figure 9-27).
3. If the difference creates an improper fraction, then reduce the fraction to its lowest terms, which will result in a mixed number.

Percents

Learning percentages isn't easy for ten- and eleven-year-olds, since they are required to think in the abstract rather than perform simple arithmetic. The best way to explain percentages is by showing a bunch of boxes, like those I drew in figure 9-28 step 1. I shaded most of the boxes and left five unshaded. A percentage problem asks the question, What percent of the boxes are unshaded? Another way to state the question is, What part of the whole is composed of unshaded boxes?

When you use the terms *part* and *whole*, you are relating a percent to something your child already knows, fractions. You'll recall that in a fraction, the numerator is the part and the denominator is the whole. In this example, there are 50 boxes, 5 of which are unshaded.

This relationship is also called a ratio. The ratio in figure 9-28 is 5 unshaded boxes for each 50 boxes. A *ratio* is a way of comparing the magnitude of two numbers and is used most often in recipes. It is typically written as 5:50 or as the fraction shown in figure 9-28 step 2.

A *percent* is a way to relate part of something to the whole thing. The whole is represented as 100 or, as we know better, 100%. The 100 is always the denominator in the fraction representing the percentage. Remember, *percent* means *per hundred*.

The challenge is for your child to create an equivalent fraction where the denominator is 100. In figure 9-28 step 2, I've created an equivalent fraction by multiplying the numerator and denominator of the ratio by 2.

Many fifth graders make the mistake of stopping the problem at step

2, thinking the equivalent fraction is the percent. The percent is the numerator, as shown in figure 9-28 step 3, which is 10%. That is, 10% of the blocks are unshaded.

Another kind of percent problem is to use a percent to find the part of the whole. Let's return to figure 9-28 and restate the problem. How many blocks are 10% of all the blocks?

Answering this question requires your child to perform a two-step process. First, she must convert the percent to a decimal. The easiest way to do this is to remove the % symbol and insert a decimal to the left of the first digit. For example 10% would be 0.10. I placed the 0 to the left of the decimal only to highlight the fact that there is a decimal before the 1.

She'll also be asked to convert a percent to a decimal equivalent by using division. Remember, a percent is another way to represent a fraction. A fraction is really another way to represent a division problem, as shown in figure 9-28 step 4.

Once the percent is converted to a decimal, your child multiplies the whole by the decimal value. I've done this in figure 9-28 step 5. The product is the part of the whole represented by the percent. Make sure your child avoids a very common mistake adults make with percentages. Display the percentage as either the percent in the decimal form or with the % symbol, but not both. The only exception to this rule is if the value is less than 1%. In that case, a decimal and the % symbol must be used together.

PROCEDURE:
Find the percent

1. Count the number of things in the whole thing.
2. Count the number of things in the part of the whole thing.
3. Create a fraction where the parts are the numerator and the whole is the denominator.
4. Create an equivalent fraction where the denominator is 100.
5. Copy the numerator of the equivalent fraction and place a percentage sign to the right of the numerator to create a percentage.

PROCEDURE:
Find the number of parts of the whole thing when you know the percent

1. Convert the percent to a fraction, then convert the fraction to a decimal.
2. Multiply the number of things in the whole thing by the decimal. The product is the number of parts represented by the percentage.

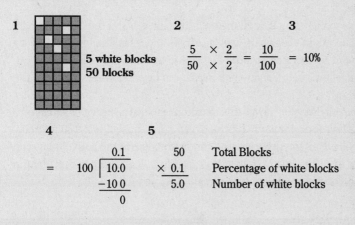

1

2   3

5 white blocks $\frac{5}{50} \times \frac{2}{2} = \frac{10}{100} = 10\%$
50 blocks

4   5

$$= \quad 100\overline{\smash{)}\begin{array}{r} 0.1 \\ 10.0 \\ -10\,0 \\ \hline 0 \end{array}}$$

$$\begin{array}{r} 50 \\ \times\ 0.1 \\ \hline 5.0 \end{array}$$ Total Blocks
Percentage of white blocks
Number of white blocks

FIGURE 9-28. CALCULATING PERCENTAGES

Geometry—Measuring Angles

Fifth graders learn to measure angles in preparation for full-blown geometry, which typically begins in the sixth grade. The curriculum in your school district may differ some, so check with the teacher to find out when more intense geometry is taught.

Angles are measured in degrees, which are symbolized by a tiny circle behind the number (45°). A *degree* is a unit of measure that can become confusing for some ten- and eleven-year-olds to understand. Here's the best way I found to describe a degree to my daughter. I begin by drawing a circle. A circle is divided into 360 units called degrees. Figure 9-29 shows a circle. I started at the top of the circle, which is both the beginning and end point. In this example, 360° is used to indicate the ending degree, but I could have used 0° for the same position to show where the degrees begin.

I counted all the degrees until I reached 90°, where I placed a tick mark on the circle. I continued counting degrees until I reached 180°, where I placed another tick mark. The process continued with a tick mark at 270° and a final tick mark at 360°.

Next, I drew a right angle using the center of the circle as the vertex (figure 9-29). Notice the angle measures 90°. I then drew an acute angle, which is less than 90°. Finally, I drew an obtuse angle, which is greater than 90°.

This explanation helped my daughter understand the concept of degrees, but didn't really answer questions about her homework. Her assignment was to measure the degrees of an angle. Another way to ask the question is, How many tick marks are between the two lines of the angle?

The only way to answer this question is to use a special ruler called a protractor. A *protractor* is like a curved ruler divided into 180 degrees. Place the 0° of the protractor on the bottom line of the angle, then read where the other line of the angle crosses the degrees on the protractor. This is the measurement of the angle.

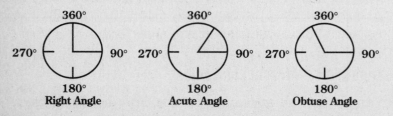

FIGURE 9-29. A CIRCLE IS DIVIDED INTO 360 UNITS. YOU CAN DRAW ANGLES INSIDE THE CIRCLE.

> **PROCEDURE:**
> **Measuring an angle**
>
> 1. Angles are measured using a protractor. The protractor is divided into degrees, which is the unit of measurement to describe an angle.
> 2. Place the 0° of the protractor on the bottom line of the angle, then read where the other line of the angle crosses the degrees on the protractor.

Geometry—Measuring Circles

A circle is one of those shapes that is difficult to measure with a ruler. I was one of those kids in the fifth-grade class who didn't like working with formulas and instead always tried to find a shortcut to avoid messy calculations. So I'd take a ruler and measure tiny, straight pieces of the circle whenever the teacher asked us to determine the circumference. The *circumference* is the distance around the circle.

It never worked, although one of the guys used a string and a ruler, which worked very well. He'd carefully place the string to cover the circle on the homework assignment, then stretch the string beside a ruler to determine the length. However, he wasn't allowed to use this method on a test.

It is better to teach your child the proper way to measure a circle so she'll be able to pass tests. Here's the way I explain the process to my daughter.

A *circle* is made up of small curved pieces called *arcs*, (see figure 9-30), which are identified with letters. In the fourth grade, she learned that a line drawn from one edge of a circle through the center to the other edge is called the diameter of the circle.

Sometimes fifth graders confuse the diameter with a chord. A *chord* is any line drawn from one edge to another edge of the circle with or without going through the center of the circle. A *diameter* is also a chord, but it must go through the center of the circle.

Another measurement of a circle is the radius, which was also taught in the fourth grade. The *radius* of a circle is a line from the center of the circle to an edge of the circle. The radius or the diameter is used to measure the circumference. Figure 9-31 shows the formula used to calculate the circumference using the diameter, and figure 9-32 is a similar formula using the radius.

Notice there are two new symbols used in these formulas: π and $\approx$. The symbol π is a Greek letter called *pi*. Your fifth grader is likely to hit you with a bunch of pie jokes once she learns about pi.

The symbol π represents a constant number, which is approximately 3.14. So whenever she sees the symbol π, she is expected to replace the symbol with the number 3.14. You'll be asked the typical "why?" Try to avoid it if you can. At this point in her education, it is only important for her to know to replace the symbol with the number.

However, here's the best explanation I can find if you must explain π to your child. π is the number of times the diameter can go around the circle to make one complete rotation.

PROCEDURE:
How to explain π to your child

1. Draw a fairly large circle on a piece of paper.
2. Cut a piece of wire the length of the diameter of the circle.
3. Bend the piece of wire so it forms an arc around part of the circle.
4. Move the piece of wire around the circle until you've completed one rotation. You'll complete one rotation by placing the piece of wire down 3.14 times.

The other symbol used in the formula is $\approx$. Although this looks like an equal sign, it isn't. This symbol means *approximately* or *about*. For example, 5 is approximately 6 ($5 \approx 6$) while 3 times 2 is equal to 6 ($3 \times 2 = 6$).

The $\approx$ symbol is used in the formula because the value of π is actually larger than 3.14. The value goes out to infinite decimal places. However, your child needs only two decimal positions to calculate fifth-grade homework problems. Therefore, her calculations will be approximately the answer to problems requiring the use of π.

Figure 9-31 uses the diameter of the circle in figure 9-30 to determine the circumference of the circle. Figure 9-32 uses the radius of the circle to find the same value. Notice the radius is multiplied by 2. The radius times 2 is equal to the diameter of the circle.

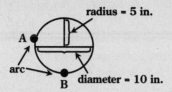

FIGURE 9-30. MEASUREMENTS OF A CIRCLE

Formula:	Circumference	$\approx$	π	$\times$	diameter
Solution:		$\approx$	3.14	$\times$	10 in.
			$\approx$ 31.4 in.		

FIGURE 9-31. HOW TO FIND THE CIRCUMFERENCE OF A CIRCLE USING THE DIAMETER

Formula:	Circumference	$\approx$	π	$\times$	(radius $\times$ 2)
Solution:		$\approx$	3.14	$\times$	(5 in. $\times$ 2)
		$\approx$	3.14	$\times$	10 in.
			$\approx$ 31.4 in.		

FIGURE 9-32. HOW TO FIND THE CIRCUMFERENCE OF A CIRCLE USING THE RADIUS

Geometry—Measuring Area

The night my daughter asked for help finding the areas of various shapes brought back memories of grammar school in Miss Gorick's class. Unfortunately for me, my daughter's questions didn't jog my memory enough for me to answer her.

I knew the area of any shape was the space between the borders of the shape, and there was a magic formula in the textbook used to calculate the answer. The solution called for my daughter to measure the shape, plug the measurements into the proper place in the formula, then perform the arithmetic to find the area.

The moment I sat down to help my daughter answer the first homework problem, I realized I was in trouble. She had already done the easy problems. The tough ones were left for me to help solve.

For example, find the area of a triangle. Sure, there's a formula in the book, but the formula called for two measurements: the base and the height. "Which side is the base?" my daughter asked. How was I supposed to know!

Questions got harder. The next problem required us to find the area of a parallelogram and required us to apply a similar formula. My daughter asked, "How can I measure the height when the sides are slanted?" Chalk up another obvious question I couldn't answer.

The final straw came when we were asked to find the area of a trapezoid. There wasn't any formula in my daughter's math book we could use. How on earth did the teacher expect my daughter to solve such a problem without a clear formula? Obviously, I was of no help.

You'll probably experience similar problems when helping your fifth grader. I called a friend of mine who is good with geometry to give me a few tips. Here's what he recommended.

The *area of a triangle* is found by using the formula in figure 9-33. Find the measurement of the base and of the height, multiply them together, then divide by two to find the area of the triangle.

The procedure to find the base and the height of a right triangle is fairly easy:

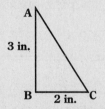

1. Find the two sides that make the right angle, sides AB and BC in this example.
2. Choose one of these sides to be the base and the other to be the height. It doesn't matter which.
   [Solution: AB (3) × BC (2) ÷ 2 = Area (3)]

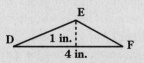

For finding areas of any other kind of triangle:

1. Pick any side to be the base. Here I chose side DF.
2. Draw a line from the vertex opposite this side (vertex E) that is perpendicular to side DF. This perpendicular line is the height.
   [Solution: DF (4) × Vortex E (1) ÷ 2 = Area (2)]

If I had chosen side DE to be the base, the perpendicular line would fall outside the triangle.

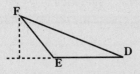

Note that this second method works for right triangles, too. In the first example, if side BC is the base, the perpendicular line through vertex A is actually side AB. But this works only with right triangles, because only right triangles have a pair of perpendicular sides.

In this example, the measurements are in inches. Notice in figure 9-33 the measurement is transformed to square inches once the base and height are multiplied. Areas always appear in square units of measure.

Formula:	Area	= (base × height)	÷ 2
Solution:	a	= (b × h)	÷ 2
		= (2 in.× 5 in.)	÷ 2
		= 10 in²	÷ 2
		= 5 in²	

FIGURE 9-33. HOW TO FIND THE AREA OF A TRIANGLE

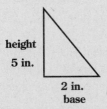

height
5 in.

2 in.
base

FIGURE 9-34. CALCULATE THE AREA OF THIS TRIANGLE.

I drew my friend's attention to the next problem, which was to determine the height of a parallelogram such as the one shown in figure 9-35. Figure 9-36 shows the formula we'll need to use to solve for the area of the parallelogram.

The height is the distance between the bottom and the top. However, the sides are slanted. This raises the question of how to measure the height. My friend solved this problem by drawing an imaginary line connecting the top and bottom of the parallelogram (figure 9-35).

This was like the missing piece that unlocked the puzzle. Once my daughter saw the imaginary line, she knew exactly how to measure the height and solve for the area of the parallelogram.

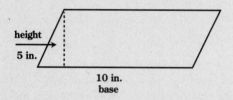

FIGURE 9-35. DRAW AN IMAGINARY LINE TO FIND THE HEIGHT OF A PARALLELOGRAM.

Formula:	Area	= base	× height
Solution:	a	= b	× h
		= 10 in.	× 5 in.
		= 50 in²	

FIGURE 9-36. HOW TO FIND THE AREA OF THE PARALLELOGRAM IN 9-35

I've found math to be like a magic trick. You wonder how a magician can make someone from the audience levitate right before your eyes. The magician even passes a hoop around the person showing there are no strings lifting her above the table.

Then the trick is revealed. The stranger from the audience is really the magician's assistant. A forklift behind the curtain lifts the wood she lies on. And the hoop never passes completely over the woman. It is an optical illusion.

The same can be said about the mystery of finding the area of a trapezoid and other irregular shapes. My friend revealed the trick: divide the irregular shape into regular shapes using imaginary lines. Find the area of the regular shapes, then add them together to arrive at the area for the irregular shape.

Let's find the area of the trapezoid in figure 9-37. My friend used two imaginary lines and divided the trapezoid into three regular shapes, which are two right triangles and a rectangle. My daughter knew how to calculate the area of both of these shapes by using the formulas shown in figure 9-38.

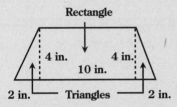

FIGURE 9-37. DRAW IMAGINARY LINES TO DIVIDE COMPLEX FIGURES INTO SHAPES YOU KNOW.

First Triangle

Formula:	Area	=	(base × height)	÷ 2
	a	=	(b × h)	÷ 2
Solution:		=	(2 in. × 4 in.)	÷ 2
		=	8 in²	÷ 2
		=	4 in²	

Second Triangle

Formula:	Area	=	(base × height)	÷ 2
	a	=	(b × h)	÷ 2
Solution:		=	(2 in. × 4 in.)	÷ 2
		=	8 in²	÷ 2
		=	4 in²	

Rectangle

Formula:	Area	=	length × width
	a	=	l × w
Solution:		=	10 in. × 4 in.
		=	40 in²

Trapezoid

Formula:
>   Area trapezoid = area 1st triangle + area 2nd triangle + area rectangle

Solution:
>   48 in²   = 4 in²   + 4 in²   + 40 in²

FIGURE 9-38. HOW TO FIND THE AREA OF AN IRREGULAR SHAPE SUCH AS A TRAPEZOID

PROCEDURE:
Finding the area of an irregular shape

1. Draw imaginary lines to divide the irregular shape into regular shapes.
2. Find the area of each regular shape using formulas shown in this chapter.
3. Add together the area of each regular shape to calculate the area of the irregular shape.

My math-whiz friend pointed out that some parents also have difficulty measuring a solid. The teacher might call the solid a *prism*.

Most fifth graders need only to find the area of a solid rectangle, also known as a *rectangular prism*. Figure 9-39 shows the formula used to determine the area of a rectangular prism, which is all the space on the six surfaces of the solid.

My friend drew a picture and labeled each side (see figure 9-40). He said most fifth graders need only to plug the measurements into the proper place in the formula to get through this homework problem. Here's his recommendation if your child wants to know more than the mechanics of using the formula.

First, point out the formula has three parts:

1. (length × width) × 2
2. (width × height) × 2
3. (length × height) × 2

Each part refers to two of the six faces of the solid. The first part determines the area of the top and bottom of the solid. The next part calculates the area of the two sides. The last part finds the area of the front and the back of the solid.

Formula:

Area = ((length × width) × 2) + ((width × height) × 2) + ((length × height) × 2)

a   = ((l   × w) × 2) + ((w ×   h)× 2) + ((l   ×   h)× 2)

Solution:

   = ((10 in. × 3 in.) × 2) + ((3 in. × 5 in.) × 2) + ((10 in. × 5 in.) × 2)

   = ((30 in²)   × 2) + ((15 in²)   × 2) + ((50 in²)   × 2)

   = (60 in²)   + (30 in²)   + (100 in²)

   = 190 in²

FIGURE 9-39. HOW TO FIND THE AREA OF A RECTANGULAR SOLID

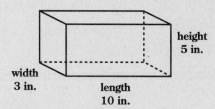

FIGURE 9-40. A RECTANGULAR SOLID

10.

Making the Grade in the Sixth Grade

- Language
- Reading
- Sixth-Grade Math
- Positive and Negative Numbers
- Exponents
- Multiplying
- Division
- Fractions
- Ratios
- Percents
- Geometry

I t starts at 6:30 every weekday morning during the school year. It's agonizing for the whole family, but there's no escaping trying to get our sixth grader and her second-grade sister out of bed.

Don't get me wrong. My kids don't mind school. It's just that school gets in the way of sleep. The worst is during the winter when temperatures dip below thirty and wind rattles the windows. You know the feeling. You're snug under a mound of fluffy comforters all warmed up by eight hours of sleep. No one in their right mind wants to put even their small toe on the floor.

My youngest holds out as long as she can, but within a minute she's awake saying a few nasty words as she ruffles the covers, which I take as a signal to move on to my next target, our oldest.

I take a different approach because her door doesn't squeak anymore. My guess is she used a can of 3-in-1 on the hinges after the last squeaky wake-up call.

Your job as a sixth-grade parent is to condition your child to attempt school assignments they don't like to do with the same motivation as those they like to do. Don't underestimate your task.

Your child is older, smarter, and knows you like a book. She can anticipate what you're going to say, what you're really saying, and when you're going to say it before you open your mouth. Think back to when you were eleven and twelve years old. You knew each rule in your house and in the school and how to avoid most of them.

This chapter is devoted to showing you how to coach your sixth grader through the toughest lessons this school year. These are the lessons she's likely to avoid because the teacher goes into the more complex details of topics taught in the previous five years.

Language

"The teacher wants me to make my writing more interesting, but I don't know how. Mom said you can show me."

"Later."

"But I need to do it now!"

Some things just aren't fair. I've written a number of books, but I don't consider myself a writer and I'm probably the least qualified to teach my daughter how to make her writing interesting to readers.

I learned that interesting writing in the sixth grade really means my daughter should use various kinds of sentences in her stories. There are four types of sentences she can choose from: simple, compound, complex, and compound-complex.

A *simple* sentence conveys a complete thought, such as in figure 10-1, and has one independent clause. No other words are necessary in this example for you to understand the actions of Jan.

Jan ran with the kite.

FIGURE 10-1. A SIMPLE SENTENCE

A *clause* consists of words that include a subject and a predicate, such as **Jan ran with the kite** in figure 10-1. There are two kinds of clauses: dependent and independent. A *dependent clause* requires other words to make it a sentence, as in **while the wind blew**. This clause cannot be a sentence because it doesn't complete a thought. An *independent clause* completes a thought and doesn't require other words to make the clause a sentence.

A *compound sentence* has two or more independent clauses and is used whenever one independent clause isn't enough to complete the idea of the sentence. Figure 10-2 is an example of a compound sentence that contains two independent clauses. The first independent clause is **Jan ran with the kite** and the second is **there was no wind**. Notice that either clause could become a sentence because each completes a thought.

Jan ran with the kite, but there was no wind.

FIGURE 10-2. A COMPOUND SENTENCE

A *complex sentence* contains an independent clause and one or more dependent clauses and is used to relate two separate thoughts. This is illustrated in figure 10-3, where the dependent clause **Although Jan ran with the kite** provides one thought and the independent clause **the kite didn't fly** provides the other thought.

Although Jan ran with the kite, the kite didn't fly.

FIGURE 10-3. A COMPLEX SENTENCE

A *compound-complex sentence* uses two or more independent clauses and one or more dependent clauses. This is shown in figure 10-4. **The wind wasn't blowing** and **the kite didn't fly** are two independent clauses. The dependent clause is **Although Jan ran with the kite**.

Although Jan ran with the kite, the wind wasn't blowing and the kite didn't fly.

FIGURE 10-4. A COMPOUND-COMPLEX SENTENCE

Learning about the kinds of sentences that are available gives you and your child a framework within which to choose the kinds of sentences to use in a writing assignment. However, knowing the kinds of sentences won't make her writing interesting. She must learn to apply this knowledge.

PROCEDURE:
How to help your child write interesting stories

1. Follow the tips I've given in chapter 8 for outlining and writing the first draft of a writing assignment.
2. Read her first draft aloud and ask her if the story sounds interesting to her. Usually, the answer is no.
3. Display sample sentences that she can use as a model for her own writing.
4. Ask her to look at each sentence in her writing assignment and see if she can change it to flow like one of the sample sentences.
5. Read the first draft again with her changes and ask if this sounds more interesting than the story without her changes. Expect to receive mixed results, because some sentences will sound better and others won't.
6. Repeat this process from step 2 until she feels her work is interesting.

Reading

"It's time for Jeopardy!" my daughter screamed as she rushed into the room.

A few years ago, my wife came up with her own version of *Jeopardy*.

She created categories based on my daughter's assignments, then pitted me against my daughter in homework Jeopardy.

"Stanza," my wife said.

The first contestant who knew the definition had to ring a bell.

"What is the car in our driveway?"

The duck call sounded.

"Wrong." She turned to my daughter.

"What is a group of related lines in a poem?"

How on earth am I expected to know that? The category for the evening was analyzing poems. I'm the first to admit I'm not much for poems and not much of a Jeopardy contestant either.

Until this school year, reading homework involved stories and poems with little analysis. My daughter had to read the material, then answer some general questions about the theme and the characters.

Sixth graders are required to read stories and poems and are also asked to analyze what they read. This can dampen any young reader's enthusiasm for reading for enjoyment. However, they must analyze the assignment to make the grade.

You shouldn't have any difficulty helping your child analyze stories. The analysis isn't too in-depth and will become apparent once you've seen the first assignment. Analyzing poems poses a different problem, because you must learn to apply the proper analytical techniques. Let me share with you some of the technical terms and concepts I had to learn so you'll be in a position to help your child analyze poems.

As you gathered from my daughter's right answer in my family's homework Jeopardy, a *stanza* is a group of related lines of a poem that are typically separated from other stanzas by a blank line (figure 10-5).

Some poems use *couplets*, which are pairs of rhymed lines of equal length. No space is left between any of these lines. You see an example in figure 10-6, where the first two lines rhyme with each other as do the third and fourth lines.

Mary had a little lamb;
Its fleece was white as snow.
Everywhere that Mary went
The lamb was sure to go.

It followed her to school one day,
Which was against the rules.
It made the children laugh and play
To see a lamb in school.

FIGURE 10-5. TWO STANZAS OF A POEM

I found a shiny nickel;
I was going to buy a pickle.
Instead I bought some pop
From the local soda shop.

FIGURE 10-6. AN EXAMPLE OF COUPLETS

I assumed all poems rhyme, but I was mistaken. Some do not and are still considered poems. However, I found my daughter was required to analyze only those poems that do rhyme.

The teacher will require your child to identify lines that rhyme using letters to form a recognizable pattern. A *rhyming pattern* is also called the *rhyming scheme* of the poem. Figure 10-7 illustrates how the teacher expects to see your child's analysis. Notice the first and third lines rhyme and are marked with the same letter. A different letter marks the second and fourth lines, which rhyme together but don't rhyme with the first and third lines.

Although the analysis appears to be easy to perform, it can become a bit more complicated for a sixth grader when many lines separate the lines that rhyme. For example, the first line might rhyme with the eighth line and the eleventh line. The distance between rhyming lines tends to confuse kids, because they expect rhyming lines to appear close together and in a regular sequence.

A The rain came falling down
B Among the flowery terrain.
A We see the funny clown
B Dancing in the rain.

FIGURE 10-7. IDENTIFYING THE RHYMING PATTERN OF A POEM

Another aspect of analyzing a poem is the *meter*. Your child will also know this as the *beat of the poem*. The meter is identified by whether or not syllables are *stressed* when reading the poem. I explained stress to my daughter as raising her voice when she speaks a syllable. When she speaks in a normal tone, then the syllable is *unstressed*.

Many sixth graders have difficulty analyzing the meter of poems because it isn't obvious where to stress syllables. The only way to overcome this obstacle is to read many poems aloud and listen to the natural places where syllables are emphasized. When your child finds a stressed syllable, she should mark it with a line over the syllable. Over an unstressed syllable, she should place a *u*.

She should begin to see a pattern form, such as a *u* followed by a line followed by another *u*, then another line, and so on. This common pattern is called *iambic*. Ask the teacher to supply you with other patterns she'll be presenting to the class so your home lessons are in sync with those taught in the classroom.

A word of warning. Not all poems have a meter, so don't allow your child to go crazy trying to analyze the meter of every poem. Take a look at the poem yourself. If you don't recognize a meter, then chances are good there isn't any.

Sixth-Grade Math

Your child finishes learning basic math this year. Many of her homework assignments will review skills learned previously and require her to work with very large and very small numbers such as trillions and thousandths. Don't expect any difficulty with these assignments, because the arithmetic is the same regardless of the size of the number.

My daughter also brushed up on the finer points of estimating values. She found it easier to solve arithmetic problems with rounded values.

In the sixth grade, your child will learn that rounding numbers to a smaller place value will result in a more accurate estimate. For example, rounding to the nearest ten is a more precise estimate than rounding to the nearest hundred.

She will also learn that decimal values should be rounded to the nearest whole number. The same holds true for rounding mixed numbers. Sixth graders occasionally become confused with the term *near-*

est. What is the nearest whole number? What is the nearest ten? Here's the rule to follow. If the number is 5 or more than 5, round up to the next whole number or ten. If the number is less than 5, then round down to the next whole number or ten.

One of the new math topics learned in the sixth grade is how to analyze data. I immediately went into one of my panic attacks when I heard this from my daughter. Statistics wasn't my best course in college. However, sixth-grade data analysis is nothing like a statistics course.

Sixth graders are required to use only four methods to analyze data: average, median, mode, and range. The *average*, also called the *mean*, is the common way to estimate a series of values. Figure 10-8 shows how to calculate the average. Add all the numbers in the series and divide by the number of items in the series.

The *median* is the middle number in the series. Sixth graders sometimes make mistakes when calculating the median because they forget two critical steps. The first is to place the series of numbers in numerical order, which is the only way they can determine the middle of the series. Figure 10-9 shows the median of the series used in figure 10-8.

The second common mistake occurs when there is an even number of items in the series, because there is no middle number. Your child is required to average the two numbers in the middle of the series to arrive at the median.

The *mode* is the most frequently found number in the series. You'll notice 40 is the most frequent number in figure 10-8. Few sixth graders have problems finding the mode, because the calculation is intuitive.

The *range* of a series indicates the breadth of values between the lowest number and the highest number. The best way for your child to determine the range in a series is to first place the series in numerical order to make it easier to find the lowest and highest numbers. The range is calculated by subtracting the lowest number from the highest, as illustrated in figure 10-9.

> **The series:** 10, 20, 40, 40, 50
> The sum of the series divided   = $10 + 20 + 40 + 40 + 50$
> by the number of items in the   = $160 \div 5$
> series equals the average.   =   32

FIGURE **10-8.** FINDING THE AVERAGE VALUE

The series: 10, 20, 40, 40, 50

median (the middle item)	= 40
mode (the most frequently occurring item)	= 40
range (the difference between highest and lowest)	= 50 − 10 = 40

FIGURE 10-9. MEDIAN, MODE, AND RANGE

You'll also find a few new math symbols on your child's homework this school year. I thought they were mistakes the first time I saw them, because the symbols aren't used in everyday calculations. Table 10-1 contains a list of these symbols.

The symbol that was most confusing to my daughter was the not-equal sign ($\neq$) because it looked as if someone tried to cross out an equal sign. The other new symbols ($\geq$ and $\leq$) were less confusing after I explained that the underline took the place of the equal sign.

TABLE 10-1
MORE MATH SYMBOLS

Symbol	Definition
$\neq$	not equal
$\geq$	greater than or equal to
$\leq$	less than or equal to

Besides new math symbols on my daughter's homework, I also found a familiar symbol missing from math problems. This school year she learned to solve complex math problems that didn't use parentheses.

A *complex math problem* contains more than one operation, such as in figure 10-10. Parentheses are used to clarify which operation is performed first. She previously learned that operations within parentheses are calculated before other operations in the problem.

However, how was my daughter expected to correctly solve the problem in figure 10-10 unless parentheses were used? The solution was to apply the order-of-operation rule to the problem. The *order-of-operation* rule is shown in figure 10-11. This is a critical rule for your child to memorize, because without parentheses, she could easily perform operations out of order, resulting in the wrong answer.

$$10 \times 5 + 3 \ = \ 53$$
$$50 + 3 \qquad = \ 53$$

FIGURE 10-10. THE ORDER OF OPERATION HELPS TO
CORRECTLY SOLVE THIS PROBLEM.

1. Multiplication and division from left to right
2. Addition and subtraction from left to right

FIGURE 10-11. ORDER OF OPERATION

Positive and Negative Numbers

I felt as if I was banging my head against the wall the evening my daughter started to learn to add and subtract signed numbers. No matter which way I explained, she couldn't comprehend the concept. We were getting nowhere until I discussed the problem with a few math teachers and found to my surprise I wasn't alone having this problem. Here's the best way I discovered to explain signed numbers to my sixth grader.

Draw a number line as shown in figure 10-12 to help your child visualize that numbers less than zero are shown with a minus sign. The number line also shows that numbers greater than zero are displayed with a plus sign, although normally we assume a plus sign if no sign is used. Zero has no sign.

Numbers greater than zero are called *positive numbers*, and numbers less than zero are called *negative numbers*. Positive and negative numbers are used in all arithmetic operations, but sixth graders use signed numbers only in addition and subtraction.

Begin with an addition problem using only positive numbers (figure 10-12) because your child knows how to calculate the problem. Plot the calculation on the number line. This will draw the connection between the concept of numbers and the familiar addition problem.

Find the first number in the problem on the number line. I marked this with the letter **A**. Add the second number by counting numbers on the number line. I marked this with the letter **B**. She'll be able to see that adding a positive number to another positive number increases the number to the right on the number line.

Negative numbers can also be added together in the same way except negative numbers are marked to the left of the zero. Figure 10-13 illustrates this technique. In this example, −3 is added to a −2.

A mental block developed. My daughter couldn't understand how the plus sign and minus sign could be used with the same set of numbers. I explained that the sign to the left of a number (−3) tells whether the number is less than or greater than zero on the number line. A sign to the left of another sign (+ −3) indicates the arithmetic operation.

After overcoming this obstacle, plot the numbers on the number line. This is similar to adding two positive numbers except the numbers go to the left of the zero, as shown in figure 10-13.

Adding positive and negative numbers can get tricky for sixth graders. Figure 10-14 shows a typical problem you'll find on your child's homework. You're asked to add a −3 to a +2. Use the same procedure to solve this problem as you used to add negative numbers. First plot the first number on the number line (**A**), then count out the other number.

Be careful. Make sure to count in the correct direction. If the second number is negative, then count to the left on the number line; otherwise count to the right as is the case in figure 10-14.

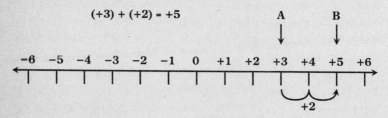

FIGURE **10-12.** ADDING POSITIVE NUMBERS

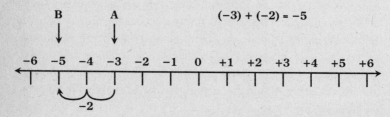

FIGURE **10-13.** ADDING NEGATIVE NUMBERS

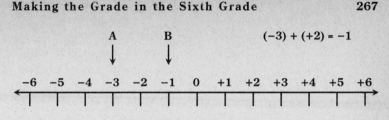

FIGURE 10-14. ADDING MIXED SIGNED NUMBERS

Once your child's class becomes proficient at adding signed numbers, teachers move on to subtracting signed numbers. Don't let your child attempt subtraction unless she has a firm understanding of addition, otherwise she'll easily fall behind the class. Speak with her teacher and devise a plan to reinforce addition using signed numbers.

Subtracting signed numbers also requires your child to use a number line and follow procedures similar to addition—with one major exception. After plotting the first number on the number line, the second number is subtracted by counting in the reverse direction of addition. In the example in figure 10-15, the first number (+3) is plotted on the number line **(A)**. The second number (+2) is used to count toward zero to arrive at the answer **(B)**.

Figure 10-16 shows a similar example: two negative numbers are subtracted. Once the first number (−3) is plotted **(A)**, the second number (−2) is counted toward zero **(B)**. Mixed signed numbers can be subtracted as shown in figure 10-17. The technique is basically the same except the count is added to the left of the first number (−3) because the second number (+2) is a positive number.

It's very likely that your child will become confused adding and subtracting signed numbers. I created a guide (table 10-2) my daughter found handy when solving signed-number problems on her homework.

First determine if the problem is addition or subtraction, then look up the sign of the first number in the first column of the guide. Next, find the sign of the second number in the second column. The third column tells which side of zero on the number line to plot the first number. The fourth column shows the direction to count from the first number using the second number.

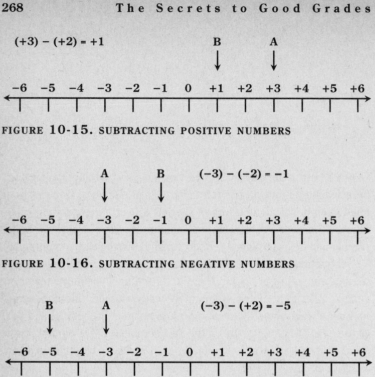

$(+3) - (+2) = +1$

FIGURE 10-15. SUBTRACTING POSITIVE NUMBERS

$(-3) - (-2) = -1$

FIGURE 10-16. SUBTRACTING NEGATIVE NUMBERS

$(-3) - (+2) = -5$

FIGURE 10-17. SUBTRACTING MIXED SIGNED NUMBERS

TABLE 10-2
GUIDELINES FOR ADDING AND SUBTRACTING SIGNED NUMBERS

If first number is	and second number is	Direction related to zero	Direction related to first number
ADDING SIGNED NUMBERS			
+	+	right	right
−	−	left	left
−	+	left	right
+	−	right	left

SUBTRACTING SIGNED NUMBERS

+	+	right	left
−	−	left	right
−	+	left	left
+	−	right	right

Exponents

Sixth graders are sometimes puzzled by exponents because of the way the exponent is referenced, such as 5^2. They recognize the first number, but the smaller number (in type size) is confused as a way to express a decimal. My daughter thought 5^2 meant 5.2, which is incorrect. An exponent is a way to express multiplication.

The *exponent* is the small number, and the larger number is called the *base*. The exponent tells your child how many times the base is multiplied by itself. For example, 5^2 means the same as 5×5. Figure 10-18 contains typical examples of exponential expressions you'll find in your child's homework.

Exponents are used as a shorthand to represent very large and very small numbers. For example, 10 million can be represented as 10^7 and 10 millionths is 10^{-7}. These are difficult for most sixth graders to comprehend, because they will rarely use exponents to represent very large or very small numbers in an expression. Instead, they'll be given an exponential number and asked to expand the number as a multiplication problem.

Special terms are used when talking about exponents. You'll hear your child say, "I raised the number to the power of two." This means the exponent is 2, as in the first example in figure 10-18. Anytime a number is used exponentially, you say the number is raised by the power of the exponent.

A base number is called *squared* when the exponent is 2, which is shown in the first example in figure 10-18. The second example shows the base number is *cubed*.

$$10^2 = 10 \times 10$$
$$10^3 = 10 \times 10 \times 10$$
$$10^4 = 10 \times 10 \times 10 \times 10$$

FIGURE 10-18. EXPONENTS

Here's a trick a math teacher showed me to help my daughter overcome the hurdles of working with exponents. The exponent tells how many zeros are after the 1 if the base number is in the series of 10s (10, 100, 1,000, 10,000, etc.). For example, 10 million is 10,000,000. Notice it has seven zeros. This number is written exponentially as 10^7.

Multiplying

Multiplying fractions is another topic you'll find on your child's homework. Until this school year, she's been multiplying whole numbers or decimals. Multiplying fractions, however, is not intuitive and doesn't follow the rules for adding and subtracting fractions. You'll recall two fractions must have the same denominator before they can be added together. This is not the case with multiplying fractions. It took a while for this to sink in for my daughter. She overcame her confusion when I segregated the rules for fraction arithmetic into the four operations: addition, subtraction, multiplication, and division. I then asked her to treat each set separately although some steps appear on more than one list. This helped her to focus on each set of rules.

The mechanics of multiplying fractions is simpler than adding and subtracting fractions because you don't need to convert the denominators to a common denominator. Set up the problem as shown in figure 10-19, then multiply the fractions. Here's how this is done.

PROCEDURE:
How to multiply fractions

1. Set up the fractions in the multiplication format shown in figure 10-19.

2. Don't convert denominators to a common denominator.

3. Multiply the numerators.

4. Multiply the denominators.

5. If the product is an improper fraction, then convert the fraction to a mixed number.

6. Reduce the product to the lowest terms.

$$\frac{1}{2} \times \frac{2}{4} = \frac{2}{8} = \frac{1}{4}$$

FIGURE **10-19.** MULTIPLYING FRACTIONS

A math teacher showed me a shortcut. The numerator of the multiplicand (first fraction) and the denominator of the multiplier (second fraction) are *cross values*. Likewise, the denominator of the multiplicand and the numerator of the multiplier are also cross values, as shown in figure 10-20.

Divide cross values by a common value to multiply the fractions. In this example, 2 and 2 are divided, as are 4 and 1. The result is the same answer as if the numerators and denominators were multiplied, then reduced to the lowest terms as in figure 10-19.

divide

$$\frac{2}{4} \times \frac{1}{2} = \frac{1}{4}$$

FIGURE **10-20.** DIVIDING BY COMMON FACTOR

Don't be surprised if your child comes home and tells you all about reciprocals. I had no idea that reciprocals were taught in the sixth grade. In fact, I had no idea what she was talking about because I never understood the concept of reciprocals. Here's what I learned.

Two numbers are reciprocals if, when multiplied, their product is equal to 1. Take a look at the example in figure 10-21 to better understand this explanation. By reversing the numerator and denominator of the first fraction, I created the reciprocal fraction. Notice, when the numerators are multiplied in figure 10-21, the product is one. The same is true when the denominators are multiplied.

divide

$$\frac{2}{3} \times \frac{3}{2} = \frac{1}{1} = 1$$

FIGURE 10-21. RECIPROCAL NUMBERS HAVE A PRODUCT OF 1.

Division

"What is 9.412 divided by 0.15?"

What a greeting when I walk in the door from work. No hello. No how are you. Just hit the old man with the first tough homework problem before he has time to take off his coat. It seems most eleven- and twelve-year-olds take for granted all the work you and I have to do to get them through the sixth grade. I imagine we did the same growing up.

Rather than start an argument, I normally drop my coat across the chair and spend the next few minutes coaching my daughter through her homework. Teachers have told me not to give in so quickly, but why postpone the inevitable?

As for this evening, there was no way I could divide 9.412 by 0.15 in my head. I actually had problems solving this with paper and pencil. Dividing by a decimal is different from the division she learned previously.

The first step after setting up the division problem in the proper form (see figure 10-22) is to move the decimal point to the right until the decimal is after the last digit in the divisor. In this example, the decimal is moved to the right two places. Likewise, the decimal must be moved the same number of places in the dividend, which changes the dividend in this example to 941.2.

Moving the decimal is a way of multiplying the divisor and the dividend. If the decimal is moved one place, then the multiplier is 10; two places, the multiplier is 100, etc. Avoid explaining this to your child since it will only confuse the calculation. All she needs to know is to move the decimal, not why she must move the decimal. Here's how I explained dividing by decimals to my daughter.

> **PROCEDURE:**
> ## How to divide by a decimal
>
> 1. Set up the problem in the division form (figure 10-22).
> 2. Move the decimal in the divisor to the right, after the last digit (from 0.15 to 15.0).
> 3. Move the decimal in the dividend the same number of decimal places to the right as you did in the divisor.
> 4. Place the decimal in the quotient above the decimal in the dividend.
> 5. Insert zeros after the last number in the dividend if there aren't sufficient decimal places in the dividend. Your child was shown how to do this in the fifth grade.
> 6. Divide as if the decimals were not present.

$$1 \qquad\qquad 2$$
$$0.15 \,\overline{)\, 9.412} \qquad 15.0 \,\overline{)\, 941.2}$$

FIGURE 10-22. DIVIDING BY A DECIMAL

Your child will also learn how to divide mixed numbers this school year. A *mixed number* consists of a whole number and a fraction, which she learned in other grades. Figure 10-23 is a typical problem you'll find on your child's homework.

Before your child attempts to solve the problem, make sure she knows how to work with mixed numbers. I found it necessary to refresh my daughter's recollection by asking her to solve old mixed-number problems found on last year's homework. We then addressed dividing mixed numbers once she got up to speed again.

Your child should recognize some of the steps used in the calculation because they are the same used to convert a mixed number to a fraction. However, there are two steps that are new to her. Once the improper fractions are created (figure 10-23 step 2), she must replace the divisor with the reciprocal of the divisor.

Just show her the mechanics of the operation without devising lessons about reciprocals. All you need to do is to reverse the numerator and the denominator of the divisor, as shown in figure 10-23 step 3.

She also has to use the inverse operation after inserting the reciprocal of the divisor into the problem. Since the operation is division, the inverse operation is multiplication. The problem is then properly set up, and she can proceed with the calculation.

PROCEDURE:
How to divide mixed numbers

1. Convert the mixed numbers to improper fractions (figure 10-23 step 2).
2. Replace the divisor with the reciprocal (figure 10-23 step 3).
3. Change the division operation to its inverse, multiplication (figure 10-23 step 3).
4. Multiply the numerators.
5. Multiply the denominators.
6. Convert the improper fraction to a mixed number.

$$1 \qquad\qquad 2 \qquad\qquad 3$$

$$5\frac{1}{2} \div 3\frac{1}{4} \qquad \frac{11}{2} \div \frac{13}{4} \qquad \frac{11}{2} \times \frac{4}{13}$$

FIGURE 10-23. DIVIDING MIXED NUMBERS

Fractions

Last school year your child learned how to change a fraction into a decimal. This year she'll learn how to reverse the process and convert a decimal into a fraction. Teachers strongly urge you not to let her attempt this lesson until she has a good understanding of place values, because place values are the key to making a decimal into a fraction.

As a precaution, my wife and I gave our daughter a place-value test before going ahead with decimal conversions. You should do the same. Don't make the test too overbearing. Instead, borrow a few problems from her old homework assignments. Avoid making this an official-looking test. I jotted down a few problems and asked my daughter if she could show me how to solve them. My daughter zipped through them. However, if you uncover difficulties, then review place values with your child.

Figure 10-24 contains a problem you'll find on most sixth-grade homework assignments. Your child's job is to convert 0.352 to a fraction. Remember the place value of the decimal is the denominator of the fraction.

PROCEDURE:
How to convert a decimal to a fraction

1. Count the place value of the decimal, which is thousandths in figure 10-24.
2. Use the value of the place value as the denominator of the fraction.
3. Remove the decimal from the decimal number and use the number as the numerator of the fraction.
4. Reduce the fraction to its lowest terms.

$$0.352 = \frac{352}{1,000} = \frac{44}{125}$$

FIGURE **10-24.** CONVERTING DECIMALS TO FRACTIONS

Ratios

Sixth graders learn that fractions are used to represent a proportion. The best way to explain proportions is by letting your child bake cookies or another goody. In our pretend recipe, the objective was to make 24 yummies that required 4 cups of flour and 12 ounces of water. I asked her to express these numbers as a fraction, which is shown in figure 10-25. This is the proportion of flour to water.

A proportion is referred to as a ratio. The proportion in figure 10-25 is read *the ratio between flour and water is 4 to 12* and is written as a fraction or as 4:12. Proportions are used to make more of the same while assuring the relation between the parts doesn't change. For example, you could make 96 yummies by multiplying each number in the ratio by 4 as in figure 10-25. You'll need 16 cups of flour and 48 ounces of water.

$$\frac{4}{12} = \frac{16}{48}$$

FIGURE 10-25. THESE TWO RATIOS ARE PROPORTIONALLY EQUAL.

The real test of proportions comes with a problem on your child's homework such as in figure 10-26. Her job is to find the missing value (y) in the ratio. Nearly all the proportion problems you'll see try to make the problem interesting by relating the numbers to a real-life situation such as baking cookies. However, I've seen problems that don't do this, which requires me to relate the numbers to real life. You'll need to do the same. Here's how to help your child solve the ratio problem in figure 10-26.

PROCEDURE:
How to find the missing ratio

1. Set up an expression where the numerator of the first fraction is multiplied by the denominator of the second fraction. Likewise, multiply the denominator of the first fraction by the numerator of the second fraction (figure 10-27).
2. Be sure your child notices the equation is unbalanced because there are two numbers to the right of the equal sign and one number on the left.
3. Multiply the numbers on the right of the equal sign.
4. Move the number on the left of the equal sign to the right side and divide. The quotient is the value of the missing ratio.

$$\frac{y}{12} = \frac{16}{48}$$

FIGURE 10-26. FINDING THE MISSING VALUE IN A RATIO

$$y \times 48 = 16 \times 12$$
$$y \times 48 = 192$$
$$y = 192 \div 48$$
$$y = 4$$

FIGURE 10-27. HOW TO FIND THE MISSING VALUE IN FIGURE 10-26.

Another kind of proportion problem I found on my daughter's homework shows two ratios and asks if they are proportionally the same. Figure 10-28 contains such a problem.

Proportionally the same means the numerator and the denominator of the first ratio have the same relationship to each other as the numerator and the denominator of the second ratio. This might be a little difficult to explain to a sixth grader. I prefer to make one attempt, then move right into the mechanics of solving the problem.

Ratios are proportionally the same if the products of cross multiplying numerators and denominators are the same. *Cross multiplying* means multiplying the numerator of one fraction with the denominator of the other, which is illustrated in figure 10-29.

PROCEDURE:
How to determine if two ratios are proportionally the same

1. Multiply the numerator of the first fraction and the denominator of the second fraction.
2. Multiply the numerator of the second fraction and the denominator of the first fraction.
3. Compare the products of both expressions. If the products are the same, then the ratios are proportionally the same; otherwise they are not proportionally the same.

$$\frac{6}{12} = \frac{2}{4}$$

FIGURE 10-28. IF CROSS PRODUCTS ARE THE SAME, THEN THE RATIOS ARE EQUAL.

$$\text{product} = 6 \times 4$$
$$= 24$$
$$\text{product} = 2 \times 12$$
$$= 24$$

FIGURE 10-29. BOTH CROSS PRODUCTS IN FIGURE 10-28 ARE
EQUAL.

Percents

Your child is familiar with percentages since she is graded on most tests based on the percentage of all the questions she answered correctly. However, many sixth graders don't understand the meaning of percents. This school year, the teacher will explain percentages in detail and expect her to solve percent problems. Here's how you can help reinforce lessons learned in the classroom.

A *percent* is a method of relating a value to the whole of something. Test grades compare the number of correct answers to the number of test questions. A 100% on the test means all the answers are correct. A 0% score means none of the questions were correctly answered.

You can say that 100% is equal to one whole thing. A value less than one whole thing is represented as a decimal. For example, 10% is 0.10 of the whole thing. Values can also be greater than the whole thing, but still be related to the whole thing by using percents. Say I have 5 whole things; then I have 500%, as shown in figure 10-30.

Avoid explaining percent as *whole things* and instead refer to an item your child can relate to, such as a pie. The pie is 1 whole thing, or 100% of the pie. When half of the pie is served to the family, then 50% or half of the whole pie is left. However, if you bought 5 pies (5 whole things), then those pies are 500% of 1 pie.

5.0	=	500%
1.0	=	100%
0.10	=	10%
0.01	=	1%
0.001	=	0.1%

FIGURE 10-30. PERCENT EQUIVALENTS

Your next job is to coach her through solving percent problems on her homework. Figure 10-31 is one such problem, where she is asked, what percent is 35 of 50? Ask her to explain the problem in terms of fractions. Remember, fractions also relate a value to a whole.

In this example, 50 is the whole thing and she knows that the whole of something is represented in the denominator of a fraction. The part of the whole is 35 and is placed in the numerator of the fraction. Once she can explain this concept, then walk her through solving the problem.

PROCEDURE:

How to determine the percent a value is of another number

1. Set up the problem as a fraction (see figure 10-31).
2. Create an equivalent fraction where the denominator of the equivalent fraction is 100. Your child learned how to create equivalent fractions last year.
3. Remove the denominator from the equivalent fraction and replace it with a percent sign.

What percent is 35 of 50?

$$\frac{35 \times 2}{50 \times 2} = \frac{70}{100} = 70\%$$

FIGURE 10-31. FINDING THE PERCENT A NUMBER IS OF THE WHOLE

Another kind of percentage problem requires your child to use a percent to find a value. You and I do this all the time when we calculate a tip or determine the sale price when an item is 10% off the regular price.

The solution requires her to convert the percent to a decimal, then multiply the whole by the decimal. This sounds confusing, but is easy once you properly set up the problem as illustrated in figure 10-32.

PROCEDURE:

How to determine the value of a percent

1. Convert the percent to a fraction using 100 as the denominator.
2. Convert the fraction to the decimal equivalent (see chapter 9). In figure 10-32, 8% is converted to 0.08, read as *eight hundredths*.
3. Multiply the whole value by the decimal equivalent of the percent. The product is the value of the percent.

$$
\begin{aligned}
\text{sales tax} &= \text{price} \times \text{percent} \\
\text{st} &= \text{p} \quad \times \% \\
\text{st} &= \$30 \quad \times 8\% \\
\text{st} &= \$30 \quad \times 0.08 \\
\text{st} &= \$2.40
\end{aligned}
$$

FIGURE 10-32. FINDING THE VALUE OF A PERCENT

Geometry

Geometry lessons your child learns this year focus on measuring shapes and finding missing measurements in homework problems. Last year, she learned how to measure the area of various shapes. This year attention is given to finding the perimeter of those shapes.

The *perimeter* is the measurement around the edges of the shape, while the area is the measurement of the space within the edges. She shouldn't have too much difficulty finding either measurement, because the teacher provides her with a formula for each shape.

You'll find most of the formulas intuitive to use when explaining the lesson. However, the formula for finding the perimeter of a parallelogram can be a little confusing because parentheses and a constant are used in the expression.

The formula is **Perimeter = 2 (base + side)** and is likely to be presented in your child's textbook as $p = 2(b + s)$. My daughter could relate the letters to the names of the sides, but was confused as to which part of the parallelogram was the base.

I explained that it really didn't matter because the base and the side are added together. Regardless of which she thought was the base, she'd still come up with the correct answer. I drew the picture in figure 10-33 to help her visualize my explanation.

She also asked why the sum of the base and the side were multiplied by two. The answer might be apparent to you and me, but it may not be to a sixth grader. I told her the sum represented one side and one base. The parallelogram has two sides and a top and a bottom, which is why the sum is multiplied by two.

PROCEDURE:

How to calculate the perimeter of a parallelogram

1. Measure one side and the base. The base is the bottom of the parallelogram (see figure 10-33).
2. Write the formula as shown in figure 10-34.
3. Insert the measurements into the formula.
4. Add the base and the side.
5. Multiply the sum by 2 since there are two sides and the base is the same measurement as the top of the parallelogram.

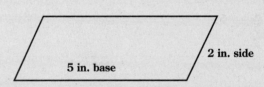

FIGURE 10-33. A PARALLELOGRAM

Formula:	Perimeter = 2 (base + side)
	p = 2 (b + s)
Solution:	p = 2 (5 in. + 2 in.)
	p = 2 × 7 in.
	p = 14 in.

FIGURE 10-34. HOW TO FIND THE PERIMETER OF A
PARALLELOGRAM

The hardest geometry problem my daughter was asked to solve required her to find the missing angle of a triangle. Until now, she had never been asked to use angles in a calculation. I could see the panic slowly set in as she read the problem and stared at the picture of the triangle (figure 10-35).

Whenever I see that expression, I remind myself that I have to do something to get my daughter thinking straight again. My job is to teach her how to approach a problem she thinks she doesn't know how to solve. This is a very important lesson to learn, because she can apply this knowledge throughout her life.

Her first step is to give herself a pep talk. Remind her that the problem can be solved and she can solve it once she learns the technique. Next, she makes two lists, one containing the facts she already knows about the problem, the other containing facts she still needs to learn.

At this point my daughter loses focus, so I start with the first lesson she learned about geometry that applies to the problem and ask her questions such as, What is an angle? This gives her a starting point from which she can take inventory of her knowledge about geometry; it shows her she knows a lot more than she thinks she knows.

Once her confidence is regained, I turn her attention to the facts about the problem she doesn't know, such as the missing angle. We narrowed the problem to a single question: How do you find a missing angle in a triangle?

PROCEDURE:
How to find a missing angle in a triangle

1. Remember, all the angles of a triangle total 180 degrees. This is the critical piece of information most sixth graders forget when addressing this problem.
2. Restate the problem in an expression like the one shown in the first line of figure 10-36.
3. Insert the angles from the problem into the expression (third line of figure 10-36).

4. Move the unknown value to the left of the equal sign and reverse the math operation from addition to subtraction (fourth line of figure 10-36).

5. Subtract the value within the parentheses first, then subtract the remaining angle from the difference to find the missing angle.

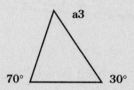

FIGURE 10-35. ONE ANGLE IS MISSING FROM THIS TRIANGLE.

$$180° = \text{angle } 1 + \text{angle } 2 + \text{angle } 3$$
$$180° = a1 \qquad + a2 \qquad + a3$$
$$180° = 30° \qquad + 70° \qquad + a3$$
$$a3 \quad = (180° \quad - 30°) \quad - 70°$$
$$a3 \quad = 150° \qquad - 70°$$
$$a3 \quad = 80°$$

FIGURE 10-36. FIND THE MISSING ANGLE.

11.

The Computer and Other Resources for Doing Homework

- Essay Homework with a Word-Processor Program
- Spelling Homework with a Word-Processor Program
- Learn Keyboarding with a Word Processor
- Math with a Spreadsheet Program and Computer Calculator
- Dressing up Projects with a Computer
- Doing Research with a Computer

Do you feel inadequate when you hear your child ramble on with jargon about computers? Press Alt-this, double-click on that. It's amazing what kids know, enough to put any parent to shame. So feel proud your child doesn't have your computer phobia, then sit down and learn a little about computers yourself. I'll get you started.

Fear is the first obstacle to overcome. The fear to let your child and the rest of the family know about your computer phobia, and the mother of all fears, the fear you're going to break the computer. This is my wife's biggest concern.

My wife honestly admits to being petrified of using a computer even though her husband teaches computer science at a college and has written more than twenty computer books. Computers are simply not her thing, yet she isn't afraid to try using a computer with a little prodding from the kids.

Let's put to rest the biggest fear. It's very difficult to break a computer. I once inadvertently left the window open next to my computer. As luck would have it, we had a storm. Rain blew in all directions including into the computer. Thousands of dollars down the drain, I thought. But I was mistaken. I let the computer dry for two weeks, then turned on the power. It worked fine.

Try this the next time your child turns on the computer. I call it the fist test. Make a fist, then roll your fist over the keyboard. You'll eventually hear beeps. This is the computer telling you it doesn't understand your typing. Stop and turn the computer over to your child. But notice, you didn't cause any harm.

Another common fear is fear of computer jargon: bits, bytes, RAM, and all the stuff that makes your kid sound like a rocket scientist. My wife has flashbacks to geometry class, memorizing strange definitions and concepts for a quiz. Forget about it. You don't need to learn this stuff to use a computer.

Here's what you need to understand. A computer is an expensive box that can do different things. It can be a typewriter, a calculator, a filing cabinet, a CD player, an arcade, and a lot more. However, nothing happens unless you tell the computer which of these things you want it to become. And you make your wishes known by running a specific program.

There is a program to make the computer a typewriter. Another program makes it a calculator, and so on. You need a separate program for each thing you want the computer to do. Without a program, the computer is an expensive paperweight.

Computers don't necessarily come with all the programs you want to use. Some computer manufacturers include a few programs in the purchase price. Others simply sell you a computer that does nothing until you purchase programs. This means you could spend a couple of thousand dollars for a computer and when you get home the computer does very little for you.

Programs can be expensive depending on what you want the computer to do. Expect to spend $200 to $300 for programs that transform your computer into a typewriter and calculator. You can spend upward of $500 if you want a program that allows you to draw fancy artwork.

Programs are sold on CDs like the CDs you buy in the music store. However, you can't simply slip the CD into the computer and run the program. First you must install the program on your computer. Let your child show you how this is done. Once installed, you'll find the name of the program on a list displayed on your computer. Simply point to the name of the program and click the mouse button twice to start the program. This is as easy as tapping your finger. Bond with your child a little and let her show you how to find and run a program.

Using a program is the most frustrating aspect of using a computer. Every program works differently from other programs. A word-processing program is a program that makes your computer a typewriter. There are many different kinds of word-processing programs, such as Microsoft Word and WordPerfect, and each works differently to achieve the same results.

This is similar to automobiles: each car takes you to your destination, but some cars are stick shift and others automatic. Some have power windows and locks, and others are manually operated.

So when you hear someone brag that he knows how to use a computer, don't jump to conclusions. He's not a whiz kid. Chances are good he only knows how to use a particular program such as Microsoft Word. He'd go into the same panic as you if he had to use a different program.

You hold a conversation with the computer, once a program is running, by giving the computer directions using the keyboard and the mouse. In response, the computer displays messages on the screen and flashes an image to prompt you to enter the next direction. The image is called a cursor. Ask your child to demonstrate how to use the keyboard and mouse to tell the computer what you want to do.

You're probably scratching your head wondering what kind of direction you're expected to give the computer. There is no simple answer. Each program has its own set of directions. This is why there are so many computer books and computer courses. You'll have to learn how to use each program you need, and there are only a couple of programs you really should learn.

Concentrate on the word-processing program and the spreadsheet program—which is like a fancy calculator and ledger book. Of course, you'll also need to learn to use a few computer games, too. My wife and I are hooked on solitaire. Playing solitaire is a good way to become familiar with using the mouse. Ask your child to show you how to run the game.

I suggest you purchase a *Dummies* book covering the programs you want to use. I've written a couple of *Dummies* books and discovered they're designed to cut out stuff you probably will never need to use. A course at your local adult school could give you a leg up, too, in learning programs.

So far I've only talked about computers. There are two other pieces of equipment that are almost required, but may not come with your purchase: a printer and a modem. Computers display information on the screen, but you'll need a printer to print that information on paper. And a printer can cost you from a few hundred dollars to more than a thousand dollars. There are various kinds of printers, but the most popular for home use is a color ink-jet printer, which costs around $250 and plugs into the back of your computer.

A modem is a $150 telephone the computer uses to make telephone calls, mainly to the Internet. The Internet is a telephone link enabling your computer to access information on computers around the world. The Internet is also used to send and receive electronic mail. I'll show you how you and your child can use the Internet for schoolwork later in this chapter.

Here are a few other things you should know about computers.

PROCEDURE:
How to buy a computer

1. Don't buy an expensive computer.
2. Look for a small computer shop that will assemble a computer to meet your needs. The parts they use are probably the same found in brand-name computers, and the price is under $1,000.
3. Know how you want to use the computer so you don't buy

more computer than you need. Most parents will do word processing, keep track of the family budget, play a few computer games, and connect to the Internet.

4. Look for a bundled price that includes the computer, a monitor, a printer, a modem, and most of the programs you'll need.

5. Avoid bringing your child to a big computer chain store. Your child will be tempted to have you buy something you don't need.

6. Buy simple books to teach you how to use the computer or how to use the programs you purchase.

7. Don't expect to learn everything about your computer and programs. Most of us, including those in the computer profession, use only 10 percent of the computer's capabilities.

8. Be a student again. Let your child teach you how to use the computer. You'll learn a lot and build her self-esteem along the way.

Essay Homework with a Word-Processor Program

I always cringed whenever the teacher assigned an essay, and it wasn't until recently that I realized why. None of us had the patience to rewrite our essays over again until we came up with a perfect paper.

I began my writing career as a reporter for a daily newspaper. I used a very old manual typewriter and two pieces of carbon paper. Reporters learned quickly to compose a story on a typewriter if they wanted to meet the deadline. There was no time for pencil and paper.

The problem I encountered as a reporter is probably the same your child runs into when writing an essay in longhand. A poorly written paragraph toward the end of the page requires me to retype the entire page just to make the correction. This is discouraging. Times have changed, and thanks to a word-processing program, I only have to correct the error and not rewrite the page.

The word processor on your computer can dramatically improve your child's essay homework because she will focus on what she wants to say and not let the drudgery of retyping the complete essay dampen her creative thoughts. Here are ways you can use your word processor to help your child write better essays.

PROCEDURE:

How your child can write better essays using a word processor

1. Have your child use the word processor in place of pencil and paper when planning the essay. Ask her to type her ideas into the word processor; from there, she can easily modify, delete, and enhance her work.

2. Outline the essay using headlines or short sentences that describe the point of the section. I use headlines for my books because they're easier to write and because they typically turn into subheadings for each chapter.

3. Use bold type to make the outline stand out from the text of the essay.

4. Enter facts beneath the appropriate headline in the outline. An advantage of using a word processor as a planning tool is that new lines can be easily inserted anywhere in your child's essay. Begin each fact with a hyphen or an asterisk.

5. Explain each fact in text. This helps to focus on the small pieces of the entire essay.

6. Work on one section of the essay at a time. Read aloud each section. Ask your child to reword the section until the words read smoothly.

7. Make stories about each fact sound like one story. Let your child take the first crack at being editor, then jump in as the coach to finish the job.

8. Avoid printing the essay until your child is finished writing. Read the essay on the computer, then make changes as needed rather than making changes on a printed copy of the essay.

9. Encourage your child to rearrange parts of the essay on the computer. She can cut and paste text using the mouse. The

computer does all the work, allowing your child to concentrate on the context of the changes.

10. Save the essay frequently. The essay will be lost if it isn't saved and someone turns off the computer accidentally.

11. Make sure your child's essay is of reasonable length. Kids quickly learn to increase the size of the characters and spaces to stretch a skimpy essay to the required page count.

12. Use all the features of the word-processor program to dress up the essay. Your child can change the size of some of the characters, use fancy characters, even add clip art to spice up the presentation.

13. Print a couple of copies of the essay. I tell my kids to do this all the time because there is always a chance a copy could get lost on the way to school.

Spelling Homework with a Word-Processor Program

Spelling wasn't my best subject, and spelling isn't the easiest subject for your child to learn either. Most words are spelled the same as they sound, but there are many that break this rule and require memorization to learn the correct spelling.

Teachers have told me there are many techniques your child can use to memorize spelling words. Flash cards and the association method all work fine, but I found another approach using a word-processing program.

Most word-processing programs come with a spell checker. A spell checker is like an electronic teacher who proofreads your work for misspellings, then suggests the correct spelling of the suspicious word.

A spell checker stores tens of thousands of words on your computer, then compares each word in your child's document against those words. A word is marked as possibly misspelled if a match isn't found on the computer.

The spell checker makes a guess as to what word you meant to type, based upon rules developed by a programmer. These rules encompass typical misspellings, transposition of letters, and rules for phonic misspellings. This is how the spelling checker knows you mean *phone* when you type *fone*.

A spell checker is not infallible. Correctly spelled words that aren't in the spell checker's reference file will be marked as possibly misspelled. Likewise, some misspellings puzzle the spell checker, making suggested corrections impossible to find. Try various phonetic spellings if you encounter this problem. The spell checker is bound to guess the word you're trying to spell.

I use the spell checker with my kids as a game to help improve their spelling. Here's how you can do the same with your child.

PROCEDURE:
How to use a spell checker to help your kids learn to spell

1. Ask your child to study the nightly spelling words, then have the computer, not you, determine if she has learned the correct spelling.
2. Have your child turn on your computer and run the word-processing program. This breaks up the homework period briefly and increases the anticipation of the computer spelling test.
3. Say a sentence using a word on her spelling list, leaving out the word. Challenge your child to guess the missing word.
4. When she guesses incorrectly, give clues to make spelling homework a game.
5. Tell her to type the word into a word-processing document, then run the spell checker if the spell checker isn't automatically running.
6. Create a scorecard for the week. Give her one point for each correctly spelled word; a half of a point for picking the correct spelling from the spell checker's recommended list; and no points for misspelled words.
7. Give a reward for improvements over the previous week's score. The reward doesn't have to be fancy or expensive.

Learn Keyboarding with a Word Processor

One of the greatest mysteries of life is why keys on the computer keyboard aren't in alphabetical order. I always wonder why this is true whenever I curse my way through typing a manuscript. You probably guessed I'm a graduate of the hunt-and-peck school of typing. Dictionaries are in alphabetical order and so are indexes, then why do computer manufacturers make computer keyboards unorganized?

The keys for the most common letter combinations are spaced farther apart. This design was developed for typewriters, and the format stuck when we moved on to word processors.

I'll admit this answer doesn't help anyone from my typing school. However, it should help to encourage your child to use the touch-typing method. Touch-typing is the skill she learns in her keyboarding class.

A touch typist can enter words into a computer very fast without looking at letters on the keyboard. Sounds impossible, but touch-typing is a skill she should master because it eliminates probably the second greatest obstacle to using a computer—using the keyboard effectively.

Learning touch-typing is similar to learning to ride a bike. It takes a while to master, but once learned you'll never forget it. The secret to touch-typing is where you place your fingers on the keyboard. They must be positioned over the home row of the keyboard.

The home row begins with the letter *A* and ends with the characters *:* and *;*. The left little finger rests on the letter *A*, and the other fingers follow in order with the first finger of the left hand positioned over the letter *F*. The left thumb rests on the space bar.

The first finger of the right hand is positioned over the letter *J* with the other fingers following in sequence, ending with the little finger hovering over the *:* and *;* characters. The right thumb also rests on the space bar. Placing your fingers on the home row will feel strange at first, but you'll get used to the feeling. Move each finger up a row, then back to the home row, then move each finger down a row. You'll notice your fingers move smoothly.

The home row is the first secret of keyboarding. The second secret is to practice! Make sure your child uses the touch-typing method every time she uses the computer. Here are some tips to get your child started.

PROCEDURE:
How to touch-type on the computer

1. Ask your child to type her homework assignments. This gives her meaningful information to use while practicing keyboard skills and helps her to learn the assignment.
2. Allow her to peck at the letters while typing. After a while she'll naturally stop looking as she picks up typing speed.
3. Purchase a typing-tutor program from your local computer store. A typing-tutor program contains exercises and games to foster touch-typing skills.
4. Don't allow your child to use the hunt-and-peck method. She'll never master keyboarding if she doesn't keep trying the touch-type method.

Math with a Spreadsheet Program and Computer Calculator

"Why do you get to use a calculator while I have to do math with paper and pencil?"

Don't you hate it when your child asks logical questions like this? She's correct. A calculator is an efficient and accurate way of solving math problems.

How do you make a convincing argument for doing math by hand? I've asked a few teachers, who had mixed opinions. Some suggest kids should use calculators to learn math. Others recommend children learn to use the grocer's calculator (brown paper bag and pencil) first, then proof their results using a calculator. I think you should also allow your child to use the computer to check her work.

The purpose of your child's math lessons is to teach her how to solve math problems and not simply to arrive at the correct answer. When you and I use a calculator or computer we're only looking for the correct answer.

You can use your computer as part of your child's math lesson by using one of two programs—the computerized calculator and the spreadsheet program.

The calculator (figure 11-1) is found typically under Accessories on the computer's list of programs. You'll notice most of the keys are similar to those found on a calculator. There are a few extra keys, but your child won't need to use them.

My daughter was confused by the asterisk (*) and the forward slash (/). She couldn't understand why × is used as the multiplication symbol in school and the asterisk is used on the calculator. The asterisk is the standard computer multiplication symbol and the forward slash replaces the division symbol. I avoid explanations and simply tell her to use the asterisk in place of the × and the forward slash for division.

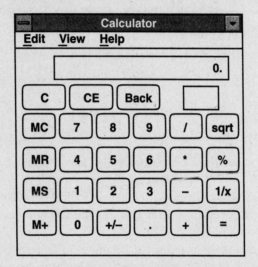

FIGURE 11-1. A COMPUTERIZED CALCULATOR

The spreadsheet program offers your child a way to check simple and complex math problems by inserting expressions into a grid (figure 11-2). Letters identify columns, and numbers identify rows. The point at which a column and row meet is called a *cell* and is identified by the combination of the column letter and the row number. A1 is the name of the first cell because the cell is in column A and row 1.

Numbers are stored in a cell by moving the cursor into a cell, using either the mouse or the arrow keys, then typing the number. I've entered the number 5 in cell A1 and 10 in cell B1 in figure 11-2.

A cell can also store a mathematical expression. You and I use expressions every day whenever we perform arithmetic. I've entered a simple addition expression in cell C1 in figure 11-2. You'll notice the expression actually appears in a box above the columns. This is where you enter numbers and expressions. The spreadsheet program places the results of the expression into the cell.

The expression $= A1 + B1$ looks a little strange. **A1** and **B1** tell the computer to use the numbers stored in those cells. The computer replaces A1 with 5 and B1 with 10, then adds them and places the results in cell C1. You can change numbers in cells A1 and/or B1, and the computer recalculates the expression. The plus sign in the expression can be replaced with other arithmetic symbols to have the spreadsheet perform subtraction, multiplication, and division.

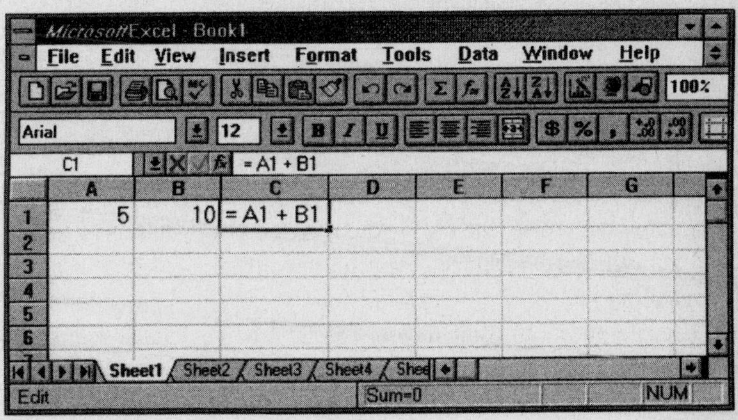

FIGURE **11-2**. A SPREADSHEET PROGRAM

Here are some tips for using the spreadsheet or calculator with your child's math homework.

PROCEDURE:
How to use a spreadsheet with your child's math homework

1. Ask your child to perform all math homework using paper and pencil since she'll need this skill to pass tests in school.
2. Create a gamelike atmosphere in which the objective of the game is for her to compete against the calculator or the computer to see who gets the most correct answers.
3. Let your child use the calculator to check homework answers. Be patient and don't rush her as she hunts and pecks her way entering numbers into the calculator.
4. Set up the expression in the spreadsheet program for your child, then let her enter the homework problem into the cells.
5. Have your child compare answers calculated by hand, with the calculator, and using the spreadsheet.

Dressing up Projects with a Computer

School projects frustrate both you and your child. First, you probably hear about the project the day before it is due, then you scurry to find text and pictures to include in the project, which are guaranteed not to be readily available.

The computer can come to your rescue. Many personal computers are equipped with programs that can spruce up any project. The most useful program I found for making any project attractive is a word-processing program in which the style of characters can be easily changed using the mouse. Text can also be positioned practically anywhere on the page by choosing a selection from the format menu.

Every project for school has pictures. Many word-processing programs come with an electronic library of pictures called clip art that your child can insert into the project at the click of the mouse. The teacher will know your child didn't draw the pictures, but will give her credit for choosing the proper picture to illustrate her project.

Your child's own artwork can be included in her project by using a graphics program or a scanner. A graphics program such as Microsoft Paint, which probably came with your computer, enables her to draw pictures on the computer screen using the mouse and keyboard. Most graphics programs have built-in shapes such as circles, squares, rectangles, and lines, which can be positioned on the screen and resized.

Images she creates can be colored. However, a color printer is necessary to print them in color. Images can also be saved on the computer and pasted into the project using the word-processor program.

A *scanner* is a gizmo that plugs into your computer and converts your child's paper drawing into an electronic image that can be pasted into the project. Practically any image can be scanned, including photographs.

There are many programs and computer hardware components you can buy to dress up your child's projects. You can read about them in computer magazines and see them at work at your local computer store. Here are a few tips to help you avoid some common pitfalls in buying graphics programs and hardware.

PROCEDURE:
How to avoid common mistakes when buying graphics programs and hardware

1. Make sure the graphics program can run on your computer.
2. Don't pay for features you'll never use. Graphics software comes in all price ranges.
3. Avoid impulse purchases. Plan your purchases carefully.
4. Don't be fooled by pictures on the program box. Very dramatic illustrations are shown, yet those images don't necessarily reflect the images you'll see on your computer. Ask to see a demonstration of the program before buying.
5. Find out if a demonstration program is available. Jot down the name, address, and telephone number of the manufacturer from the program's box. Call and ask for a demo ride.
6. Ask about a return policy. Don't be afraid to return the product if you are dissatisfied.

Doing Research with a Computer

"I had to walk a mile, through ten feet of snow, carrying my schoolbag to the library where I spent hours and hours poring over books, taking notes for my report."

So I have a good imagination. My kids don't believe me anyway, but they get the point. Researching a report for school takes effort, especially if you want to make the grade. Until now the local library was the only resource for research material. Today your kids can flip on a computer and sift through research material in libraries located literally around the globe.

Technology is mind-boggling, especially for you and me. I include myself even though I'm heavily involved in computer technology because I'm astonished by the capabilities of computers. You've heard about the Internet and how information stored in computers around the world can be displayed on your computer. If you're like most parents, you're utterly confused. I'll try to clear up the confusion and give you enough information to speak intelligently with your child.

The Internet is an informal group of computers linked together using the telephone network. I use the term *informal* because no one owns or runs the Internet. This is hard to believe, but it is true. The Internet began decades ago as an alliance among defense contractors, universities, and the government so information could be easily shared by their computers. No one ever dreamed of the revolutionary impact the Internet would have on the world.

Many computers linked to the Internet contain information available to your child for her projects. These computers are called Web sites. Your computer can't directly call a Web site, because your computer does not have the special telephone line to make the call. Instead, you need to make the call through the services of an Internet provider.

An *Internet provider* is typically a corporation, such as America Online, or a school system that has a direct link to the Internet telephone lines. For a fee, they'll let your computer connect to the Internet via their larger computer and Internet telephone lines.

The Internet provider supplies you with a local telephone number to call and a program to allow your computer to talk with their computer. The software is called a *browser*.

So if you want your child to connect to the Internet, you'll need a computer, a modem, and a subscription to an Internet service that will supply you with the necessary program to complete the connection.

Each Web site has its own Internet telephone number, which is in the form of a name. You've probably seen this as something like **www.onlinenj.com**. After you've subscribed to an Internet service, you can dial the Internet provider's computer, then enter the Web site you want to visit. The browser and the Internet provider make the connection for you.

Your job is to find Web sites that contain research material to help your child with her projects. Where do you find these Web sites? Table 11-1 contains a few Web sites I found geared to students. I suggest you preview these Web sites and determine if they are appropriate for your child.

Another way to locate Web sites is through the use of a special Web site called a *search engine*. A search engine prompts you to enter key words to identify the topic you're researching, then takes a few minutes to find Web sites that might meet your requirements. I use the **www.lycos.com** search engine Web site.

Web sites are also published in books. However Web sites come and go frequently, so a Web site mentioned in a book may no longer be operational.

In addition to the Internet, your child can use reference material available on CDs. You'll find a multitude of them in your local computer store. You'll find dictionaries; thesauruses; encyclopedias; specialty programs on space, anatomy, and physiology—the topics are almost endless. You don't require any connection to the Internet to use these CDs.

You should use caution whenever you subscribe to an Internet service or purchase reference software on CDs. Here are the guidelines I follow.

PROCEDURE:
How to make sure the Internet is appropriate for your child

1. Subscribe to an Internet service that offers a low, flat monthly or annual fee. Stay away from any Internet service that charges

by the minute or hour or that charges separately for other services such as chat rooms and discussion groups.

2. Use toll-free, local telephone numbers to connect to the Internet provider. Some Internet providers supply you with telephone numbers that are within your area code but are not considered a local telephone call by the telephone company. You incur a per-minute charge from the telephone company to connect to the Internet provider. Call your local operating company to be certain your call will be billed as local.

3. Preview Web sites and other Internet services used by your child. Keep your computer near the family room. Pop in and see what your child is doing on the Internet from time to time.

4. Don't permit your child to copy research found on the Internet or from reference books on CDs. Text and pictures displayed on your computer can be copied and pasted directly into your child's project. This defeats the purpose of the assignment.

5. Find out which Web sites your child visited.

6. Check E-mail received by your child. Call your Internet provider and ask for directions on how you can review *all* the E-mail your child received and sent.

7. Visit your school or local library if you don't have a computer or if your computer is not connected to the Internet. These locations typically have Internet connections and computers available to students.

TABLE 11-1
HELPFUL HINTS FOR STUDENTS

ASKERIC@ERICIR.SYR.EDU
E-mail the U.S. Department of Education Resource Information Center (ERIC) which offers a national system for accessing many education-related resources, such as electronic books, an on-line dictionary, and the CIA *World Factbook*.

CHILDREN'S LITERATURE WEB GUIDE
WWW.UCALGARY.CA/~DKBROWN
You'll find literary discussion groups for kids, children's books, children's stories, and connections to the Web sites of authors and publishers of children's books.

DAN'S WILD WILD WEATHER PAGE
WWW.WHNT19.COM/KIDWX
Let your child explore weather, cloud formation, rain, and weather forecasting, and take a peek at the U.S. weather radar, all from your home computer.

MAD SCIENTIST NETWORK
WWW.MADSCI.ORG
Stumped with a science question you can't answer for your child? Connect to this Web site and ask the staff from Washington University for help.

MEGA MATHEMATICS
WWW.C3.LANL.GOV/MEGA-MATH
Math can be fun when your child uses math to win a game. This Web site is filled with interactive projects that make learning math a game.

REED INTERACTIVE
WWW.REEDBOOKS.COM.AU
You'll find newsgroups for kids, bulletin boards, discussion groups, and interactive projects, along with connections to other educational Web sites.

WHITE HOUSE FOR KIDS
WWW.WHITEHOUSE.GOV/WH/KIDS/HTML/KIDSHOME.HTML
Let your child roam around the White House (without worrying about getting caught by the Secret Service) by visiting this Web site.

WHY FILES
WHYFILES.NEWS.WISC.EDU
The hardest question asked by any child is Why? Why is the sky blue? Why do the clouds move? Most of those questions are hard for parents to answer. However, you'll find answers to all the why questions at this Web site.

Index

ABOUT THE AUTHOR

For more than a decade, JIM KEOGH has been in the forefront confronting the problems of the public school education system. He is one of those persons who is behind the headlines and the two-minute sound bites. He is a school leader who has dealt with the tough issues of today, such as setting curriculum; hiring teachers; negotiating union contracts; dealing with teachers' strikes and school financing, and angry parents who demand to know how their child can get good grades and a good education. *The Secrets to Good Grades* is his answer to this last issue.

Keogh is also the author of *Getting the Best Education for Your Child*. He is a professor of computer science at Saint Peter's College in Jersey City, New Jersey, and a member of the faculty of Columbia University in New York.